THE MIGHTY EIGHTH
IN THE
SECOND WORLD WAR

Graham Smith

COUNTRYSIDE BOOKS

NEWBURY, BERKSHIRE

First Published 2001
© Graham Smith 2001
Reprinted 2003

COUNTRYSIDE BOOKS
3 Catherine Road
Newbury, Berkshire

To view our complete range of books,
please visit us at
www.countrysidebooks.co.uk

ISBN 1 85306 709 1

*This book is humbly dedicated to all those young airmen of the
Eighth Air Force who served during the Second World War,
in honour of their determination, courage and sacrifice.*

The cover painting by Colin Doggett shows B-17Gs
of the 350th Bomb Squadron of the 100th Bomb Group
in early 1945.

Designed by Mon Mohan

Produced through MRM Associates Ltd., Reading
Typeset by Techniset Typesetters, Merseyside
Printed by Woolnough Bookbinding Ltd., Irthlingborough

CONTENTS

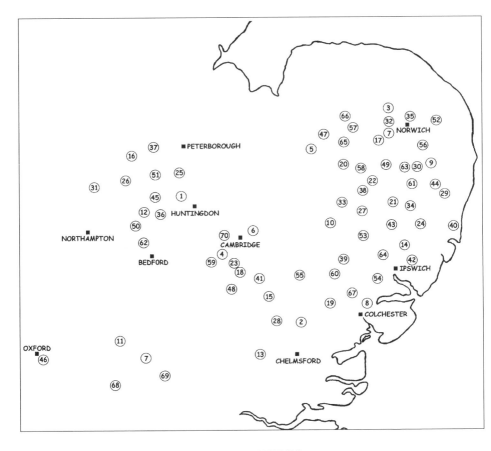

KEY TO AIRFIELDS

1. Alconbury.	20. East Wretham.	39. Lavenham.	58. Snetterton Heath.
2. Andrews Field.	21. Eye.	40. Leiston.	59. Steeple Morden.
3. Attlebridge.	22. Fersfield.	41. Little Walden.	60. Sudbury.
4. Bessingbourn.	23. Fowlmere.	42. Martlesham Heath.	61. Thorpe Abbotts.
5. Bodney.	24. Framingham.	43. Mendlesham.	62. Thurleigh.
6. Bottisham.	25. Glatton.	44. Metfield.	63. Tibenham.
7. Bovingdon.	26. Grafton Underwood.	45. Molesworth.	64. Wattisham.
8. Boxted.	27. Great Ashfield.	46. Mount's Farm.	65. Watton.
9. Bungay.	28. Great Dunmow.	47. North Pickenham.	66. Wending.
10. Bury St Edmunds.	29. Halesworth.	48. Nuthampstead.	67. Wormingford.
11. Cheddington.	30. Hardwick.	49. Old Buckenham.	
12. Chelveston.	31. Harrington.	50. Podington.	*Also*
13. Chipping Ongar.	32. Hethel.	51. Polebrook.	
14. Debach.	33. Honington.	52. Rackheath.	68. 8th A.F. H.Q.
15. Debden.	34. Horham.	53. Rattlesden.	69. 8th F.C. H.Q.
16. Deenethorpe.	35. Horsham St Faith.	54. Raydon.	70. Military Cemetery
17. Deopham Green.	36. Kimbolton.	55. Ridgewell.	& Memorial,
18. Duxford.	37. Kings Cliff.	56. Seething.	Madingley.
19. Earl's Colne.	38. Knettishall.	57. Shipham.	

ACKNOWLEDGEMENTS

I am deeply indebted to a number of people for assisting me during the preparation of this book, especially with the provision of illustrations.

First and foremost, I must thank Norman G. Richards of the Archives Division of the NASM. Over the last six years, Norman has been unstinting with his time and patience in answering all my enquiries regarding the USAAF, particularly concerning the selection of illustrations. From being a most reliable and diligent correspondent, 'Norm' has become a true friend.

I would also like to thank Rusty Bloxom, Chief Historian of the Mighty Eighth Heritage Museum for his assistance, along with Tom Lubbesmeyer of the Historical Archives of Boeing Co. The Staff of Galleywood Library have again willingly helped in obtaining specialist books. The 398th Bomb Group, via Wally Blackwell in Rockville, Maryland, has kindly granted me permission to reproduce the verse that appears on their Group Memorial at Nuthampstead.

Graham Smith

Lieutenant James and some of his crew of B-17 'Home James' of 457th Bomb Group at

6

Glatton, after completion of their 25th mission on 31st May 1944. (USAF)

INTRODUCTION

Military aviation in the United States can be traced back to March 1898 when the War Department allocated $50,000 to fund Professor Samuel P. Langley's experiments to build a manned 'flying machine' which would have practical application in war. On 8th December 1903 Langley's machine, *Aerodrome*, powered by a petrol engine, failed for a second time; the US Government withdrew its support and the project was abandoned. Just nine days later the Wright brothers completed their epic flight in *Flyer* entirely without any military or government funding.

By 1907 the Signals Corps of the US Army had decided that powered flight might indeed have some military potential. On 1st August it established an Aeronautical Division under Captain Charles Chandler, 'to have charge of all matters pertaining to military ballooning, air machines and all kindred subjects', heralding the birth of American military aviation. The next step was to obtain a suitable 'heavier-than-air flying machine' that could be developed for military purposes. The US Army specified that it should be able to carry two airmen with sufficient fuel to remain in the air for 125 miles and be capable of flying at least ten miles at a speed of 40 mph. Three tenders were received but only the Wright brothers delivered an aeroplane for testing. During September 1908 Orville Wright demonstrated the Model B biplane to Army officers and Government officials at Fort Meyer, Virginia. On 17th September Lieutenant Thomas E. Selfridge of the Signals Corps was taken up as a passenger. The biplane suffered a propellor failure and crashed; Wright was seriously injured and tragically Lieutenant Selfridge became the first passenger to die in an aircraft crash. Nevertheless the conviction in powered flight and its potential for military use had not weakened. In August 1909, the Aeronautical Division obtained its first Wright biplane at the price of $25,000 plus a $5,000 bonus because it exceeded 40 mph! As a precursor of all those 'personalised' American Second World War aircraft, this aeroplane was later called *Miss Columbia*.

Over the next two years a number of Army personnel were taught to fly at the Wright brothers' school, but it was not until March 1911 that Congress approved the first funds ($125,000) specifically for 'the purchase of flying machines'. During April 1912 aeroplanes were used on US Army manoeuvres for the first time, and in March 1913 several aviators and aeroplanes moved to Galveston Bay, Texas, ready for possible service along the border with Mexico. They were provisionally formed into the First Aero Squadron, later officially established as an Army squadron at San Diego, California, where the Signal Corps Aviation School was formed. On 18th July 1914 the renamed Aviation Section of the Signals Corps was given full responsibility for all US Army flying, with 60 officers and 260 enlisted men and a budget of $250,000.

Military aviation and aircraft production in Europe was given a massive boost with the outbreak of war, whereas US Army flying lagged far behind; it then ranked 14th in the world. When the United States declared war on Germany on 6th April 1917, the Aviation Section had fewer than 300 aeroplanes, none of which could be considered suitable for combat, and merely 35 qualified pilots, with only seven squadrons.

Since March 1916 a number of American pilots had been flying in France with the French *Aviation Militaire* in a unit originally named the *Escadrille Américaine*, later changed to *Escadrille Lafayette*. These airmen pre-empted the volunteer American pilots that served in the three RAF 'Eagles' squadrons in World War II. In February 1918 the *Escadrille Lafayette*, as the 103rd Pursuit Squadron, was incorporated into the Aviation Section, which on 24th April was renamed the Army Air Service.

Although the US Government had boldly announced that it would build 40,000 military aeroplanes in one year, they never materialised and no American-designed aeroplanes flew in combat during the First World War. General Dunwoody, responsible for aviation procurement, remarked, 'We never had a single plane that was fit to use'! The nascent US aircraft industry concentrated on trainers, including the famous Curtiss *Jenny*. The British de Havilland 4 was built under licence in the States powered by the American Liberty 12 engine; the first 'Liberty' machine was completed in February 1918, but only 20% of 3,225 D.H.4s built in the US actually went to the Western Front; Handley Page 0/400 and Caproni night-bombers were also built under licence.

In September 1917 the Ist Aero Squadron arrived in France to serve as an observation unit, and in the following February the first US pursuit squadron, 95th, arrived in France. But the first to see action, on 3rd April, was the famous 94th Squadron, known as the *Hat-in-the-Ring* from its emblem. The legendary Captain Edward V. 'Eddie' Rickenbacker, the most famous and successful American pilot of the war, served in and commanded the 94th. At the end of May the Air

Katheleen – one of the 3,225 D.H.4 'Liberty' aircraft.

Service was separated from the Signals Corps and gained, albeit briefly, a small measure of autonomy.

Perhaps the most influential American airman of the war was Colonel William 'Billy' Mitchell, who, in May 1918, had been appointed Chief of the Air Service for the US Army's 1st Corps. In the previous year Mitchell had led the first American air patrol over the lines; he also planned and led bombing missions and even organised the first large aircraft operation, almost 1,500 American and French aircraft – fighters, bombers and observation – bombing and acting as support for ground troops. In October Mitchell was given operational command of all the US air units serving in France.

At the end of the First World War the Air Service had forty-five squadrons in France with almost 200,000 personnel of which some 800 were pilots. American airmen claimed 780 enemy aircraft, 73 balloons destroyed and 14 tons of bombs dropped in 150 raids, so although relatively late onto the scene, the Air Service had made its contribution. The Army speedily disbanded most of its aero squadrons and the immediate post-war years saw a considerable reduction in defence spending, and the Army Air Service suffered severely. Only twenty-seven out of the proposed eighty-seven squadrons were authorised and the Air Service was firmly back under the direct control of the Army, although recognised as its combat arm.

In the immediate post-war years Brigadier General Mitchell was the

General Mitchell standing before his DH-4B Airplane that he used in directing the bombing of the German warships off the Virginia Capes, July 1921. (Smithsonian Institution)

most vigorous and vociferous advocate for the creation of an independent air force after the style of the newly formed RAF, but he was bitterly opposed by Army and Navy chiefs. In 1921 Mitchell dramatically demonstrated the potential of aerial bombing when eight Martin MB-2 bombers destroyed the captured German battleship *Ostfriesland*, then considered unsinkable, along with two other warships in the Atlantic off the Virginia Capes; a most significant event in American military aviation.

Mitchell continued to voice his strong opinions but overstepped the mark in 1925, when he accused the War Department of 'criminal negligence and almost treasonable administration of the country's defence' over the loss of the Navy's airship, *Shenandoah*. Mitchell was court-martialled, found guilty and suspended from the Air Service for five years. He resigned his commission and American Army aviation had lost its most ardent and passionate champion and its foremost 'airpower strategist'. However, Mitchell's beliefs in 'strategic' bombing

Lt. Col. H.H. 'Hap' Arnold with a B.10 of the 'Alaska Flight'. (Smithsonian Institution)

were shared by a number of senior officers within the Air Service. Perhaps one of the most prominent was Henry H. 'Hap' Arnold, an ex-West Point infantry officer who had transferred to the Aviation Division in 1911 on obtaining his pilot's licence. Arnold lobbied Congress for greater funding for the Air Service and he was a powerful advocate for a heavy bomber force especially during the late 1930s.

In December 1925 a Special Board convened by the President rejected the idea of a separate air service but recommended that it should be upgraded to Corps status; with effect from 2nd July 1926 the Army Air Corps (AAC) was established with an Assistant Secretary of War for Air. A modest expansion programme over five years was planned – 1,800 aircraft and 17,500 officers and men – although it would be twelve years (1938) before the target was achieved. The majority of aircraft within the Air Corps were training and observation aircraft, only seventy-six were pursuit fighters and fewer than sixty bombers. The control of training and operations of the Air Corps was still resolutely held by the ground forces.

By the early 1930s the accepted doctrine of air-warfare, in Europe and America, was that the future of air-power lay in the employment of

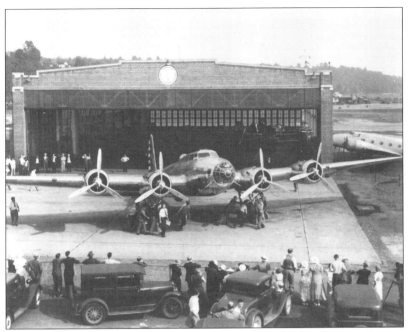

Model 299 at Boeing Field, Seattle – 17th July 1935. (Boeing Business Services Company)

an all-powerful bomber force with fighters playing a minor role. The precept that 'the bomber will always get through' became the fundamental principle within the AAC; one senior officer maintained 'a well-planned and well-conducted bombardment attack, once launched cannot be stopped.' This dictum was taught at the Corps' Tactical School at Maxwell Field, Alabama and especially in its Tactical Bombardment Section. It was here that the cherished concept of long-range heavy bombers with strong defensive armament, organised in large formations, became central to American air strategy, which would reach its apogee with the Eighth Air Force. In 1933 Brigadier General Oscar Westover, who became Chief of Army Air Corps two years later, even proposed that pursuit fighters should be abandoned because of their recent poor performance in air manoeuvres!

In 1933 forty-eight B-10A twin-engined bombers were ordered from the company founded by aviation pioneer, Glenn L. Martin. They were of all-metal and mid-wing construction with enclosed cockpits, retractable landing gear and internal bomb-carrying capacity. In the

B-17s 'intercepting' the Italian liner Rex, 776 miles at sea – 12th May 1938.

(National Archives)

following summer ten left Washington to fly to Alaska and then returned to participate in Army exercises. By the time the 'Alaska Flight' was completed, the US Continent had been spanned four times and over 18,000 miles had been flown in close formation without a major incident; a striking demonstration of the strategic bombing concept. The Flight Leader was none other than Lieutenant Colonel H. H. Arnold!

Two years later, in July, the B-17 flew for the first time in the guise of 'Model 299', and in 1937 the first B-17s entered the AAC with the 2nd Bomb Group. These aircraft would also show their potential when, in May 1938, three 'intercepted' the Italian liner *Rex* when it was over 770 miles from New York. Earlier in the year six B-17s had flown to Buenos Aires and covered over 12,000 miles without any mishap. The future of this aircraft was assured, as indeed was the concept of a long-range bomber force.

There was a major advance for the AAC in March 1935, when the War Department established a General Headquarters Air Force with Brigadier General Frank M. Andrews as its first Commander. He reported to the Army's Chief of Staff and was responsible for all the training and operations of the air force. Three years later, because of the deteriorating political situation in Europe, President Roosevelt wanted to strengthen the country's air defence, which he considered 'totally inadequate'. The AAC then comprised just 14 Groups with some 2,100 aircraft, and 21,000 personnel plus another 3,200 in the Air Reserve. It was not until April 1939 that Congress agreed to a maximum total of 5,500 aircraft for the Air Corps. A group of officers, led by Lieutenant Colonel Carl A. Spaatz, was given the task of planning the expansion, which became the impetus for the rise of US Army aviation to its ultimate position of pre-eminence.

From the outbreak of the Second World War the AAC used the time wisely, making sound preparations for a future involvement in the air war. Technical developments such as an excellent aircrew oxygen system and superchargers to boost engine performance especially at high-altitude had been introduced, and considerable investment had been made into the 'wonder' Norden bombsight. Many senior officers had spent time in the UK to observe RAF operations. Back home training facilities were reorganised and greatly increased to cater for the planned massive influx of airmen.

On 21st June 1941 the AAC was renamed the Army Air Forces, as a new autonomous Army Division with Major General Arnold as its first commander. He exerted a powerful influence on the USAAF in the

Second World War and guided the US strategic bombing offensive of Germany and Japan. By the end of 1941 the USAAF comprised 67 Groups (although many were in the process of being formed) with over 354,000 personnel. Since 1940 it had been provided with over 23,000 aircraft by a rapidly developing aircraft industry. Undoubtedly it was now far better equipped and prepared than it had been two years earlier. Its complement of B-17s had grown considerably from a mere handful in 1939, and the other heavy bomber, the B-24, was well into production. Many of the USAAF's famous wartime aircraft entered the Service during 1941.

The growth of the USAAF during the Second World War was dramatic in the extreme and nothing short of meteoric. By 1944 it had become the most powerful air force in the world, with over 2.4 million personnel and a front-line strength of some 24,000 aircraft, with the massive B-29 Superfortress as a symbol of its might and awesome power. This accelerated rise of American air-power to a position of unassailable dominance had been achieved in barely three years.

On 7th December 1941 Pearl Harbor was attacked and four days later Germany declared war on America; as Winston Churchill famously remarked, 'The United States was in the war, up to the neck and in to the death.' The USAAF would fight alongside the RAF in all theatres of war but it would face its harshest test in the daylight skies over Europe. Just three days after Pearl Harbor the first USAAF mission of the war was flown, when five B-17s attacked Japanese ships near Vigan in the Philippines. However, its first famous air-strike came on 18th April 1942 when Lieutenant Colonel James H. Doolittle led sixteen B-25 Mitchells from an aircraft carrier to make a spectacular low-level attack on Tokyo. It would be another four months almost to the day before the Eighth Air Force's B-17s took to the air in anger.

I
THE EIGHTH
AIR FORCE

In just two years the Eighth Air Force developed from a mere handful of aircraft and airmen to a massive and powerful force of heavy bombers and fighters, described by one USAAF General as 'the greatest striking force the world has ever known'. Even allowing for a certain hyberbole the number of heavy bomber squadrons ultimately operating in the Eighth was over double that available to RAF Bomber Command. The Eighth richly deserved its label 'Mighty', not solely on account of its sheer size but also because of the many valiant and determined operations it mounted, sometimes at a great loss of men and machines.

The Eighth was one of sixteen separate air forces that formed the USAAF during the Second World War. Not only was it the largest, but it served in the European Theater of Operations (ETO) for the longest period. The Eighth suffered harshly for its time operating in 'The Big League', as the American media was fond of describing the ETO. Half of the USAAF's total casualties occurred in the Eighth, its losses at certain times were said to be as high as the infantry and they were more than the entire US Marine Corps in the Pacific.

Its origins can be traced to the dark days of December 1941. Less than three weeks after 'the Day of Infamy', as President Roosevelt memorably called the Japanese attack on Pearl Harbor, Churchill and Roosevelt met in Washington, DC for the first time as war leaders. From 23rd December until early in the New Year they and their military advisers 'discussed all questions relevant to a concentrated war effort'. Decisions taken at this *Arcadia* Conference had far-reaching implications for the future conduct of the war, and none was more

The 'Mighty Eighth': B-17s of the 303rd over Molesworth. (USAF)

decisive than the announcement that the US Government would treat Germany as 'the *first* and most dangerous enemy'.

The first step would be the build-up of US forces and material in the UK under the code-name *Bolero*, in preparation for an Allied cross-Channel assault on Hitler's *Festung Europa* (Fortress Europe) in late Spring of 1943; the projected operation would be known as *Round-Up*. The establishment of the Eighth in the UK can be directly attributed to these vital decisions taken in Washington.

On 8th January 1942 the War Department activated the establishment of US forces in the British Isles (USAFBI), including a USAAF Bomber Command; the first US ground troops landed in Northern Ireland on 26th January. Meanwhile on 2nd January the Fifth Air Force was established to act as the air support for a projected Allied landing in French North Africa – *Gymnast* – another decision to come out of *Arcadia*. However, four days later the embryonic Air Force's number was altered to the Eighth because the three air forces operating in the Philippines, the Caribbean and in Hawaii were redesignated the 5th to 7th respectively. Thus on 19th January the new force was constituted as the VIII Bomber Command and nine days later activated at Savannah Army Air Base in Georgia under the command of Colonel Isa N.

Daws Hill Lodge, High Wycombe: the Headquarters of the Eighth. (Buckinghamshire County Council)

Duncan. Within weeks the VIII Bomber Command found itself without a specific purpose when *Gymnast* was shelved because of a worsening situation in the Pacific. At this stage General Carl A. Spaatz, the designated overall Commander of the 'American Air Force in Britain', proposed to General Arnold that the VIII Bomber Command should now form the basis of the USAAF in Europe. It was by this somewhat circuitous route that the Eighth became established in the UK.

The initial steps were taken to prepare the way for the establishment of the first USAAF units to serve in Europe. In February a coterie of USAAF officers under Brigadier General Ira C. Eaker were sent to the UK, specifically tasked with the acquisition and preparation of suitable airfields and installations, to advise on the equipment and deployment of USAAF units, as well as the operational training programmes necessary for service in the ETO. They were instructed to liaise closely with RAF Bomber and Fighter Commands and more especially to study Bomber Command's operational methods.

Eaker, with six fellow officers, arrived at Hendon on 20th February. They had flown across the Atlantic via Bermuda to Lisbon and from thence directly to England in a Douglas DC-3 transport. Within days Eaker and his staff were accommodated in RAF's Bomber Command headquarters at Walter's Ash near High Wycombe whilst a permanent home was sought. The Air Ministry secured a country mansion, Daws

Hill Lodge, which had recently housed Wycombe Abbey Girls' School; it was conveniently situated about five miles away from Bomber Command headquarters. On 15th April Eaker and his fast growing staff moved into Daws Hill Lodge, which became the VIII Bomber Command headquarters, code-named *Pinetree*.

Eaker was not the most senior USAAF officer in the UK at that time. He reported to Major General James E. Chaney, who had headed the US Army's Observer Group in London since its formation in May 1941, and had recently been appointed the commander of USAFBI. Sadly the General's Aide, Lieutenant Colonel Townsend Griffis, can be considered the first USAAF airman to lose his life on active duty in the ETO; on 15th February 1942 he was a passenger in a RAF transport aircraft that was shot down in error by friendly fighters. The Eighth's headquarters at Teddington would become known as Camp Griffis.

On 20th March Eaker submitted a comprehensive report to General Chaney on all the problems involved in establishing a large US Air Force from scratch. Chaney made some pertinent comments on Eaker's list of nineteen officers to augment his headquarters staff. He would have preferred 'officers more senior in age and rank', most 'had only pursuit experience rather than bomber', and many had come directly from civilian life with little or no military background. Chaney expressed his misgivings to Washington, but Eaker's nominees were appointed, and most arrived in early May.

In the light of Chaney's comments it is interesting to examine Eaker and his six initial officers. Eaker was aged 46 years and perhaps could be considered slightly young for such a senior command, furthermore he was a pursuit 'expert' having recently commanded the 20th Pursuit Group. His right-hand man, Lieutenant Colonel Frank A. Armstrong Jr was a 'bomber man' and would lead the Eighth's first heavy bomber operation. Both Captains Frederick Castle and Beirne Lay Jr would later command Bomb Groups. Castle, Major Peter Beasley and Lieutenant Harris Hull had been executives in the aircraft industry prior to the war; Hull would later become the Senior Intelligence Officer at the Eighth's headquarters. The previous experience of the seventh officer, Lieutenant William Cowart Jr is not known. So perhaps there was a certain validity to General Chaney's comments at least as far as Eaker and his initial staff. Although it should be noted that General Arnold later stated that he selected Eaker to lead the VIII Bomber Command because he wanted him 'to inject the aggressive pursuit spirit into his bomber force'!

Despite Chaney's views both Eaker and Major General Spaatz, who

*Major General Carl A. Spaatz and Brigadier General Ira C. Eaker at Polebrook –
December 1942. (via M. Green)*

in early May was formally appointed the Commander of the Eighth,
were utterly dedicated to the USAAF's policy of daylight strategic
bombing. Both men had spent time at the Air Corps Tactical School and
had been strongly influenced by the experience and its doctrine.
Perhaps not surprisingly considering the small Army Air Corps of the
1920s/30s, Spaatz and Eaker were well acquainted. They had been
members of the crew of *The Question Mark*, an AAC aircraft which, in
1929, had set an endurance flight record of 150 hours. Their close
working relationship would greatly help the Eighth through its first
faltering steps and early development.

In early April Eaker was aware he was preparing the way for the
Eighth, known as 'The Winged Eighth' because of its insignia. The

22

original planned build-up was not only ambitious but quite staggering in its immensity. It would comprise four Commands – Bombardment, Fighter, Ground-Air-Support and Composite – with a complement of 60 Combat Groups, made up of 33 Bombardment (Heavy/Medium/Light) of which 17 would be heavy, 12 Fighter, 8 Transport and 7 Observation; all units to be in place by April/May 1943. This would comprise over 220 squadrons containing some 3,500 aircraft

The 'Winged Eighth'.

along with multifarious units to support this massive force. At this time the *raison d'être* of the Eighth was to give air support for the projected invasion of Europe under *Round-Up*.

Although this original blue-print was not realised due to changes in the war situation in the Pacific and North Africa, and a changed role for the Eighth, it was nevertheless a herculean and daunting task that faced Eaker and his staff. The Eighth owes a huge debt of gratitude to Eaker for his drive and determination in not only establishing it in Europe but also for his purpose and courage in guiding and directing it through its testing and painful period of growth.

During May the VIII Fighter Command was established with Brigadier General Frank O'D. Hunter appointed its first Commander. His headquarters were based at Bushey Park, Watford not far from RAF Fighter Command's headquarters at Bentley Priory. Hunter was another First World War 'veteran', who during 1940 served as Assistant Air Attache in Paris, and after escaping from France witnessed the Battle of Britain first-hand. Hunter, nick-named 'Monk', was described as 'a handsome, swashbuckling playboy ... fond of parties, women and fishing' but whether his extrovert personality helped to establish a close working relationship with his opposite numbers in RAF Fighter Command is open to conjecture! Perhaps more than Eaker he needed harmonious accord because until March 1943 RAF Fighter Command held the planning and operational control of his meagre fighter forces.

From the outset Eaker formed a strong and close working relation-

Brigadier General Frank O'D. Hunter at Bushey Hall – June 1943. (USAF)

ship with RAF Bomber Command. He based his own headquarters structure closely on that at Southdown (the Command's headquarters), which eased and facilitated the exchange of information and the co-operation between the two staffs. With hindsight Eaker can be seen as an ideal choice to introduce the USAAF into the UK. He was a soft-spoken Texan with a reserved and reticent manner, belying the British pre-conceived image of the brash and outspoken American. Eaker was unfailingly courteous and proved to be a fine ambassador for his young Air Force. He also gained the reputation of a calm, efficient and very determined commander.

Senior RAF officers expressed the gravest doubts about the USAAF's proposed daylight bombing operations, as Bomber Command's costly operations with unescorted bombers back in 1939/40 had forced the change to night-bombing. The brief but unhappy experience of No 90 squadron with Flying Fortresses in 1941 only added to their misgivings. One senior officer expressed the hope that 'the flower of America's regular Army Air Force is not to be squandered on a type of operation that our experience would judge unwise.' It was felt the American aircraft would be better used in assisting Coastal Command in their battle against the U-boats!

Despite harbouring such strong doubts the RAF and the Air Ministry nevertheless gave full co-operation and help to the USAAF to get its fledgling Air Force into the action. Precious airfields were handed over, experienced airmen were detached to USAAF units to help with operational training, and intelligence officers were trained by the RAF and allowed to question crews returning from operational missions. USAAF airmen trained with RAF operational squadrons; it was almost Lend-Lease in reverse. Eaker was fulsome in his praise and appreciation of the assistance he had received: '[they] have co-operated one hundred per cent in every regard ... they have housed and fed our people, and they have answered promptly and willingly all our requisitions ... allowed us to study their most secret devices and documents ... We are extremely proud of the relations we have been able to establish between our British Allies and ourselves ...'

A close working relationship grew up between Eaker and his counterpart at Bomber Command, Air Chief Marshal Arthur T. Harris, who had recently been appointed its new AOC-in-C. Harris, recently returned from a spell in Washington, was well acquainted with many senior USAAF officers, and fully understood and appreciated their different methods of operations but nevertheless he too harboured serious reservations about their efficacy. He was well aware and sensitive of the Eighth's needs and gave Eaker his utmost support. The two commanders became personal friends, which augured well for the combined Allied bombing offensive of Germany. Both were convinced of its ultimate success and they worked towards the goal of 'round the clock bombing', although it was rarely achieved.

On 18th June General 'Tooey' Spaatz arrived in London and set up his headquarters at Bushy Park, Teddington, code-named *Widewing*. He was a First World War airman, a pursuit pilot with three enemy aircraft to his credit and had previously held staff appointments in Washington, where his administrative skills proved vital in the rapid expansion of the Army Air Corps. Spaatz was quiet and very reserved, taciturn with a strong dislike of public speaking. His manner was curt and direct but he became one of the finest air commanders of the Second World War, as his subsequent successful military career proved. With his arrival it could be said that the Eighth was at least up and running, if not quite in business yet – all it needed now were the aircraft and the airmen to fly them!

Also in June another senior US Army officer arrived in the country to take command of what had been renamed ETOUSA (European Theater of Operations US Army) – Major General Dwight D. Eisenhower;

Chaney had returned to the States to command the First Air Force. General Arnold in Washington informed Spaatz that Eisenhower should 'recognize you as the top airman in all Europe', and on 21st August Spaatz was given the added responsibilities of Air Officer for ETOUSA and head of the air section of Eisenhower's staff. General Eisenhower would leave for North Africa and Operation *Torch* in November, and indeed Spaatz would accompany him.

It would be difficult to find four senior Allied air commanders more committed to an all-out bombing offensive; Harris and Air Chief Marshal Sir Charles Portal, the Chief of the Air Staff, were in complete accord on the use of the RAF's growing force of heavy bombers now being augmented by Lancasters. However, there was a sharp dichotomy between the two Services on the methods to be used; in simple terms, daylight as opposed to night-bombing and specific industrial targets against 'area bombing'. Only days before Harris had taken command of Bomber Command, Portal, with Churchill's blessing, had given Bomber Command the green light for 'area' bombing. Whereas Spaatz and Eaker were completely convinced and determined that the USAAF could wage a successful daylight bombing offensive directed solely against 'strategic' targets.

Back in the summer of 1941 the Air War Plans Division of the USAAF had produced its plans (AWPD/1) for such a bombing offensive, listing 154 'strategic' targets in primary or intermediate importance – aircraft and light-metal industries, electric power plants, transportation centres and petroleum and synthetic oil industries – and in its early days the Eighth would use AWPD/1 (later amended to AWPD/42) as its *vade-mecum*. The two USAAF Generals were confident that the Eighth possessed the right heavy bombers, well equipped technically to operate at high-altitudes, which would mitigate most of the enemy's anti-aircraft batteries. They believed that these strongly armed bombers flying in close formations would be able to counter the Luftwaffe. Furthermore they had a complete faith in their crews' ability to achieve accurate and precise bombing with the aid of the Norden bombsight. There was perhaps also a 'hidden agenda' in the USAAF's determined prosecution of daylight strategic bombing: if indeed the Eighth succeeded with this policy then a strong case would have been proven for the establishment of an independent US Air Force. However, it was readily accepted that this bombing strategy was as yet theoretical and both men had to wait patiently until the middle of August before the theory would be tried and tested in combat conditions.

2
THE AIRFIELDS

Of all the tasks facing General Eaker and his staff on arrival in the UK, none had greater priority than the acquisition of airfields, not only for operational and training units but also to provide bases for the supply of materials and the maintenance and repair of aircraft. This demand came at a time when the Air Ministry was already stretched providing new airfields for a burgeoning RAF. Ultimately 92 airfields would be used by the Eighth, albeit some only briefly; additionally several units also 'lodged' at a number of RAF airfields.

During 1941 valuable initial work and negotiation on airfields had already been undertaken by the US Special Observers Group in London, and as a result, in November, the Air Ministry tentatively assigned eight new bomber airfields to the USAAF, most nearing completion. A number of sites in Northern Ireland had been considered because there were plans in hand for the USAAF to provide fighter cover for the shipping lanes into north-western ports. With the agreement of the Ministry of Aircraft Production two sites for the supply, maintenance and repair of aircraft had been ear-marked for the USAAF – one in Northern Ireland and one in Lancashire. The Lockheed Aircraft Corporation, which was already operating an assembly plant at Speke near Liverpool for the RAF, was asked by the US Government to develop the site in Northern Ireland. Langford Lodge, a large country estate on the banks of Lough Neagh would become the Eighth's first base air depot. It was one of eleven airfield sites in the Province allocated to the USAAF, though only seven were ultimately used – mainly for operational training. The other depot site at Warton near Lytham St Anne's was first occupied by the USAAF in June 1942. However, due to a likely delay in its final completion, Burtonwood near Warrington was approved for joint USAAF/RAF occupation as a base air depot; but in May it was transferred to the USAAF and became the largest military base in Europe with over 18,000 officers and men.

In late January 1942 the Air Ministry was notified that the first four heavy Bomb Groups for the Eighth were scheduled to arrive in the UK during the Spring. In the event these Groups did not arrive but nevertheless the original eight bomber airfields were allocated for their occupation. This was based on the provision of two airfields per Group because each comprised four squadrons and RAF bomber stations normally housed two heavy squadrons. In practice this division of a Group between two airfields proved to be unsatisfactory and the policy was quickly changed in favour of a single airfield for each operational Group.

The eight airfields were planned to accommodate units of a new Bomber Command Group, No 8, which was swiftly disbanded, although it would reform in August as the famous Pathfinder Force. Chelveston, Grafton Underwood, Kimbolton, Little Staughton, Molesworth, Podington, Polebrook and Thurleigh were situated to the north of Bedford and the east of Northampton, an area that saw the inception of the Eighth's strategic daylight bombing offensive. Little Staughton would be used as a strategic air depot for the 1st Bomb Wing, which established its headquarters at Brampton Grange, Huntingdon, mainly because the airfields had been provided with a communications network based on Brampton Grange. In May new airfields at Bovingdon and nearby Cheddington were also handed over; both were close to Eaker's headquarters at High Wycombe. They would become involved in operational training and operate as Combat Crew Replacement Centers (CCRCs). Bovingdon became a high profile base, used as a major staging post for aircraft arriving from and leaving for the States, as well as testing and trialling technical improvements for its Fighter Command.

By the end of May a major decision had been made; it was deemed that East Anglia was the most appropriate area to accommodate the planned expansion of the Eighth. It was considered sufficiently distant from Bomber Command's heavy squadrons, mainly based in Lincolnshire and Yorkshire. Thus the 2nd Bomb Wing would set up its headquarters at Ketteringham Hall, Norfolk and the headquarters of the 3rd Bomb Division would ultimately be based in Suffolk. Early in June another 36 airfields were allocated to the Eighth and most of the bomber stations were situated in East Anglia. In total the Eighth occupied 53 airfields in the region, so it is not surprising, considering the number of RAF airfields also in the area, that an American pilot maintained, 'I guess if you just switch off and glide in you'll find you're more likely to have gotten on an airfield than any other place'!

On 10th August the Air Ministry released a further list of 65 possible airfields and sites, of which 36 were ultimately used by the Eighth. Ten were RAF fighter airfields largely in the West Country but their allocation was rescinded in favour of existing fighter stations in East Anglia – Coltishall, Debden, Duxford and Wittering along with their satellites. However, only Debden and Duxford, both famous Battle of Britain airfields, would be transferred to the Eighth.

By the end of September 1942 the airfields used operationally by the Eighth during the war had been effectively decided and sealed save for minor amendments. Eight were established pre-war RAF stations, of which probably the most notable were Bassingbourn, Honington, Martlesham Heath and Wattisham. A number had been built during the early war years and were already occupied by RAF units, but the majority were either in the throes of construction or merely approved virginal sites. A list of the operational airfields used by the Eighth Air Force can be found at Appendix A.

In August each allocated airfield or site was given an official USAAF 'Station Number'. Those in the 100 range were for designated bomber stations whereas fighter stations were numbered in the 300 series. This station number appeared on all official reports and correspondence. It had been the Air Ministry's practice to name a new airfield from the nearest village or the parish in which it was situated, but there were some exceptions, most notably in the case of Great Saling in Essex. Shortly after its official opening in April 1943, the name was changed to Andrews Field in memory of Lieutenant General Frank M. Andrews, a celebrated US airman who had recently been tragically killed in a flying accident over Iceland. The term 'field' was universally used for landing grounds in the United States. Andrews Field was the only British wartime airfield to be named after an airman.

The development of airfields during the Second World War was a monumental construction project on a massive scale, possibly the most ambitious ever undertaken in such a short time – well over 400 were built. At its peak, in 1942, one third of the construction industry was dedicated to the operation, and the airfield building programme received top priority in the allocation of scarce manpower resources, often to the detriment of the clearance of bombed buildings and sites. Most of the well-known names in civil engineering were engaged in the immense enterprise, as well as hundreds upon hundreds of small sub-contractors. Each wartime airfield cost on average £1 million, and in

US Engineers (Aviation) at work on an airfield in Essex – September 1943.

1942 alone £145 million (probably equivalent to some £3½ billion in today's values!) was expended on new airfields and improvements. The US Government contributed £40 million in total, really a drop in the ocean considering the total wartime expenditure on airfields – estimated at over £600 million.

From the summer of 1942 the severely hard-pressed construction industry was assisted by eighteen battalions of the US Aviation Engineers. They were allotted fourteen airfield sites, all but one allocated to the USAAF; nine would be used by the Eighth. The first airfield to be completed by US Aviation Engineers was Great Saling and the last – Birch, also in Essex – was ready in the Spring of 1944.

Once the legal formalities had been completed, hundreds of building workers moved in to camp alongside the site, bringing their large earth-working equipment, heavy tractors, lorries and cement mixers. Roads in the area were either clogged with heavy traffic or closed; some would not reopen for the rest of the war. The peace of the rural countryside was utterly shattered, especially when the work carried on day and night, such was the urgency. The average construction period was twelve months and during that time the conditions for local residents were most uncongenial. Many later recalled that it was their worst experience of the war.

Aerial view of Station 167 – Ridgewell in Essex. Hard standings in the foreground.

For months the surrounding area resembled a battleground; land was flattened, trees removed (usually with explosives), hedges uprooted, ditches and hollows filled in, trenches were dug for water mains, sewerage pipes and telephone lines. In no time at all the site would become a sea of thick mud. One American engineer remarked, 'where there's construction, there's mud; and where there's war, there's mud and where there's construction and war, there's just plain hell'! Another remembered the conditions at an airfield site in Essex as, 'mud, rain, leaky tents, rain and more mud, along with nightly air-raid alerts'.

The first real construction work was the provision of a concrete perimeter road. Normally fifty feet wide with thirty feet each side levelled and cleared of obstructions right around the extent of the airfield, this road or 'track' could stretch for three miles or more to give access to the aircraft dispersal points, more generally known as hard standings. These were of two types – 'frying pans' or 'loops', and most of the Eighth's bomber airfields would have up to fifty loops built in linked clusters.

They were part and parcel of what was known as a Class A Standard Bomber station layout. The main runway measured 2,000 yards by 50 yards wide with two subsidiaries, each 1,400 yards long, and normally with a cleared area of 100 yards at each end as an 'overshoot'. They were sited to be as near $60°$ to each other as possible, and invariably laid in the pattern of the letter 'A'. The main runway, where possible, was aligned to run from south-west to north-east. By 1942 virtually all runways were constructed of concrete. However, at several of the Eighth's fighter stations where grass airfields had been inherited, several types of 'temporary' metal runways were laid down to cope with the heavy P-47 fighters. Sommerfeld Track, Pierced Steel Plank and Square Mesh Track were used not only for runways but also for taxi-ways and dispersal points.

Class A Standard airfields were normally provided with two T2 hangars. They had been developed and built by Tees-Side Bridge and Engineering Works and were of galvanised corrugated iron construction, specially designed to be simple and speedy to erect – 'T' stood for Transportable. The T2 hangar was 240 feet long with an opening span of $113\frac{1}{2}$ feet and a door height of 25 feet – formidable structures, many of which have survived to the present day.

But perhaps the most recognisable feature of any wartime airfield was the watch-house or watch office, later universally known as the

A wartime control tower, built to a standard design.

Colonel C.B. Overacker takes over Thurleigh (Station 111) from the RAF – December 1942.

control tower. This was the airfield's nerve centre of air traffic control and was fully equipped with telephone lines, radio, radar and tele-printer apparatus, as well as housing the meteorological section. It was often sited on the inner side of the perimeter track or road, and by 1942 a fairly standard design had been developed; a functional and almost square two-storied building approximately 35 feet by 34 feet, constructed of brick and rendered with cement. The tower had a railed balcony in addition to railings on its flat roof, and many were provided with an external iron stairway. There are many poignant wartime film images of the balcony crowded with senior officers waiting in apprehension for the first sound and sight of the returning aircraft. Several of these wartime towers have survived at old Eighth Air Force airfields, some converted into offices or private houses, such as at Attlebridge, Lavenham, Little Walden, Podington, and Rackheath. Whereas some accommodate Memorial Museums, notably at Bassing-bourn, Framlingham, Seething and Thorpe Abbotts.

Close to the control tower and inscribed in large white letters was the airfield's unique identification code – two capital letters about 10 feet in size. These date back to pre-war days when it became the practice to display the name of the aerodrome in white letters sufficiently large to be visible from an altitude of about 2,000 feet. For security reasons this method was suspended during the war and the letter code was substituted. They became more commonly known as the 'Pundit Code' from the mobile beacon unit (known as a 'pundit') which flashed the airfield's code in red morse signals at night. With so many airfields clustered so close together in East Anglia, the pundit codes became an essential and speedy means of identification. The codes of most of the Eighth's airfields were self-evident – 'AY' for Alconbury and 'GU' for Grafton Underwood – although a few were not, 'UT' for East Wretham and 'JO' for Bungay, for instance.

The airfield required a vast number of administrative and technical buildings from the armoury through to the vehicle repair shops. Most were constructed of pre-cast concrete slabs – 'Orlit' and 'Maycrete' being the most prevalent, whilst others were built of light timber materials and plasterboard sheets. Many were protected from blast by exterior earth walls. The operations room was usually set aside from the main site, and was substantially constructed of concrete without windows to offer maximum protection. For the welfare of personnel there was usually a dental surgery, hairdresser, gymnasium/theatre, cinema, PX or Post Exchange store (the US equivalent to NAAFI) and a multi-faith chapel. The bomb stores, a series of narrow roadways protected by earth bankings, were positioned, if possible, in a wooded area away from the main buildings and technical site. Two large and partially underground aviation fuel tanks were placed adjacent to the perimeter road. The firing butts were normally sited by one of the loop hard standings and some distance from the main airfield sites.

A winter scene at Station 152 – Debach, Suffolk.

You have been warned! (USAF)

Behind the main airfield buildings and dispersed around the surrounding countryside were the accommodation huts, mess halls and clubs, communal sites, and sick quarters, grouped in separate domestic sites perhaps six to twelve in number. They afforded a spartan existence usually in the omnipresent Nissen huts in spans of 16, 24 and 30 feet. The Americans knew them as 'Quonsets', from Quonset Point, Rhode Island where they were first built in the States. These famous curved sheet constructions perhaps more than any other single feature epitomise wartime airfields. The design dated from the days of the First World War and they were the brainchild of a Canadian – Colonel Peter Nissen. The huts had a reputation for being oppressively hot in the summer and bitterly cold in the winter, their only form of heating being small coke stoves.

Because the sites were some distance away from the main airfield buildings and technical sites, bicycles were essential and highly valued, although many American airmen recall that during the winter especially, the constant presence of thick mud meant they spent more time carrying their bikes than riding them! One airman recalled that on an East Anglian airfield 'the raw and damp North Sea cold ... was nothing like we had experienced before. It cut through six blankets at night and we lay around the small coke stoves like wolves about a dying doe ...'! Several of the Eighth's airfields acquired nicknames, which reflected the mud, rain and harsh living conditions, 'Duckpond' for Duxford, 'Goat-hill' for Goxhill, and 'Grafton Under*mud*'!

The majority of the Eighth's airfields were planned to accommodate some 2,800 officers and men, which meant they would greatly outnumber the local residents. The airfields became established as 'Little Americas', enclaves of American life, customs and food comprehensively transferred into the English countryside. Living sites were given names to remind the servicemen of home, some tinged with a certain cynicism and black humour – such as 'Dodge City', 'Greenwich Village', 'The Alamo', 'Sun Valley', 'Tombstone', and even 'Alcatraz'! Certainly the 'Stars and Stripes' held sway in large areas of East Anglia and Eastern England.

Several airfields quickly acquired the reputation of being show places and were frequently visited by the 'Top Brass', politicians and the American and British press, in addition to a variety of celebrated show business people. These visits provided ample opportunities for publicity, which the USAAF encouraged far more than the Air Ministry; Captain Beirne Lay Jr, one of Eaker's original officers, was a very active Public Relations Officer.

Many of the Eighth's operational airfields have long since disappeared, reverting to farmland, and others have been turned into industrial estates. A few are still under the control of the Ministry of Defence, though not necessarily for their original use, and several are used for private flying or gliding. Some airfields have survived under a different guise, for instance Podington as Santa Pod for drag racing and, of course, Duxford, where the Imperial War Museum opened its American Air Museum in August 1997 – a splendid memorial to the USAAF in the Second World War.

3
THE AIRCRAFT

The B-17, flown by twenty-six Groups, really epitomised the Eighth Air Force during the war. They filled the skies over East Anglia, flying in close formations and indicating their presence with white contrails. Their design dated back to 1934 and was born out of a private venture by Boeing Aircraft Company. The prototype made its first appearance in July 1935 at a cost of $432,000, a large investment for what was then a relatively small company. A *Seattle Daily News* reporter dubbed the aircraft 'a 15 ton Flying Fortress', not because of its defensive armament but rather for its specific role in defence of the US coast against enemy vessels. This concept captured Boeing's imagination and 'Flying Fortress' became the registered name.

Despite its size – over 74 feet long and 19 feet high with a wing span of almost 104 feet – the sleek and slender design made it visually rather elegant, a marked exception to contemporary military aircraft. It was also the first all-metal four-engined military monoplane. The first of thirteen YIB-17s (the AAC's designation) was delivered to the Service in March 1937 and Major Barney M. Giles flew the initial operational trial from Langley Field; the B-17 legend was born. By July 1940 Boeing had developed a B-17C powered by four 1,200 hp turbo-supercharged Wright R-1820-65 engines and armed with seven .30 inch machine guns. Twenty were ordered for the RAF, specially fitted with self-sealing fuel tanks and .50 inch guns. They served with No 90 squadron as Fortress 1s, and commenced action on 8th July 1941 in a daylight operation to Wilhelmshaven. The Fortress experiment was not a success, eight were lost in action and accidents for just fifty-two operational sorties. One British air correspondent thought 'they might not be suited to operations in northern Europe'! The crews liked the aircraft for its handling qualities, its comfort and spaciousness. One

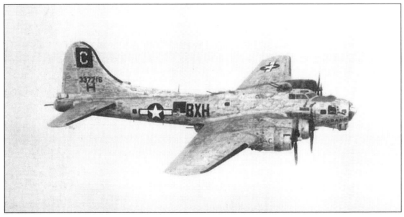

5 GRAND – the 5,000th B-17 off Boeing's production line and signed by all the workers. It completed 78 missions with the 96th Bomb Group. (via G. Ward)

pilot reckoned that it was 'a lady and a graceful and elegant one at that.'

As a result of the RAF's experiences, B-17s already on order for the AAC were modified with additional armour-plating and armament, self-sealing fuel tanks and a new bomb release system; they were designated B-17Ds. Boeing also completed a major redesign of the aircraft and the first B-17E flew in September 1941. Outwardly the most striking differences were the enlarged vertical tail surface to provide better stability at high altitude and the provision of one manual and two power-operated turrets, along with a tail gun position. Over 800 were ordered but after some 500 had been produced, the remainder were converted to B-17Fs.

The new model that appeared in April 1942 was similar in appearance except for a larger frameless Plexiglas nose and improved broad-blade propellors. Over 400 modifications had been made, notably an increased fuel capacity; the B-17F was the first to be mass produced with some 4,500 being built by Boeing, Douglas and Lockheed-Vega. The final version – B-17G – first flew in May 1943. It was provided with a Bendix twin-gun 'chin' turret in the nose section, to counter the Luftwaffe's destructive frontal attacks; subsequent models were powered by improved turbo-superchargers for their Wright R-1820-97 Cyclone engines. In total over 8,600 B-17Gs were produced, making it the most prolific model. The aircraft had a maximum speed of 302 mph at 25,000 feet, although it cruised at around 160 mph with a normal bomb load of 4,000 pounds. The B-17G perhaps deserved the name 'Flying Fortress' because of its formidable armament – eleven/thirteen .50 guns with twin mounts in the chin, top (dorsal), ball (dorsal) and tail turrets and single guns in both sides of the nose and the waist, with another in the radio room firing upwards.

Perhaps the B-17's greatest merit was its capacity to be regularly upgraded to maintain its currency. General Eaker considered it 'the best combat airplane ever built', and another famous USAAF General, Curtis LeMay, said, 'The Air Force grew up with the B-17. It was as tough an airplane as was ever built. It did everything we asked it to do, and it did it well.' Certainly 'Forts' or 'Big Ass Birds' inspired a tremendous loyalty and confidence in their crews. They were convinced that their 'ship' would get them back however severely damaged, and time after time the B-17 demonstrated its remarkable durability. Without doubt it was one of the classic bomber designs of all time and when production ceased in April 1945 over 12,700 had been built.

The Eighth's other heavy bomber, B-24, owed its inception to an AAC request, in January 1939, to Consolidated Aircraft Corporation for a design specification of a long-range bomber with a superior performance to the B-17. At the end of March a prototype of 'Model 32' was ordered with the proviso that it should be completed by the end of the year, and XB-24 first flew on 29th December. The aircraft was marginally smaller than its rival, except for its wing span, which was over six feet longer although the wing area was 26% less. The XB-24 had several unique features for a heavy bomber. It was the first to employ a tricycle undercarriage and its high wing aspect ratio was a new concept. The wing was designed by David R. Davis and was of a very slender section, which gave the aircraft its remarkable operational range.

The B-24 was not an attractive aircraft; its deep and slab-sided fuselage, allied to its large twin-tails appeared cumbersome. However, the AAC were pleased with the prototype and ordered seven YB-24s for trials. The French government had already ordered 120 straight from the drawing board but before they could be delivered France had fallen, so the Air Ministry took over the order and contracted for another 165. The first B-24A made its maiden flight on 17th January 1941 and had acquired the name 'Liberator' as a result of a competition amongst the workers at Consolidated's plant at San Diego. The first Liberators arrived in the UK in March and were diverted to transatlantic transport duties. Consolidated improved its defensive

B-24 of 389th Bomb Group, November 1944. (National Archives)

fire-power, and armour-plating was added, as well as self-sealing fuel tanks. The newly designated B-24Bs entered RAF service in June as Liberator Is in an anti-submarine role with Coastal Command, where their long operational range proved vital.

The first true bomber version was the LB-30 or Liberator II, of which there was no USAAF equivalent; its fuselage nose section had been slightly extended and Boulton Paul power-operated gun turrets installed in the mid-upper and rear fuselage positions. In June 1942 Liberator IIs were first used by the RAF as bombers in the Middle East; one, *Commando*, became the personal transport of Winston Churchill. Consolidated was already modifying the prototype B-24 for the USAAF and ultimately developed the B-24D. It had four 1,200hp exhaust-driven turbo-supercharged Pratt & Whitney R-1830-65 Twin-Wasp engines, was armed with ten .50 machine guns, and provided with a larger fuel capacity. In addition to its normal bomb load of 5,000 pounds, it could also carry two 4,000 pounds externally on wing ranks. The B-24D was the first model to be mass produced, mainly at San Diego and later with Consolidated-Vultee at Fort Worth; North American produced B-24s at Dallas as did Douglas at Tulsa, and Ford Motor Company built a special plant at Willow Run in Michigan.

The two major marks – H and J – were essentially the same but for details of equipment and minor differences associated with the production companies. The first of over 6,600 B-24Js appeared in August 1943. They were powered by four Pratt & Whitney Twin-Wasp engines giving a top speed of nearly 300 mph at 30,000 feet and a cruising speed of 200/215 mph. The ten .50 inch guns were located in the nose, upper, ventral 'ball' and tail turrets and in beam positions. By the autumn of 1944 two modified models – L and M – began to enter service with the Eighth. Both were attempts to lighten the aircraft and improve the weight distribution with changed tail armament.

At its peak the USAAF had over 6,000 B-24s in service, 25% more than its B-17 force. It was the most versatile American aircraft of the war and produced in greater numbers than any other – over 18,000. Besides its bombing and anti-submarine roles, the aircraft was modified as a transport carrier, fuel tanker and for photo-reconnaissance duties. Production ceased on 31st May 1945 and the B-24 passed quickly into aviation history as one of the outstanding American aircraft of the Second World War.

There was a keen debate in the Eighth as to which was the better aircraft. The B-24 was dubbed the 'Banana Boat' or 'Boxcar' by B-17 crews, or more harshly as 'the crate that ours came over in'! They also maintained that B-24s were 'the best escorts we ever had', on account of the heavier losses suffered, largely because of their lower operational altitude and the Luftwaffe's firm but mistaken belief that the B-24 was easier to set on fire. The B-24 airmen retaliated by calling the B-17 a 'Medium Bomber' or 'Grenade Carrier' and the 'Glory Bird' because of its lighter bomb load and the greater publicity accorded it. However, the fine operational record of the B-24 in its many varied wartime roles spoke volumes and really the aircraft required no defence.

Both bombers were equipped with the technical support for their high-altitude bombing role. They had an effective and generally efficient oxygen system, but the most famous item of equipment was the Norden precision bombsight. It had been first developed by Carl L. Norden for the US Navy in the early 1920s and after considerable development the Mark 15 had emerged. This greatly improved version was famously tested by the AAC in 1940 over Muroc Dry Lake in California's Mojave Desert with impressive results; thus the legend of the 'wonder' bombsight was born. It was claimed that bombs could be dropped into 'a pickle barrel' from as high as 20,000 feet! These results were obtained by hand-picked and experienced crews testing in the clear air of California, and not operating in the adverse weather and fierce combat conditions faced by the Eighth's crews in Europe.

A further advance was the Automatic Flight Control Equipment,

Flak Bait – B-26 of 322nd Bomb Group. It completed over 200 missions. (Smithsonian Institution)

which enabled the bombardier to take over flying the aircraft on the bomb run with the Norden bombsight connected to the aircraft's autopilot system. This gyro-optical sight had a timing device to indicate the precise moment to release the bombs. By late 1943 the Norden Mark 9 was the standard bombsight in the Eighth and considered to be far more accurate than the RAF's Mark XIV bombsight.

Briefly during 1943 the Eighth operated a force of medium bombers – Martin B-26 Marauders. The aircraft had first appeared in November 1940 in response to a specification for a fast and heavily armed medium bomber. It had sharp clean lines and was very streamlined, which led the press to name the aircraft 'the flying torpedo'. The AAC had been so impressed by the design specification that they ordered 1,100 directly from the drawing board, then a unique departure. The B-26 was a rather difficult aircraft to handle with its high landing and take-off speeds, and early into the training programme an alarming number of accidents occurred. As the accident rate rose steadily the aircraft gained the name of 'widow maker' or the 'Baltimore Whore' (Glenn Martin's plant was at Baltimore). The position became so grave that the AAC set up a Board of Enquiry to investigate the design, and production of the aircraft was halted. However, the Service retained its faith in the aircraft and with a number of design modifications, production was resumed.

When the first B-26Bs arrived in England in March 1943 they had already seen action in the Pacific and North Africa. They were powered by two Pratt & Whitney R-2800-43 Double Wasp engines, producing a maximum speed of some 280 mph, and a cruising rate of 195 mph. The bomb load had been increased to 4,000 pounds and its total armament to twelve .50 inch guns, although later this was reduced. Despite its early grim reputation the B-26 proved to be a most successful medium bomber with an amazingly low loss rate, and perhaps the aircraft never received the renown that it deserved.

The only American fighter to operate briefly with the Eighth during 1942 was the Lockheed P-38 or Lightning. This large twin-boom and twin-engined fighter was revolutionary back in 1937 when 'Model 22' was designed in response to a Service competition for a long-range interceptor fighter. The prototype, XP-38, first flew in January 1939 and the early trials were so impressive that the AAC placed an initial order, but because of development problems the first production P-38s did not appear until March 1941. One of its advantages was the operational range – about 450 miles – but it was also fast, in excess of 400 mph at

P-38 coming in to land after a mission over Germany. (via H. Brown)

43

P-47D of the 78th Fighter Group with a 'bubble' canopy. (USAF)

25,000 feet, and well-armed with four .50 inch guns and two .20 mm cannons. However, its Allison V-1710 turbo-charged engines proved to be temperamental and rather unreliable in the cold and damp air of northern Europe. Although a formidable fighter it did not make the same impact with the Eighth as it did in North Africa and the Pacific; its prowess in North Africa gained it the name, *Der Gabelschwanz Teufel* or the 'Fork-tailed Devil'!

The next fighter to serve with the Eighth, in March 1943, was the Republic P-47 Thunderbolt, which had originated in 1939 at the behest of the AAC for a lightweight interceptor. But the air battles of 1940 clearly demonstrated that any new fighter of merit would need to be more rugged and heavier in order to carry armour plating, greater firepower and self-sealing fuel tanks. Alexander Kartveli of Republic Aviation responded with an almost completely redesigned fighter – P-47B. It had a new engine – 2,000 hp Pratt & Whitney R-2800-21 Double Wasp with a turbocharger – and was almost twice as heavy as the original XP-47. In September 1940 an order was placed for 171 P-47Bs and 602 P-47Cs, the latter having a slightly longer fuselage to improve manoeuvrability.

This large, robust and heavily armed fighter became the workhorse of the USAAF and was variously described as the 'Jug' (Juggernaut), or 'Flying Milk Bottle'. Despite its bulk, the P-47 had a top speed in excess of 420 mph, a frightening rate of dive and was armed with eight .50 machine guns. It was capable of sustaining heavy damage, but its biggest drawback as an escort fighter was its limited operational range, although later improved with the use of drop tanks. Not only was it a most destructive fighter, but it also became a successful fighter/ bomber and ground attack aircraft, able to carry 2,500 pounds of bombs. The most prolific mark by far was the 'D', most of which were fitted with a teardrop moulded cockpit hood for improved rear vision. In early 1945 P-47Ms came into service with the 56th Group, as a high speed or 'sprint' version to counter the Luftwaffe's jet-fighters, perhaps the fastest airscrew-driven fighter in operation. The P-47 was built in greater numbers than any other American fighter – 15,683.

By early 1944 its thunder had been stolen by the North American P-51, ultimately operating in all but one of the Eighth's Groups. This fighter, destined to have such a dramatic influence on the European air war, owed its existence to the British Air Purchasing Commission in Washington. In April 1940 North American Aviation took up the challenge to design a new fighter for the RAF as a 'substitute' P-40 (Tomahawk), and in less than 102 days a prototype – NA-73X – was produced. In the light of its ultimate triumph over the Luftwaffe, it is ironic that its co-designer was Edgar Schmued, a German-born Austrian, who had previously worked for Fokker and Messerschmitt!

The British were most impressed with the design and specification; it had clean fine lines, an ideal cockpit layout, and good performance. An immediate order was placed and the first Mustang, as it had been named, arrived in the UK during October 1941 just a year after its maiden flight. At that stage the AAC had not taken a great interest in the new fighter as it was considered primarily to be of 'foreign design' and its pursuit budget was committed to the production of P-38s and P-47s; it had been supplied with a number of trial aircraft, which were designated XP-51s. The Air Ministry soon discovered that although the Mustang had an impressive speed at low altitudes, its performance fell away markedly at over 15,000 feet, thought to be due to its under-powered and 'asthmatic' engine – the Allison V-1710 – which was similar to that of the Tomahawk. Like that aircraft the Mustang did not fit the bill as an escort fighter and was also 'relegated' to reconnaissance and army support duties.

The salvation for the P-51/Mustang came in May 1942 when, as an experiment, Rolls-Royce substituted one of their Merlin engines for the Allison engine, which produced an all-round improvement in performance, especially at high-altitude. In the States the aircraft was being produced for the USAAF as a dive-bomber (A-36) and also as a tactical reconnaissance aircraft (F-6A) fitted with cameras. The USAAF followed suit and installed US-built Packard Merlin V-1650-3 engines into two P-51 airframes, and they were designated XP-51Bs. They were impressed with the aircraft's rate of climb and top speed and ordered almost 2,000 P-51Bs, most of which had a higher powered engine. These were built at the company's plant at Inglewood, California, with

P-51Ds awaiting delivery in late 1944. (San Diego Aerospace Museum)

an additional order for 1,750 to be produced at Dallas, which were provided with a British-designed Malcolm sliding hood and increased fuel capacity.

The most numerous was the P-51D; over 7,950 were produced, and it first appeared in November 1943. It introduced a teardrop canopy as standard, as well as a modified rear fuselage and six .50 inch machine guns, with a top speed just short of 440 mph at 25,000 feet. The P-51 ranked alongside the Spitfire as a classic fighter, Air Vice-Marshal J. E. 'Johnnie' Johnson considering it the 'finest combat fighter of the Second World War'. Over 14,810 P-51s were produced. They operated in the Korean War and were still in use with the National Guard in the States until March 1957.

The Eighth operated a number of British aircraft. On arrival in the UK the Air Ministry supplied its first aircraft – Airspeed Oxfords – for general communications duties. Besides Spitfire Vs that equipped its first Fighter Groups, a number of Mark XIs were allocated to 7th Photographic Group from October 1943. The 15th Bomb Squadron (Light) would be the first Eighth unit to go into action on 4th July 1942 with RAF Boston IIIs (or Douglas DB-7s). In April 1944 25th Bomb Group was equipped with de Havilland Mosquito PR XVIs. The Eighth's Gunnery and Tow Target Flights were originally equipped with Westland Lysanders to act as target towers.

A number of small American aircraft were used for communications, liaison and light transport duties. Many could be seen around the

46

operational airfields, where they were used by the Groups' staff officers. Amongst them were Beech UC-45s, Cessna UC-78 Bobcats, Piper L-4 Grasshoppers, Fairchild UC-61-A Forwarders and Noorduyn UC-64 Norsemans. Probably the latter two were the most numerous. It was in a UC-78, a Canadian-built transport aircraft, that Major Glenn Miller went missing in December 1944 on a flight to Paris.

Except for P-38s, the fighters along with the small transport and liaison aircraft were shipped across by sea. They would then be transported to either Warton (P-51s) or Burtonwood (P-47s) for processing and modification for service in the Eighth, prior to being transferred to the Groups. The bombers were flown across the Atlantic by their crews, either in complete Groups or more frequently as replacement aircraft. Two ferry routes were used – Northern and Southern. The former would take the crews from Presque Isle in Maine, to Goose Bay in Labrador, thence to Bluie West One in Greenland and on to Meeks Field in Iceland for arrival at Prestwick in Scotland. Some Groups would make a direct flight across the Atlantic from Gander Lake in Newfoundland – an eleven-hour flight of some 2,100 miles. The Northern ferry route could vary and if the crossing was made via Greenland and Iceland it totalled almost 3,000 miles, and was normally used during the summer months; all of the original Bomb Groups arrived by this route.

The Southern route was longer, taking the crews from Florida to Trinidad, then to Belem in Brazil before crossing the Atlantic to Dakar and/or Marrakesh. The final leg was for initial landfall in Cornwall, avoiding the Spanish and French air spaces for obvious safety reasons. Most of the B-24 Groups arrived by this route, because their assignment to the Eighth largely occurred during the winter of 1943/4. One B-24 pilot well recalled his first sight of England at the end of the long flight: 'as we approached we were given an unusual greeting ... out of nowhere I spotted two beautiful Spitfires on each wing, which escorted us to the nearest airstrip ... this was my first introduction to the fine English hospitality'! Considering the strain of these long ferry flights relatively few aircraft were lost *en route*, although a few Groups were unfortunate in losing a couple of crews on the way over.

When Groups flew across en bloc, the crews would ultimately fly their aircraft to their allotted operational airfield. The replacement crews would have to leave their brand new aircraft at air depots for the necessary modification work to be completed before delivery to Groups. When these crews then arrived at their appointed Groups they would usually find that they were allocated the oldest and most battle-scarred aircraft!

Besides the National insignia – a white five-pointed star on a dark blue disc with two white rectangles outlined in blue at either side of the blue rondel – the Eighth's aircraft carried a number of regulation markings. The aircraft's serial number appeared on the nose and was also emblazoned on the tail fin. Its radio call sign – a single letter from the phonetic alphabet – was painted on the tail fin in the case of bombers, but on the fighters' fuselages. From late 1942 Group and squadron markings were introduced for easier identification when flying in combat formations. Each Bomb Group was allocated an individual identification letter within the Wing (later Division) and this would appear in a geometrical shape on the vertical tail plane and upper right wing; for Groups in 1st Wing it was placed within a triangle, the 2nd in a circle, and a triangle identified the 4th. Most Fighter Groups, but not all, adopted group markings, usually plain or chequerboard colours emblazoned on the aircraft nosebands. Every squadron was allocated a two letter code, later some would have a letter and a number; these squadron codes appeared on the aircraft's fuselage normally to the left of the National emblem. Fighter squadrons would also carry different colour markings on the tail fins. The aircraft were now ready for action, but what opposition would they encounter during the next three years?

Bf or Me 109G – Gustav. (via J. Adams)

In their first forays over enemy-occupied territory the bomber crews had to contend with the Jagdwaffe, the Luftwaffe's fighter arm. It was organised into Wings – Jagdgeschwader abbreviated to JG – with a Gruppe (I,II,III ...) as the basic unit. The two main day-fighters were the Messerschmitt 109 and Focke-Wulf 190; both were single-seated and single-engined aircraft. The Bf or Me 109 dated back to 1939 when it was designed by Willy Messerschmitt for Bayerische Flugzeugworke (hence 'Bf'), which was later taken over by Messerschmitt. German records show both abbreviations but 'Me' will be used for ease of identification. The Me 109 was a quite amazing and formidable fighter that served with the Luftwaffe throughout the war in many variants, and maybe over 35,000 were ultimately produced. It was the aircraft's final major production model – the 109G or 'Gustav' – that first tackled the Eighth's heavies. The model began to appear in 1942 and had a top speed of over 420 mph at 24,000 feet. Armed with one Mauser MG151 cannon and two Bersig MG131 13 mm machine guns, it could also carry two 210 mm air-to-air rockets. By 1944 it was out-classed by the current Allied fighters, although in that year alone 14,000 were produced.

The Focke-Wulf 190 first flew in June 1939 and made its operational entry in September 1941, immediately demonstrating its superiority over the Spitfire V. It was the Luftwaffe's most potent day-fighter, more robust than the Me 109, and its pilots took a heavy toll of the Eighth's bombers especially during 1943. It was produced in over fifty variants and maybe some 20,000 were built, though no firm production figures have survived. The Fw 190A-8, which first appeared in early 1944, had a top speed just in excess of 400 mph and was armed with four MG151 20mm cannons plus two MG131 13 mm machine guns. Another version known as the *Sturmbock* or 'Battering Ram' was produced specifically as a bomber destroyer with extra armour and heavier cannons. These fighters would attack *en masse* and from close range. However, their increased weight meant that they were no match for American fighter escorts and they required their own escorts.

In January 1943 twin-engined German fighters entered the fray and they carried sufficient fire-power to destroy a heavy bomber. Hitherto these fighters had been mainly used for night-operations against RAF Bomber Command. The Messerschmitt 110 or famed *Zerstörer* or 'Destroyer' dated back to May 1936, and had taken quite a beating during the Battle of Britain. The Me 110G, armed with 30 mm or 37 mm cannons, could be most destructive, although it was vulnerable to US fighters. Its replacement the Messerschmitt 210 proved to be a dismal

Fw 190A-8 – Sturmbock or Battering Ram of IV. (Sturm)/JG 3. (via J. Adams)

failure, so Me 110s were produced beyond their 'sell-by-date'. Nevertheless, over 6,100 were built.

Faced with a shortage of day-fighters the Luftwaffe was forced to use other twin-engined night-fighters, such as the Junkers 88, probably the most versatile German aircraft of the war. The Messerschmitt 410 *Hornisse* developed from the unsuccessful Me 210, did make an impact as a heavy and well-armed day-fighter. The Me 410A-1 carried four MG151 20 mm cannons, two forward MG17 .31 inch machine guns and another two rear MG131 .51 machine guns. Although they had some successes against the Eighth's bombers, they suffered harshly at the hands of US fighters.

A concern for the Eighth was the appearance in July 1944 of the rocket-propelled Me 163B or *Komet*. It had a top speed of 590 mph but its main drawbacks were its short operational range and its unstable and dangerous fuel; fewer than 400 were produced and they made little impact on the Eighth's bomber formations. The same could not be said for the Messerschmitt 262A, *Schwalbe* or Swallow, the world's first turbojet-fighter. It was an impressive aircraft with quite devastating fire-power, and considerable speed advantage over the US fighters. Since it had first flown in 1941, its development had been dogged by technical problems and political interference – even as late as November 1943 Hitler ordered that it be developed as a 'Super-speed bomber'! It was not until late August 1944 that Me 262s appeared on the scene as bomber interceptors, and armed with four 30 mm MK108 cannons they were most destructive. Despite their speed advantage, a

Me 262B-1a. (via J. Adams)

number were destroyed in the air by the more manoeuvrable P-51s. In total 1,433 were produced and had they arrived earlier and in greater numbers, it is now accepted that they might have made some difference in the bitter battle for air superiority.

The bomber crews also faced anti-aircraft fire or flak (*Flieger-abwehr Kanone*), really their greatest fear and the reason why so many of the aircraft were named *Flak* ... They could only fly through it and hope and pray. Their fear was justified; during 1944 3,500 aircraft were destroyed by flak, some 600 more than fell to fighters. Although fighter attacks were frightening enough, at least the airmen could see their enemy and fight back. The light flak – 20 and 37 mm – came streaming up in the form of tracers, which was probably more spectacular than harmful, but the heavy and legendary 88 mm flak was lethal.

During 1944 when the Luftwaffe was being defeated in the air, flak batteries at the major targets in Germany were greatly strengthened. They were operated by *Würzburg* fire control radar. Their shells were time-fused and took about 25 seconds to reach the bombers, which by then had travelled some $1\frac{1}{2}$ miles, so the batteries had to predict where the formations would be at that time. As one young airman recalled, 'They always seemed to know where you were going – I don't know how the hell they knew, but they always did.' Often the crews met a constant and almost solid wall of hot metal – 'the flak was so thick you could walk on it.' On the Eighth's final bombing mission of the war, six bombers did not return, all victims of flak.

4
THE AIRMEN

The Eighth was a young Air Force in more senses than one; in late 1944 the average age of its bomber crews was twenty-one years with the air gunners invariably being the junior hands, many in their late teens. As a direct contrast their senior commanders and staff officers were by and large 'career airmen', having served for a number of years in the AAC and many were 'West Pointers', graduates of the famous US Army Military Academy. The Group Commanders were always called the 'Old Man' irrespective of age and normally held the rank of Colonel (Group Captain); they regularly flew alongside 'their boys', often leading the Group formation.

When the USAAF entered the war, unlike the RAF, it did not have a large cadre of qualified airmen to call upon. It did, however, have the Air Reserve but like the AAC itself, it was a relatively small force, with the result that the vast majority of Eighth airmen were civilians in uniform, who had volunteered for flying duties, and but for the war would certainly not have considered the USAAF as a career. They were from all walks of life, every level of society, and descendants of immigrant families from all corners of the world – 'a microcosm of America'. They came from farms, small and large towns and the big cities, representing every state and every creed. Workers from the land, offices, factories, shops, garages and schools joined actors, artists, musicians and cab-drivers, to name but a few, as well as college students and many direct from high school. Quite a number would gain fairly rapid promotion and would remain in the USAAF to make it their career.

With the rapid expansion of the USAAF, it faced a training programme on a massive scale, which, in under three years, produced 27,000 bomber crews and 35,000 fighter pilots – over 300,000 fully trained airmen! One American aviation historian has suggested that 'the bomber crews were, like their aircraft, a mass produced but quality product.' Certainly the USAAF produced qualified airmen at a prodigious rate but without doubt they were, like their RAF counterparts, thoroughly trained and well qualified for the demands placed upon them by the Eighth Air Force.

The principal source for flight officers – pilots and co-pilots, navigators and bombardiers – was the Aviation Cadet Recruiting Programme; this also provided candidates for the specialist ground officers. The other members of a heavy bomber crew – flight engineer, radio operator and air gunners – were 'enlisted men' or Sergeants, from Staff/Technical/First to Master. Although in July 1942 the grade of Flight Officer was established to enable enlisted men to qualify as pilots.

All airmen, whatever their flight category, passed through basic military and physical training courses before moving on to the various stages of flying training (primary/advanced and conversion) for pilots and specialist training for the other flight categories. All bomber crew members, other than pilots, undertook a gunnery course. On the successful completion of their respective courses, all would receive their silver 'wings'. The style of these coveted badges varied according to their flight category and they were, in the case of service in the ETO, mounted on a blue, rectangular patch to denote that they belonged to a 'combat crew'.

It was normally at the first phase base B-17/B-24 training that the ten airmen – pilot, co-pilot, navigator, bombardier, flight engineer, radio operator, and four gunners – first came together as a crew to begin to train and work as a close and co-ordinated team; although personnel might well change before the crew finally went into action. It was a general policy not to include more than two airmen from the same State in a crew.

Perhaps it could be said that in the early days the operational training was the one weakness in the USAAF's long programme. Indeed, one of the Eighth's early Bomb Commanders, Colonel Charles B. Overacker of 306th, voiced his opinion to Washington that inadequate operational training was the main cause of the poor bombing results during the winter of 1942/3. His Group experienced a torrid introduction to the air war in late 1942, and Eaker rather smartly removed him from his command on the grounds that he 'lacked the stamina for the hardships and rigors of war'! However, because of all the problems of providing operational training in the United Kingdom,

Cycles were essential at the bases. Ground crews ride along the perimeter track at Alconbury – May 1943. (Imperial War Museum)

mainly on account of the crowded air space and limited airfields, the School of Applied Tactics was established at Orlando, Florida. This was a massive combat training centre known as the 'War Theater' and the School greatly improved this aspect of the crews' flying training.

On arrival in the UK the fresh crews would spend time at one of the CCR Centers for instruction in the flying control systems and landing procedures used in the ETO as well as assembly and formation procedures. The fighter pilots were familiarised with the operational demands of the Eighth's Fighter Command at either Atcham or Goxhill. Even when the new crews and the fighter pilots finally arrived at their designated Groups, they would be engaged on a number of training flights – assembly skills, navigation exercises, simulated bomb runs and escape procedures – before they left on their first operational mission; these depended on the operational schedules of the Groups and the availability of crews and pilots.

Originally there was no prescribed limit to the number of missions to be flown by the crews and fighter pilots. However, in early 1943 Colonel Malcolm C. Grow, the Eighth's Chief Surgeon, considered that this situation was greatly adding to the stress suffered by bomber crews and was thought to be a major contributory cause of low morale. He recommended that matters could be improved by the introduction of a limit of 15 missions to comprise a combat tour. When more replacement crews began to be available in the spring of 1943, General Eaker directed that a combat tour would comprise 25 missions for bomber crews and 200 hours operational flying for fighter pilots. This change immediately offered the promise of ultimate relief from the treadmill of operations, that is if one was fortunate to survive 25 missions; during 1943 there was about a one in three chance of this happening.

In early April 1944 when the Eighth's losses had eased somewhat, the tour was extended to 30 missions. It was then calculated that the survival rate had increased to over 40%, although aircrew still only had a 33% chance of surviving without being wounded. During 1943 the Air Ministry estimated that the chances of RAF bomber crews reaching their tour of thirty sorties was 44%, and a second tour of twenty sorties as 20%. On completion of a tour the Eighth airmen would return to the United States to be deployed on training duties, although some stayed in the UK in staff posts. Relatively few volunteered for a second tour. Later in 1944 the combat tour was extended to 35 missions, and fighter pilots to 300 hours, on the premise that individual missions appeared to be getting less hazardous. Now because of the increased number of operations being mounted, a crew could expect, or at least hope, to return home within three or four months.

Each airman would be awarded the Air Medal after five missions and the Distinguished Flying Cross on completion of their tour. They would also automatically qualify for 'The Lucky Bastard Club'

Main briefing for the 467th Bomb Group at Rackheath. (via D. Hastings)

55

Publicity photograph of gunners in full operational gear. (USAF)

receiving an 'unofficial' certificate from the Group to prove that they had in fact survived in the 'toughest theater of air-war'. These certificates were greatly treasured by the 'lucky' airmen and were given pride of place in the home or office. One pilot later recalled, 'the euphoria when you hit the runway at the end of 30 missions, it was heaven ... sheer, sheer heaven. I remember thinking this was the beginning of the rest of my life.'

Equally most Eighth airmen also vividly remembered their first mission. The planning and logistics involved in mounting any bomber operation was a complicated affair. The crews, awoken at 3 am or even earlier depending on the selected target, would make their way to the mess halls for breakfast, usually fresh eggs (a rare commodity in wartime Britain), bacon, pancakes, fruit juice and coffee; although many later recalled that their nerves diminished their appetites. The ground crews had, since late the previous evening, been busy preparing the aircraft for the mission; testing engines, fuelling, bombing-up, checking the oxygen supplies, testing the gun turrets and cleaning the guns etc, a routine meticulously carried out for every mission.

After breakfast the crews would attend the pre-flight briefing. There they would be confronted with a large map of Europe covered by a black curtain. The 'Old Man' would be present to give his 'pep talk' before the Operations officer rather dramatically revealed the map showing a red ribbon marking the selected route to the day's target. The disclosure of their destination would either be greeted by groans if it was, say, Berlin or Merseburg, or cheers for a 'milk run' to a lightly defended target in France. Details of the formations, route, target, known heavy flak areas, weather etc were related by a variety of 'paddlefeet' – the term universally used to describe non-flying officers. At the end of the briefing there would be a synchronization of watches, before the individual members separated for their specialised briefings.

The crew later foregathered at the flight equipment store to collect their heavy flying clothes, body armour, Mae Wests (life-jackets), escape kits and parachutes. The bombardier would be issued with his bombsight. All personal effects and jewellery were required to be handed in, the airmen's only identification was the two 'dog tags'. The heavily laden airmen were transported to their aircraft at the hard standings perhaps an hour or less before the scheduled departure time. Each member completed a number of pre-flight checks and made a full inspection of their equipment. Many recalled that this tense period of waiting was the worst part of a mission. The firing of a bright two-star green flare from the control tower was the signal for the engines to be started, and according to the pre-planned order the aircraft would taxi along the perimeter track, to await the second green flare, the signal for the first aircraft to take-off, to be followed by the other aircraft at one-minute intervals.

Once airborne, the intricate assembly procedures were made into the prescribed combat formations. First squadron, then Group, followed by Combat Wing and ultimately into the Division formation, only then would the massive phalanx of heavy bombers head out at an altitude of 10,000 feet and climbing; from now onwards the crews would be on oxygen and their mission had begun. Perhaps some eight hours or so later, depending on the target and weather conditions, the crews would thankfully land back home. Trucks brought them back to hand in the bomb sight, machine guns, cameras, flight equipment and escape kits, before they were taken for a mission de-briefing. Sandwiches, dough-nuts, coffee or hot chocolate, along with whisky were readily available, whilst the Intelligence officers asked questions about the operation – the route, bombing accuracy, extent of flak, fighter attacks and any claims, also reports of any friendly aircraft going down and the number

Post-mission briefing. A bottle of whisky is close to hand. (USAF)

of parachutes seen. After the de-briefing the machine guns would be cleaned in the armament room before the crew was finally free to go for an evening meal. By now they had been awake for fouteen hours or longer but another successful mission had been completed.

High-altitude operational flying imposed considerable physical demands on airmen. Operating their aircraft and its equipment in temperatures ranging from -30°F to -45°F, depending on the season and the altitude, was rigorous and uncomfortable in the extreme. Sweat froze and turned to ice and icicles formed inside their oxygen masks, while frost-bite was common despite heated gloves. Their electrically-heated flying suits, known as 'blue bunny suits' were not particularly effective. Furthermore any movement imposed additional physical strain, especially as they were on oxygen and laden with all their heavy and cumbersome flight clothing. Most crewmen also wore an infantry steel helmet for protection against flak and metal splinters; it was later adapted with hinged ear protectors to allow the use of radio earphones.

Besides the physical rigours, there were all the additional anxieties and emotional stresses associated with operational duties and the ever-present thought that on this mission it would be 'their turn to buy it'. Assembly procedures where the margin of error was so slender, close formation flying often in unfavourable weather, enemy fighter attacks, and dreaded flak; as one crewman remarked, 'Five miles above the earth, there was no place to hide.' Then the return flight in maybe a

Armament personnel often painted bombs with personal messages – Bassingbourn 1943. (USAF)

damaged aircraft with the attendant fears of shortage of fuel, ditching in the sea or an emergency landing – all took a heavy toll on mental reserves. During 1944 the bomber crews were surveyed on their feelings about operational flying; 40% admitted to being 'frightened almost all of the time', with another 44% for 'most of the time'. The majority claimed that what kept them going was 'a sense of duty to America' and also a desire 'not to let their crew down'. Other than at periods of heavy losses at a Group level, the morale of the crews was usually fairly buoyant and their Commanders and senior officers strove desperately hard to maintain this standard. They continually stressed the discipline of close formations and 'the tighter you fly, the lighter you fall' became the guiding principle.

The airfields, which had become their home from home, were provided with as many American diversions and comforts as the sites and wartime conditions would allow – baseball, soft ball, basketball, movies, swing bands, and weekly dances. The 'clubmobiles' and US

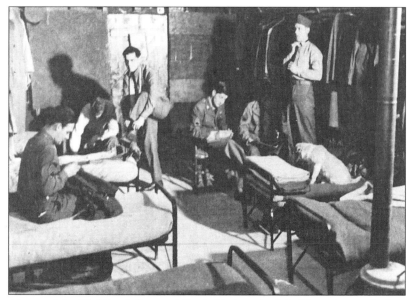

Airmen of the 93rd Bomb Group at Hardwick dress in their Nissen hut ready for a three-day pass. (USAF)

Red Cross wagons provided coffee and an endless supply of dough-nuts to remind the men of home. These were especially appreciated by the ground crews, who worked long and exhaustive hours, often in cold and difficult conditions to keep the aircraft flying. US Red Cross clubs in the local large towns provided American comforts and special celebrations for the traditional American holidays. Visits and concerts by show-business celebrities were notable highlights and a release from the stress of operations. A Group's important milestones – 100th, 200th or even 300th mission – were celebrated in style with a large party and a stand down from operations for a day or so. From July to October 1944 Glenn Miller and his famous AEF Band made an exhaustive tour of many Eighth Air Force bases.

There was the V-mail from home – letters photographically reduced to allow more to be carried by the limited air traffic from the States. The US Army produced its own newspaper *The Stars and Stripes*, which was avidly read. From July 1943 the US Army authorities, with the help of the BBC, created the American Forces Network mainly comprising recordings of favourite American shows sent over from the States. However, it was the local public houses, of which there was no equivalent in the States, that became the favourite place of recreation. These forays into the local countryside to sample 'the warm, flat and weak British beer' became known as 'low-level missions'! It was here that the two different cultures met. Many US servicemen used the 'Welcome Clubs', many were 'adopted' by local families and the Americans' kindness and generosity to local children, orphanages and hospitals was legendary.

Depending on the availability of crews, operational schedules and the British weather combat crews would usually get a break of a day or so before their next mission and every three to four weeks they were given a three day pass. This was usually spent in London at one of the numerous hotels and hostels. Nevertheless in spite of all these distractions, many showed the signs of combat stress or were known to be 'flak happy' – utter mental and physical fatigue, listlessness, memory loss, battle nightmares, lack of appetite and insomnia. Early on the Eighth's chiefs had acknowledged the problem and Colonel Grow had recommended the use of 'Rest Homes'. The first opened in January 1943 and by late 1944 there were fifteen. These were mainly old country houses where the airmen could go for a week of 'rest and recuperation' and relax in the peace and quiet of the English countryside. They were afforded a high standard of comfort, recreation and food; these homes were quickly dubbed 'Flak Houses' or 'Flak Shacks'!

Major Glenn Miller and his AEF Band.

A Christmas party for nearly 400 local children given by the 401st Bomb Group at Deenethorpe – 23rd December 1944. (National Archives)

The flight personnel were really the 'elite' of every Group and probably numbered less than 20% of the Group's strength. To get them into the air and to keep their aircraft fully maintained and serviced, involved a large number of officers and airmen of a wide variety of trades and categories. This was besides all the other necessary personnel needed to keep the Group and airfield running effectively and safely. These airmen went under the general name of the 'ground echelon' and they had come across the Atlantic by boat, the majority arriving either on the *Queen Elizabeth* or *Queen Mary*, their passage having taken perhaps five to six days. Most of the ground echelon would remain in the United Kingdom for the duration of the war.

The Eighth's aircraft, be they bombers or fighters, were very efficient mass-produced war machines, and their crews and pilots felt the need to personalise their 'ship' to make it special to them. The pilot, who was the crew commander, normally had the right to endow the aircraft with a name, which was illustrated on the nose of the aircraft. This 'nose art' of the Eighth has become famous and John Steinbeck described it as, 'The best writing of the war'. Cartoons, insignia, and many portraits were depicted but the most notable and eye-catching examples were those of scantily clothed females in a variety of poses, some of which were sexually quite explicit; just how much largely depended on the attitude taken by the Commanding Officer. Mostly the paintings were copies of the pin-ups by George Petty and Alberto Vargas that appeared in the *Esquire* magazines and calendars.

Many paintings were of a high standard, their quality depending on the artistic talent available at each airfield. Perhaps the most famous 'nose art artist' was Corporal Anthony L. Starcer of 91st Bomb Group at Bassingbourn. His artistic output was quite prolific and included such famous B-17s as *Memphis Belle, General Ike, Yankee Doodle* and *Nine O Nine*. Various combat positions on B-17s and B-24s also carried the names of wives, girl-friends, towns and states. A bomb symbol to represent each successful mission would be stencilled on the nose of the aircraft along with any enemy aircraft destroyed. Fighter pilots also added a swastika for each accredited victory.

It was fully recognised in the USAAF that operational service in the ETO was the hardest, but also the 'most glamorous' of all the theaters of war. Air Chief Marshal Harris later acknowledged the young Eighth airmen as 'the bravest of the brave'; and they were awarded the highest number of bravery and gallantry medals of any US Air Force. However, there was a strong belief in the RAF that American airmen received medals 'along with their rations'. This was a fallacy, but it was a fact that over 41,000 DFCs and some 122,000 Air Medals were awarded to members of the Eighth, which might suggest that the USAAF was perhaps more liberal in this respect than the Air Ministry. These medals were for 'extraordinary achievement in aerial combat'. Above these in prominence were three decorations for special acts of heroism – the Medal of Honor, Distinguished Service Cross and the Silver Star. The Medal of Honor was the American equivalent of the Victoria Cross and whatever may be said of the American distribution of minor awards, the MOH was certainly not bestowed lightly. Only 37 were awarded to airmen during the Second World War; seventeen were bestowed on Eighth airmen and ten of these posthumously.

Every member of the Eighth was utterly convinced that his own Group was 'the damn'd finest fighting unit in the whole of the Eighth'. Each Group had its own individual badge, as did most of the squadrons; many are on display in the Imperial War Museum at Duxford. Quite a few of the Groups adopted unofficial names, for example the 56th Fighter Group was known as 'The Wolfpack', 44th Bomb Group as 'The Flying Eightballs', 303rd Bomb Group as 'Hell's

Angels' and 92nd Bomb Group as 'Fame's Favoured Few'. This strong Group identity and pride can be seen in the number and strength of the various Group associations still flourishing in the United States. Often a Group's claim of superiority was justified by the award of a Distinguished Unit Citation (DUC). This highly prized commendation was awarded for a Group's meritorious performance on a single mission or a series of operations. Just sixty-six were awarded, so they were greatly honoured, and formally presented to the Group with full and due military ceremony. Only the 95th Group at Horham was awarded three DUCs, with several Groups receiving two.

The demand in America for information and news about the Eighth's operations and airmen was quite insatiable. The American public was well aware of the thousands of aircraft and airmen that were being sent across to the UK to fight over Europe. Really until D-Day, the Eighth was in the forefront and limelight of what has become known in the United States as the 'Good War'. Early on it was quickly recognised by the US Government that the brave exploits of the men and aircraft of the Eighth could provide a great boost to public morale and the war effort in the States and they could also be used to promote and increase the sales of War Bonds.

The USAAF also appreciated the promotional and propaganda value of their expert fighter pilots, especially those accorded the title 'ace' for five positive victories in air combat; ultimately 261 of the Eighth's airmen were acknowledged as 'aces'. This term dated from the days of the First World War and was first introduced by France quickly followed by Germany and Britain. However, it is the heavy bomber crews that have provided the lasting and most potent image of the Eighth Air Force at war. They were seen to represent an almost idealised cross-section of young American manhood operating closely together as a team – providing a PR dream scenario! This abiding impression was first, and probably best, captured by William Wyler in his fine wartime documentary film, *The Memphis Belle*, later given further impetus by *Twelve O'Clock High* and other films and books.

These young airmen arrived in the UK with a confident sense of purpose and strong determination, utterly convinced of the superiority of their aircraft, equipment and the might of the USAAF. This belief can be partly attributed to the inherent self-confidence of US servicemen generally; but more especially it had been largely fostered and bolstered by reports in the American media, which had somewhat exaggerated the Eighth's successes, and had been economical with the truth over its losses of men and machines.

The plaque in honour of Lt. Col. Lewis 'Lew' E. Lyle in the memorial garden of the Mighty Eighth Heritage Museum at Pooler, Georgia.

This young Air Force was probably best captured by Major General Lewis E. Lyle, himself a celebrated Eighth commander. 'They came out of the wheatfields, the factories in the cities. They were guys just off the streets. Some of them only had a few weeks training, a few months at the most. As soon as the commander said "I think you can make it", they sent them out.' And so these young airmen 'went out' and many of them never returned, and those who did return, soon realised that they were involved in a harsh and very brutal war, far, far different to that portrayed by the media back home in the States.

5
YANKEE DOODLE GOES TO WAR

The manner in which the Eighth Air Force finally went to war might be considered a bit of an anti-climax and certainly low-key. It went into action not with its vaunted B-17s but rather with RAF Boston IIIs. Nevertheless the day itself could not have been more appropriate – 4th July 1942, Independence Day; the USAAF later maintained that it was a 'symbolic mission'.

The six Bostons were manned by American crews of the 15th Bomb Squadron (Light), which had arrived in the UK on 13th May, based first at Grafton Underwood and then Molesworth. The squadron had been part of the 25th Bomb Group but had remained in the United States when the Group was posted to the Philippines in late 1941; the original intention was for the 15th to move to Britain and train as a night-fighter unit, but this role changed to one of daylight intruder bombing. Since the squadron's arrival in England the crews had been training under RAF guidance.

In late June nine crews moved to Swanton Morley to work alongside airmen of No 226 squadron. Captain Charles C. Kegelman and his crew flew the Eighth's first bombing sortie of the war when, on the 29th, they accompanied eleven RAF Bostons to marshalling yards at Hazebrouck in northern France. On 4th July six crews joined six RAF crews in a bombing attack of four airfields in Holland. The Bostons set off in four flights, each with an experienced RAF crew in the lead. At De Kooy airfield intense flak was encountered and one Boston crewed by American airmen was shot down in flames, whilst another, flown by Captain Kegelman, was severely damaged but he brought the aircraft back on a single engine. Another two, one with an American

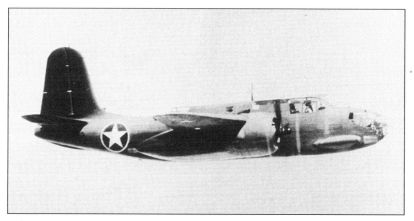

F for Freddie – DB-7 of No 15 Bomb Squadron (Light).

crew, also failed to return. It was not an auspicious start but the RAF airmen admitted that it was the 'worst flak' they had experienced.

The operation resulted in the award of the first American decorations in the ETO – three DFCs and a DSC for Captain Kegelman, who would lose his life in 1944 whilst serving in the Pacific. Another joint mission was made on 12th July to Drucat airfield; all twelve Bostons arrived back safely. The Squadron began to receive its own DB-7Bs and when the crews next went into action – 5th September – their aircraft carried the famous American white star.

Meanwhile other Groups were making their way across the Atlantic. The first B-17E of 97th Bomb Group landed at Prestwick on 1st July and the rest followed to occupy their new homes at Polebrook and Grafton Underwood. P-38s of 1st Fighter Group also made their way across 'the Big Pond' to settle into Goxhill. It was the 'elite' pursuit unit of the USAAF, able to trace its origins back to May 1918. The other P-38 Group, 14th, arrived at Atcham towards the end of July, but these fighters required certain modifications, delaying their entry into operations. The 31st Fighter Group was already at Atcham but without its P-39s (Airacobras) and the pilots were converting to Spitfire Vs. The 52nd Group, also to be equipped with Spitfire Vs, would not arrive at Eglington in Northern Ireland until August.

The second Bomb Group, 301st, was on its way; its first B-17s landed at Chelveston on 9th August. This airfield had recently housed C-47s (Douglas Skytrains) of 60th Troop Carrier Group, which along with the other C-47 Groups, 62nd and 64th, would not serve operationally with the Eighth, moving to North Africa in November. The 92nd Bomb Group, also equipped with B-17Fs, made the first direct Atlantic crossing on 12th August and was initially based at Bovingdon. The forces were gathering and the Eighth was slowly becoming a reality rather than just a 'paper' Air Force.

Spitfire Vs of the 31st first went into action on 26th July, when six pilots joined RAF squadrons in a fighter sweep from Biggin Hill. Lt Col Albert P. Clark was shot down and taken prisoner. During the next few weeks, the Group, under RAF stewardship, would fly *Rodeos* (fighter sweeps to entice the Luftwaffe into the air), defensive and convoy patrols from RAF airfields in south-east England. On 9th August Major Harrison Thyng in *Mary-James* was engaged in the Eighth's first aerial combat when he damaged a Junkers 88.

The Eighth's daylight bombing offensive was confirmed by a Joint Directive issued in August: 'American day bomber forces under British fighter protection reinforced by American fighter forces ... will attack suitable objectives within the radius of British fighter cover'. The die had been cast.

The crews of the 97th were busy training to bring them up to operational readiness under their new Commander, Colonel Frank A. Armstrong Jr. On 1st August, *King Konder* overshot the runway at Grafton Underwood. It hit a lorry, killing its civilian driver; the first B-17 to be written-off due to accidental causes. Eight days later another B-17 was only fit for salvage after a heavy landing at RAF Church Lawford. A serious accident occurred on the 11th when a B-17 of the 303rd crashed into Llanthwadr mountain in Wales and all on board were killed. Three days later another B-17 was salvaged after a crash landing at Elveden in Suffolk. Four B-17s 'lost' without a bomb being dropped, just the first of many hundreds of heavy bombers that inevitably came to grief due to accidental causes.

Colonel Armstrong now had thirty-five B-17Es on hand with forty-seven combat crews, of which he considered about twenty-four were ready for operations. Missions had been planned for the 10th and 12th but were cancelled due to poor weather conditions; the north-west European climate was a constant bugbear for the Eighth throughout the war. The culmination of six months' patient build-up and planning came on 17th August when twelve crews were detailed for the Eighth's first heavy bombing mission to the Sotteville marshalling yards at Rouen. Another six would be sent out on a diversionary flight to Dunkirk and the Channel Islands as a feint for the main mission. The Eighth used this ploy of diversionary missions on many major

Yankee Doodle – B-17 of 97th Bomb Group – General Eaker flew in this aircraft on the Eighth's first heavy bomber mission. (USAF)

operations and new Groups often had their first experience in the ETO on such flights.

Twelve B-17Es left Grafton Underwood at 15.26 hours and the lead aircraft, *Butcher Shop*, was flown by Major Paul W. Tibbets, who would pilot the B-29, *Enola Gay*, to drop the first atomic bomb. Tibbets had Colonel Armstrong as co-pilot. The second flight of six aircraft was led by *Yankee Doodle* with General Eaker on board as a passenger. Only eighteen tons of bombs were dropped on or near the target from a height of about 23,000 feet and some moderate but accurate flak was encountered. The Luftwaffe made a token appearance, and a gunner, Sgt Kent West, of *Birmingham Blitzkreig*, claimed an enemy fighter destroyed, later classified as a 'probable'. The escorting RAF fighters claimed two victories but for the loss of two pilots. At about 17.00 hours all the B-17s arrived back safely, their return eagerly awaited by senior USAAF officers and representatives of the British and American press. The Eighth Bomber Command had successfully completed 'Mission 1'!

Euphoria greeted this first heavy bombing mission. It became front-page news in America and Eaker received a message from his friend 'Bomber' Harris: 'Congratulations on the highly successful completion of the first all American raid by the big fellows ... Yankee Doodle certainly went to town and can stick another well-deserved feather in his cap.' At a celebratory dinner at High Wycombe, Eaker tempered

B-17Es of the 92nd and 97th Bomb Groups. (USAF)

such praise with, 'We won't do much talking until we've done more flying. We hope that when we leave, you'll be glad we came.'

Two days later the Eighth made a contribution to Operation *Jubilee* – the ill-fated Dieppe landings. The 31st Group was involved in the massive air battle and during the day its pilots flew 123 sorties in eleven missions. Lieutenant Sam S. Junkin Jr shot down a Fw 190; shortly afterwards he ditched in the English Channel but was rescued. Eight Spitfires were destroyed with four pilots missing in action, but two victories were claimed. The 97th was given the task of bombing a major airfield at Drucat, the home of II./JG 26, an elite force dubbed the 'Abbeville Kids' by RAF pilots. The airfield was put out of action for a couple of hours and one RAF pilot engaged in escorting the B-17s reported that he 'watched some superb American bombing at Abbeville.' All twenty-four B-17s arrived back safely.

On 20th August twelve crews were dispatched to the Longeau railroad yards at Amiens. All but one bombed through moderate flak and all survived. The crews were now becoming a trifle confident, three missions had been completed without loss and no fatalities. Nevertheless the Eighth's chiefs were only too aware that their heavies had barely penetrated into hostile skies and the Luftwaffe had yet to come to terms with their formations. At this stage the Eighth's senior staff, along with the bomber crews, under-estimated the quality of the opposition.

The Wilton shipyards at Rotterdam were the target on the next day. The dozen B-17s were about 15 minutes late for their rendezvous with the escort fighters with the result that the Spitfires could only escort them halfway across. The force had been reduced to nine because three had developed mechanical problems and were recalled before crossing the enemy coast. Twenty or so Fw 190s attacked the small and ragged formation. The battle lasted about twenty-five minutes, and *Johnny Reb* (a veteran of Rouen) was severely damaged. The co-pilot was killed and Lieutenant Richard S. Starks, the pilot, seriously injured, but Lieutenant E. T. Sconiers, the bombardier, managed to bring the stricken aircraft down safely at Horsham St Faith. The rest returned with the gunners claiming seven fighters destroyed, later reduced to two and five 'probables'. It would appear that B-17s could operate in daylight and still hold their own against the Luftwaffe fighters. Eaker and his staff at Pinetree could feel quite satisfied with the outcome, although it was still very early days.

A greater concern was looming on the horizon for General Eaker. Only the day before (20th) the Twelfth Air Force had been formed and activated in the States to act as the air support for Operation *Torch* – the Allied invasion of North Africa. Soon its combat units would arrive in the UK and the Eighth would be required to prepare and train them. Within the next month or so the Twelfth increased in size, although it would be dubbed 'Junior' by the Eighth's airmen. It was given the priority of aircraft, crews, spares and training facilities, largely to the detriment of the Eighth. 'You can't have that; it's for Junior,' became a standard catch-phrase. Eaker later ruefully commented that the Twelfth was a bigger worry to his Air Force than the Luftwaffe!

In the last week of August four missions were mounted; the crews

Spitfire VB of the 309th squadron of the 31st Fighter Group. (USAF)

were sent to shipyards at La Trait, then Rotterdam, before attention was directed to Aviens Potez, a major aircraft depot at Meaulte. Finally on the 29th, Wevelghem airfield at Courtrai in Belgium was attacked, and on this occasion Spitfires of 31st joined the large fighter escort. In these missions forty-eight bombers had been dispatched but the accuracy of the bombing was erratic; no B-17 had been lost but then the Luftwaffe had been conspicuous by its absence.

Due to operational training problems Eaker was forced to convert one of his precious Groups, 92nd at Bovingdon, into a operational training unit or CCRC, although it was still called upon for some missions over the next month or so. The 92nd relinquished its new B-17Fs to the 97th and in return received their older and battle scarred B-17Es. September was a significant month for the Eighth. It suffered its first bomber losses in action, managed to dispatch over fifty B-17s on a mission, and its complement of B-17s almost reached two hundred. It would also effectively lose, at least on paper, the majority of its operational units to the Twelfth. However, it was not quite all doom and gloom – the first B-24s of 93rd Group arrived during the month, P-38s entered the fray along with Spitfires of 52nd Group, and the Eighth was allocated the newly formed 4th Fighter Group.

Weather intervened in a mission planned for 3rd September, but two days later the crews returned to Sotteville rail yards. The force was augmented by twelve B-17s of 301st Group making their debut; also twelve crews of 15th Bomb Squadron returned to the battle with their DB-7Bs, attacking the port of Le Havre. There were no losses on the day's operations. The following day (6th) airfields at Abbeville and St Omer were attacked by B-17s and DB-7s, whilst the main force of fifty-one B-17s of 92nd and 97th made a second strike on the air depot at Meaulte, with the 92nd flying its first mission. The Luftwaffe opposed the formations continuously from the French coast, and one of 97th's B-17s was shot down. Lt Clarence C. Lipsky and his crew were the first to be lost in action; he and five of his men were later reported as POWs. A B-17E from 92nd ditched in the Channel for the total loss of its crew. These losses created some despondency. As one pilot recalled, 'Now at last the war was a bloody reality for all of us.'

The Rotterdam shipyards were attacked on the 7th, or at least by four out of twenty-nine crews – five bombed Utrecht and the rest had responded to a recall signal. The Luftwaffe was in action and severely damaged a B-17 from 97th, and although it staggered back to Polebrook, it was salvaged – the first as a direct result of enemy action. The Eighth was now removed from operations in order to concentrate on the organisation and training of the units of the embryonic Twelfth Air Force. Two B-17 Groups, 97th and 301st, were formally allocated to the Twelfth along with the Fighter Groups, although they would continue to operate with the Eighth for the next six weeks. The three Groups were active with fighter sweeps, and on the 22nd Major Thyng shared in the destruction of a Junkers 88 off Selsey.

Towards the end of the month the Eighth was released from its training commitments and returned to operations. On 26th September forty-five B-17s were sent to Maupertus airfield at Cherbourg and Poujean airfield at Morlaix, with the 92nd flying a diversion. It was a futile mission, the Cherbourg force was recalled because it could not locate its escort, and the 97th failed to bomb because of cloud and navigational errors. An uninspiring performance despite almost three weeks break from operations. In four missions over two hundred and ten bombing sorties had been flown of which less than half were effective. However, two new Groups, 93rd and 306th were engaged in training flights and would be available in October.

On 12th September the 4th Fighter Group was allocated to the Eighth. It was made up from the three RAF 'Eagles' squadrons, Nos 71, 121 and 133, which mainly comprised American volunteer pilots. They were transferred to the USAAF to become the 334th to 336th Squadrons respectively. A premier fighter airfield – Debden in Essex – was earmarked for the Group and the pilots would, for the present at least, retain their Spitfire Vs. The RAF squadrons were formally handed over at Debden on 29th September by the head of Fighter Command, Air Marshal Sir W. Sholto Douglas, in the presence of Generals Spaatz and Hunter. He said, 'We of Fighter Command deeply regret the parting. In the course of the past eighteen months we have seen the stuff of what you are made. We could not ask for any better companions with whom to see this fight through to the finish ... We shall watch your future with confidence.'

The pilots were given the option of remaining with the RAF or transferring to the USAAF and most opted for the latter. They were allowed to retain their RAF 'wings', which were worn on the right side of their new uniforms with their US 'wings' on the left. Perhaps the most marked change for them was financial. As Pilot Officers they had received $76 a month, now as 1/Lieutenants they would be paid the princely sum of $276! General Hunter would later tell them, 'You will never know what it meant to us to receive a group of fully trained operations pilots. You have formed a nucleus around which we have built our fighting machine'. From the end of October until the middle of April 1943 the 4th, known as 'The Eagles', was the only Fighter Group operating in the Eighth.

Only three bombing missions were mounted during October due to unfavourable weather. On the 2nd the 15th Bomb Squadron flew its final mission with the Eighth, when twelve DB-7Bs attacked shipping in Le Havre without loss; in mid-November it left for North Africa. Over forty B-17s returned for the third time to Avions Potez depot at Meaulte; in the escort were P-38s of 1st Group and one pilot failed to return. A small B-17 force had flown a diversionary mission to Longuenesse at St Omer and was outnumbered by twenty-three Spitfires of the 4th, making its first appearance with the USAAF; an auspicious day as four victories were claimed, the first of over five hundred in the air. The Group was led by Wing Commander Raymond M. Duke-Woolley, DFC, Bar, a most experienced RAF pilot, who greatly assisted the Group during its pioneer days. He was later appointed RAF Liaison Officer at the Eighth's headquarters, and was the first RAF airman to be awarded the American DFC.

Time was passing for Eaker to utilise the two experienced B-17 Groups before they left for North Africa. Two targets at Lille offered the opportunity for a large bomber strike – the Ateliers d'Hellemmes engine and carriage works and the Compagnie de Fives steel and locomotive plant. According to official sources they were targeted because of their accessibility (about forty miles south-east of Dunkirk) and the enemy's known shortage of railway rolling stock. Eaker was able to call upon 108 heavy bombers – an impressive effort considering only seven weeks previously just a dozen B-17s had taken to the skies. Sadly this total would not be bettered until April 1943.

On 9th October this relatively large force, augmented by two 'freshmen' Groups, 306th and 93rd, the latter with B-24s, left for Lille. In the event only sixty-nine crews bombed the primary targets and perhaps because of the inexperienced crews, the bombing accuracy was not impressive; many bombs fell outside the targets causing French civilian casualties. Less than half of the B-24 crews bombed, and they jettisoned their bombs over the English Channel on the return flight, which caused them to be derisively named 'Chandeliers' by certain B-17 crews!

The mission encountered fierce fighter opposition – as one gunner recalled, 'Lille was our first real air brawl'. Crews reported no fewer than 248 encounters with enemy fighters and four heavies were lost.

B-24 of the 93rd Bomb Group – the first B-24 Group to serve in the Eighth.

The 93rd lost *Big Eagle* near Lille, and another, *Ball of Fire*, although heavily damaged, made a safe emergency landing at Northolt. The operation was acclaimed in the British press as a great success, but the reports implied that the gunners' claims of fifty-eight aircraft destroyed and thirty-eight probables were rather exaggerated – 'typical American hyperbole' suggested one newspaper! Although the claims were later reduced to twenty-one destroyed and twenty-one probables, they were still well in excess of the actual Luftwaffe losses of two! In fairness it must be said the Luftwaffe were not always strictly accurate in recording their true losses.

The whole question of gunners' and fighter pilots' claims was to be a contentious issue for the Eighth throughout the war, although at this stage of proceedings it was not overly concerned. The very nature of the Eighth's air battles with close and large bomber formations resulted in many gunners claiming in all good faith the same fighter destroyed, and the speed and ferocity of the fighter attacks made accurate claims almost an impossibility. To add to the confusion some Luftwaffe pilots after attacking would turn their aircraft over and plunge straight down with smoke pouring from their exhausts; it was thought that some aircraft carried smoke pots under their engine cowlings to add to the illusion. Despite all the valiant efforts of the Intelligence officers to arrive at reasonably accurate figures, it is generally accepted that the gunners' claims were well in excess of the actual Luftwaffe losses. However, whether the claims were accurate or not, the numbers of

A ditched crew – happy at being rescued. (RAF Museum)

enemy aircraft thought to be destroyed did wonders for the crews' morale, *they* were convinced that they were making serious inroads into the Luftwaffe's fighter force, which helped them bear the losses of friends and colleagues.

Two B-17s had come down in the English Channel or 'the Ditch', which was described as 'the shortest stretch of water in the world when you're going out – the longest when you're coming back.' It was thought that a B-17 would float for about $1\frac{1}{2}$ minutes. During the war over 450 of the Eighth's bombers ditched and some 1,540 airmen were rescued, a survival rate of about 35%. On this day just one crew was rescued by a RAF Air/Sea/Rescue launch; the saving of the fortunate ten airmen of the 301st became the first successful rescue of an Eighth bomber crew.

Another operational hazard manifested itself on the Lille mission – the mid-air collison of friendly aircraft. Two B-17s of 92nd collided, both sustaining extensive damage. It was the first of over one hundred such incidents during the war, a harsh and costly penalty that had to be paid for the Eighth's dedication to tight formation flying, often conducted in poor weather conditions. Not only bombers but friendly fighters sometimes collided in the heat and fury of combat, indeed in November two Spitfires of the 4th collided and one pilot was killed. The two B-17s collided over the Channel about twenty miles from Dunkirk on the flight out; one crew coaxed their aircraft back to

Bovingdon and the other made an emergency landing at Detling. Both were fortunate as such collisions were usually fatal for men and machines. This was the last mission for 92nd until May 1943.

Despite the losses the operation was considered a moderate success, and it appeared to justify the policy of daylight bombing; indeed Eaker told General Spaatz that his crews 'could cope with the German day-fighters'! Over one hundred bombers had been dispatched, and some 160 tons of bombs dropped, intense fighter attacks had been faced without undue losses, and some serious damage had been inflicted on the enemy's fighter force. This conclusion was somewhat flawed in that the bombing was conducted in clear weather and in theory it should have been more accurate. Also the enemy's day-fighter force was still relatively small and had not yet devised the best tactics to deal with the massed firepower of the bombers. Finally, the Luftwaffe had suffered far lighter losses than the USAAF believed.

Again frustrated by unfavourable weather, before the Eighth's heavies ventured out again on the 21st, the goalposts had been moved. The previous day Brigadier General Asa N. Duncan, Chief of the Air Staff, issued a new directive: 'until further orders every effort of the Eighth's Bomber Command will be directed to obtain the maximum destruction of the submarine bases in the Bay of Biscay.' Thus throughout the winter it would be engaged in bombing the U-boat shelters at Brest, Lorient, St Nazaire, La Pallice and Bordeaux.

During 1942 the Battle of the Atlantic reached a critical stage, with the U-boats, now over two hundred, taking a harsh toll of the vital Atlantic convoys. RAF Bomber Command had made a number of ineffective attacks during 1941 and in early 1942 a night-bombing offensive was considered but the Air Staff doubted whether it would have much effect on U-boat operations. Furthermore there was a serious risk of heavy French casualties, which was thought to be politically 'unacceptable'. Thus the U-boat ports had escaped serious attacks and during this respite the TODT organisation had constructed massive shelters with twelve foot reinforced concrete roofs and eight foot thick blast walls, which were considered bomb proof and virtually indestructible.

The Eighth's first attempt to neutralise the U-boats was made on 21st October when Keroman, about eleven miles from Lorient, was the target. This entailed a flight of over 300 miles, and for much of the time the bombers lacked fighter escort. Ninety bombers were dispatched on a route taking them on a long sea flight over the Bay of Biscay to reduce the Luftwaffe threat. However, thick cloud at the bombing altitude of

22,000 feet precluded bombing and only fifteen B-17s of 97th found a break in the clouds; they carried on to the target, bombing at a height of 17,500 feet. Although the bombing was accurate, the small high-explosives inflicted only slight damage on the U-boat shelters. On return the formation was attacked by a force of Fw 190s and three B-17s were shot down with another two subsequently written-off – the heaviest Group loss so far. The 'veteran' crews had paid a high price for their determination, and it proved to be their swan song for the Eighth – their fourteenth and final mission. Over the next few weeks they would transport senior US Army and USAAF officers out to Gibraltar in preparation for Operation *Torch* before leaving to serve with the Twelfth.

At the end of October Spaatz informed Washington that because of the poor bombing results he planned to send in his bombers as low as 4,000 feet if necessary and would accept the expected heavy casualties as a result! Certainly over the next few weeks the bombing altitude was reduced but never as low as 4,000 feet. During November the Eighth bombed Brest, La Pallice, Lorient and St Nazaire, with the latter port coming in for special treatment on no fewer than five separate days, although not always as the primary target. Already seventy-five heavy flak guns were in place at St Nazaire and were ultimately strengthened to over a hundred making the port the heaviest defended area outside Germany, and fully justifying the name, 'Flak City', bestowed upon it by the Eighth; it became the bane of its crews in the coming months. As one gunner said, 'You always get good trouble over St Nazaire; they got postgraduates at them flak guns'!

During November the Eighth lost all its Fighter Groups, except the 4th, to the Twelfth Air Force, along with the experienced 97th and 301st; well might Spaatz rhetorically ask, 'What is left of the Eighth Air Force after the impact of *Torch*?' The answer was two B-24 Groups, 44th and 93rd, and four B-17 Groups, 91st, 303rd, 305th and 306th; the latter became known as the 'Four Horsemen' or the 'Pioneers' because for the next six months they would manfully lead the way and suffer harshly in the process. Soon Spaatz would leave for warmer climes to command the USAAF in North Africa, leaving Eaker in charge of the Eighth. The importance of the Eighth and its presence in Britain, however meagre its resources, was acknowledged on 13th November when HM King George VI made his first visits to a number of its airfields; a recognition of his country's appreciation of the American airmen engaged in the air offensive.

Eight operations were mounted in November, all but one to U-boat

B-17 of the 306th Bomb Group, Man O'War, named after a famous American racehorse. The aircraft was lost in action on 9th November 1942. (USAF)

bases, the busiest schedule since August. Four new Groups were 'blooded' during the month – 44th, 91st, 303rd and 305th, and for these inexperienced crews their baptism of fire could not have been much sterner. Brest was attacked for the first time on the 7th with the 91st and 44th crews joining the battle. 'The Ragged Irregulars' (91st) had a daunting time, five crews had to return early with their guns frozen solid, eight managed to bomb and although all its B-17s survived eleven were damaged.

Two missions to St Nazaire on the 9th and 23rd proved to be the most costly so far. For the Eighth's first attack on this 'infamous' target, the bombing altitude had been reduced to 10,000 feet with the last Group, 306th, coming in at about 7,500 feet and it lost three B-17s. Although the lead Group, 91st, did not lose an aircraft all were heavily damaged. The harsh experience of the port's flak batteries had been assimilated, and on the 23rd when fifty B-17s were in action over 'Flak City' they were back to 'four miles high', but they suffered at the hands of the Luftwaffe.

Hitherto the enemy fighters had mainly attacked the bomber formations from the rear, but on this mission their pilots made head-on frontal attacks. It had been decided that the American bombers were more vulnerable to such attacks because of their relatively weak nose armament and restricted field of fire. These new tactics are credited to Oberstleutnant Egon Mayer, the commander of III./JG 2. They were highly dangerous; with closing speeds of 600 mph there was a real risk of collisions and the Luftwaffe pilots had just a few precious seconds to sight and fire before pulling up and over the bombers. Two B-17s from 91st were shot down, another two were severely damaged and made forced landings in England; only one, *Quitchurbitchin*, managed to return to Bassingbourn. The 91st was particularly unfortunate in losing two squadron commanders in action. The 306th lost another aircraft, *Snoozy II*, and only three crewmen were seen to bail out; it was suffering a harsh time with seven aircraft lost in action, then the highest loss rate. One of its B-17s *Banshee*, piloted by 1/Lt William 'Wild Bill' Casey, went to the assistance of a damaged B-17 and suffered in the process; Casey managed to make it back to Thurleigh with claims of seven Fw 190s shot down in just twelve minutes. This was a record for a single heavy bomber and would remain so until well into 1943.

The 305th made its mark on this mission, and it was the only B-17 unit to escape unscathed. On the previous day it had been in action for the first time over Lorient but the crews had returned without bombing due to 10/10 cloud cover. It was commanded by Colonel Curtis E. LeMay, who became one of the most astute bomber tacticians and able commanders in the Eighth. He was a tough, brusque and most determined leader, known to his airmen as 'Old Ironpants' or 'Hard Ass'! Many of the innovations in bomber formations and bombing techniques were instigated by him. He instructed his crews to fly a straight course on the bomb run rather than weaving every ten seconds

H.M. King George VI visits Chelveston – 13th November 1942. (M. Smith)

or so in an attempt to avoid the flak, thus maintaining a greater speed and so minimising the time of vulnerability. Fourteen out of twenty crews managed to bomb, and strike photographs later revealed that they had been far more accurate than any other Groups. The 305th, which adopted the sobriquet 'Can Do', developed into a very effective fighting unit under LeMay's strong and positive leadership.

There was a break of thirteen days before the Eighth was able to launch its next mission; the weather had lived up to its 'evil reputation' and day after day operations had to be 'scrubbed'. Only four were completed in December. Two familiar targets were attacked on the 6th and 12th – Lille and the Sotteville marshalling yards. Even these were hindered by the weather, when heavy cloud over the targets reduced the bombing and four aircraft were lost. Conditions also frustrated the planned strike on a large aircraft park and repair depot at Romilly-sur-Seine to the south-east of Paris, but finally the forecast for the 20th was favourable.

The Eighth dispatched one hundred and one B-17s and B-24s from its five Bomb Groups (the 93rd had been detached earlier in the month for service in North Africa). Unfortunately nine B-24s of 44th Group were forced to abort because of failures with the oxygen systems and machine guns. Once over enemy territory the formations came under heavy attack from Fw 190s; one gunner recalled that 'sixty fighters ripped through our formation and made decisive hits.' Nevertheless over seventy crews managed to bomb the target with good results. On the homeward flight the Luftwaffe struck again and a total of six B-17s were shot down, three from the luckless 306th and two from 91st with a third crash landing in Sussex. The gunners originally claimed fifty-three 'kills', this was whittled down to twenty-one but actually the Luftwaffe lost only five fighters. This mission was quite a milestone for the Eighth. It had penetrated over one hundred miles into enemy airspace, 70% of the crews had bombed and they had fought off fierce and determined fighter opposition without escorts, at a loss rate of 6%. The accepted 'tolerable' or 'sustainable' loss rate in both RAF Bomber Command and the Eighth was considered to be 5%.

The final mission of 1942 was mounted on the 30th when U-boat pens at Lorient were the target. The 306th, which had suffered so harshly in recent weeks, was in trouble once again, most crews abandoning the mission before the start point thus weakening the whole formation. LeMay's Group experimented with another combat framework, opting for a basic three aircraft formation staggered within squadrons and further staggered into a total Group 'box' formation. To save involved bombing procedures, he introduced the concept of a lead bombardier with the rest of the crews releasing their bombs on his signal. In the early days of the Eighth the precise make-up of combat formations and bombing practices within a Group resided with its Commander. After considerable experimentation the Eighth introduced standard operational procedures.

About fifty fighters attacked and the 91st lost another squadron commander. The solitary remaining B-17 from 306th had tacked onto the 305th's formation and when it left the formation for no apparent reason, was set upon by enemy fighters and shot down. The crew bailed out but were then attacked by two Fw 190s and a B-17 of 305th went to their aid in an attempt to distract the enemy fighters, only to be also shot down. Lone bombers that had fallen out of formation stood little chance of survival in such hostile skies. Indeed crews were directed not to break formation to assist and defend a lone and damaged bomber, however distressing it was for the crews to witness their colleagues being doomed to destruction.

As the year ended the Eighth's daylight bombing offensive was barely four months old, and even Eaker would have to admit that it was still very much in the 'kindergarten' stage. Some 1,550 bombing sorties had been made, of which 52% had been effective but this relatively low figure was due mainly to adverse weather and inexperienced crews. Over 1,700 tons of bombs had been dropped for the loss of thirty-two bombers, another fifteen or so written-off with battle damage and over 320 airmen killed/missing in action. In the process some harsh lessons had been learned. Nevertheless the Eighth had shown that it was capable of maintaining its daylight bombing offensive without too heavy losses (under 2%) and that it was also able to fight back strongly. Eaker and his senior staff were 'absolutely convinced that 300 bombers can attack any target with less than a 4% loss.'

However, not everybody held such strong convictions. In Washington there was already concern about 'the general lack of urgency and progress of the bombing offensive'. After all, the Eighth had yet to attack a German target. At the end of November Winston Churchill had expressed his misgivings of the Eighth's performance so far: '[They] have not shown themselves possessed of any machines capable of bombing Germany by night or by day ... it would be the greatest pity to choke up all our best airfields with more Americans ... I would prefer to have a half-a-dozen extra American Army divisions'! Without doubt the future of the Eighth Air Force and its daylight bombing offensive hung precariously in the balance. In January General Eaker would be called upon to defend the performance of his Air Force and to justify its very future.

6
EAKER'S
'PIDDLING
LITTLE FORCE'

The New Year opened in the same vein as the old one had closed – with U-boat shelters; on 3rd January the crews were back over 'Flak City'. Individual bombing had been abandoned for bombing on the signal of a Group leader and Brigadier General Hayward S. Hansell, recently appointed Commander of 1st Bomb Wing, accompanied the 305th to St Nazaire to evaluate their staggered formation and bombing procedure.

Again the place lived up to its reputation, seven B-17s were lost. Only eight of the thirteen B-24s of 44th managed to bomb but they survived intact. On the return flight thick fog was encountered and running short of fuel, three made emergency landings at Dale and Talbenny airfields in Pembrokeshire; all were salvaged. The year had not started very propitiously. The losses were the heaviest so far; although the bombing was reasonably accurate the operation could not be considered a success, but at least General Hansell conceded that the new bombing procedure 'showed promise'.

Severe weather prevented operations until the 13th, when the Eighth returned to a favourite target, the Fives locomotive works at Lille. The force was well-escorted by RAF Spitfires but the 306th suffered again when two aircraft collided. The bombing accuracy was of a high standard and the Eighth never returned to this target. General Eaker was summoned to attend the Allied Conference at Casablanca – a meeting of Roosevelt and Churchill with their military chiefs and advisers. The performance of the Eighth thus far would be put under close scrutiny.

Eaker left on 15th January in *Boomerang*, a B-17F of 305th, flown by Captain Cliff Pyle. Within hours of his arrival at Casablanca, General Arnold informed him that Churchill was pressurising the President to convert the Eighth to night-bombing of German cities, and added 'only you can save us'. He also handed him a list of prepared questions requiring his replies. They queried the relatively few missions mounted by the Eighth, the high rate of abortive sorties and the choice of French rather than German targets. Eaker argued that poor weather and the low rate of replacement crews were factors in its progress. He stressed that valuable maintenance time and replacement spares had been devoted to the Twelfth; but he maintained that as his crews gained in experience and operational lessons were put into practice the rate of abortives would fall. French targets had been partly dictated by priority of U-boat pens and the absence of long-range fighters. However, he now considered that his crews were ready to attack Germany!

Eaker was also required to justify the daylight bombing offensive. He argued persuasively that it permitted the destruction of relatively small strategic targets, which would be difficult by night; furthermore because it was more accurate than night-bombing, a smaller force could destroy a given target. Also daylight operations kept the enemy's defences on the alert for twenty-four hours, imposing a serious strain on its strength. He even averred that his bombers were 'knocking the ears off the German day-fighters'! Operating by day reduced the congestion on British airspace and the communications systems, which would become more acute as the two bomber forces grew. In addition his crews were neither equipped nor trained for night-bombing, and a change would necessitate a long training programme with a high accident rate, maybe more than in action. In his opinion daylight bombing offered a unique opportunity for combined bombing, the two types being complementary. He concluded by submitting that daylight bombing was the boldest and most aggressive method to use, and furthermore it was the USAAF's speciality.

Eaker's arguments finally won the day. The Eighth's biggest critic, Churchill, told him, 'Young man, you have not convinced me you are right, but you have persuaded me that you should have a further opportunity to prove your contention. How fortuitous it would be if we could, as you say, bomb the devils round the clock.' Eaker had gained the Eighth a reprieve. He was promised further aircraft and

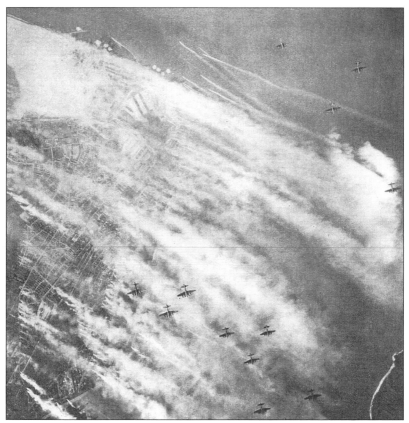

Wilhelmshaven: the Eighth's first mission to Germany – 27th January 1943. (USAF)

men but clearly his Force was still under trial. The Conference produced a Combined Bombing Offensive (CBO), code-named *Pointblank*. It stated that 'the primary object will be the progressive destruction and dislocation of the German military, industrial and economic system and the undermining of the morale of the German people to get to a point where their capacity for armed resistance is fatally weakened.' Within this general concept the primary objectives were to be 'the German submarine construction yards, the German aircraft industry, transportation, oil plants and other targets in the war industry, in that order.' Each of the Allied heavy bomber forces interpreted the directives to suit themselves, and were left relatively free to pursue their own ends.

86

Eaker arrived back on 25th January and two days later fifty-five of his crews were blooded over Germany. The target for this auspicious mission was the U-boat construction yards at Wilhelmshaven. Colonel Frank A. Armstrong, the 306th Commander, led the formations and thus it proudly claimed to be the 'first USAAF Unit over Germany', which is inscribed on its memorial. Low cloud obscured the targets and effective smokescreens had been laid, the bombing was considered 'fair . . . and the flak attentive, if not too accurate'. Some sixty enemy fighters were in action, including for the first time twin-engined fighters, although on this occasion they did not attack. Many crews reported that the Luftwaffe pilots seemed somewhat inexperienced compared with those faced over French targets. Three bombers were lost, two B-24s from 44th. One collided with a Fw 190 – the first recorded incident. The mission was not a shining success, nor was it a dismal failure, but the Eighth had taken a big step forward.

January was a critical month for Eaker's young Air Force, which he famously called his 'piddling little force'. Replacement crews and aircraft were far fewer in number than losses and just ninety operational B-17s were on hand, the lowest figure since the previous September. Indeed in February he was told by a maintenance officer that the lack of replacements meant that the last B-17 would take off in March. He is reputed to have replied, 'Okay, I'll be on it.' Adding to these problems the February weather – rain, sleet and freezing banks of clouds – restricted the number of operations to a mere five.

Despite temperatures falling to -45°, Emden was attacked on the 4th. The contrails left by the bombers helped to direct the Luftwaffe onto them and five B-17s were lost. A crew of 91st flew their eleventh and final mission; Lieutenant W.J. Crumm's crew of *Jack the Ripper* were the first to return to the States, specifically to work on an aircrew combat manual. At Bassingbourn, Major William Wyler, the Hollywood producer, was making a documentary film on the Eighth's operations. He used one of the Group's aircraft, *Bad Penny*, for the aerial photography of actual combat, although his film would be called *The Memphis Belle*.

St Nazaire was bombed on 16th February, and the locks of the U-boat protective basin suffered considerable damage. Eight bombers were lost to the experienced Luftwaffe units – JG 2 and JG 26 – and there were a number of unsuccessful attempts to drop bombs onto the formations. Ten days later the Eighth returned to Germany – Bremen – but as it was obscured by heavy cloud, the crews returned to Wilhelmshaven as an optional target. Major J.J. Preston, who led the

B-24s of the 44th Bomb Group at Shipdham. Texan II was lost on 13th February 1943. (via V. Jenkins)

305th, considered that they encountered the strongest fighter opposition so far. Three of the seven shot down came from the Chelveston outfit. One gunner, S/Sgt Lee S. 'Shorty' Gordon survived as a POW but he escaped from prison twice before successfully returning to the UK in March 1944, becoming the first Eighth airman to receive the Silver Star for escaping.

This was the first operation in which air correspondents were allowed to fly as passengers. The journalists had undergone a high-altitude survival course at Bovingdon, where they called themselves 'The Writing 69th'! Seven correspondents went out and Robert B. Post of the *New York Times* was lost in a B-24 of 44th Group. Three months later a British correspondent was killed over Kiel whilst flying with the 91st.

In March, Air Chief Marshal Harris was preparing to launch his massive bomber force into its 'Battle of the Ruhr', which would commence on the 5/6th. The Eighth had planned its first attack on this industrial complex, known to RAF crews as 'The Happy Valley' or more grimly 'The Valley of No Return', but twice in February operations to the Ruhr were frustrated by weather. The forecast for the 4th seemed promising, so Eaker dispatched seventy-one B-17s to the Hamm marshalling yards, a vital railway junction in the Ruhr. The four Groups encountered heavy cloud over the North Sea and two opted to attack Rotterdam with the 306th aborting. Only the 91st, led by Major Paul Fishburne, found a break in the clouds and the young Squadron Commander, only 22 years old, now had the choice of whether his sixteen aircraft should carry on alone. In his words, 'nothing would be said if I turned back, so we went on'.

The handful of crews soldiered on to the target and their bombing was excellent – 'right on the button' – but they did suffer the full fury of the Luftwaffe. As one gunner said, 'These fighters came closer than I've ever seen them in the movies. I could have almost shook hands with one of those fellows.' Four were lost and another B-17 was written-off, but the gunners claimed thirteen enemy aircraft. Major Fishburne in *Chief Sly II* arrived back at Bassingbourn and was awarded the DFC. In March 1945 when Allied troops were engaged in the land battle for the Ruhr, a radio broadcast in the States recalled the Hamm mission, under the title *Lest We Forget*, reminding listeners that the Eighth had been fighting over the Ruhr two years earlier. The Group was awarded a DUC for this mission two years after the war had ended. The long delay was perhaps because the USAAF did not want to encourage Groups 'to go it alone', with all the attendant risks.

As the 91st had shown over Hamm, the operation to the Rennes marshalling yards on 8th March gave further proof that the Eighth was coming of age as a bomber force. General Hansell, flying with 306th, was impressed with the standard of bombing and all for the loss of two B-17s. On the same day a small force of B-24s went to Rouen, heavily escorted by Spitfires, both RAF and USAAF, which was quite a change.

Stormy Weather of 91st Bomb Group comes to rest outside Bassingbourn airfield after the Hamm mission – 4th March 1943. Extinguisher foam saved the aircraft. (USAF)

B-17s of 305th Bomb Group over Lorient – 6th March 1943. (Imperial War Museum)

The B-24 crews were disappointed with the number of diversionary operations they had flown. They felt that they were being used as 'fighter bait' to allow the B-17 crews to gain 'all the glory'!

Changes were afoot at Debden. The 4th's pilots had spent most of the year on fighter sweeps and patrols, but now they were training on their new aircraft – P-47s. Many viewed the impending change with mixed feelings, most felt that the Spitfire was the best Allied fighter in service. However, somewhat to their surprise they found the P-47 was 'a lot better than we had been led to believe.' The first P-47 operation was mounted on 10th March, a fighter sweep over Holland, and their last with Spitfires on 1st April; a Spitfire was retained at Debden purely for sentimental reasons.

Two missions to French targets on successive days were accomplished without loss, but on 18th March it was back to Germany. The Eighth mustered one hundred and three heavies, its highest total since September 1942; the target was the Bremer Schiffbau Vulcan yards at Vegesack, the fourth largest U-boat yard in Germany. Over 268 tons of high explosives rained down, causing 'extremely heavy damage', putting the yards out of action for two months. It was probably no coincidence that Automatic Flight Control Equipment was used for the first time.

The crews encountered heavy flak especially during the bomb run, and the 303rd, flying in the low box position, suffered the worst of the barrage. The leading aircraft, *The Duchess*, received a direct hit about a minute before reaching the bomb release point. The bombardier, 1/Lt Jack W. Mathis, a twenty-one year old Texan, was hurled some nine feet to the rear of the nose compartment by the explosion. Despite being mortally wounded he managed to drag himself back to his position to release the bombs on time and also to close the bomb doors. Captain Harold Stouse nursed his damaged aircraft back to Molesworth. Lt Mathis was posthumously awarded the Medal of Honor, the first Eighth airman to receive the highest award.

Without doubt Vegesack was the most successful operation so far. Eaker, normally circumspect in his comments, was moved to say, 'The men and the machines have proved themselves ... it was a successful conclusion to long months of experimentation in daytime, high-level precision bombing. After Vegesack comes a new chapter.' Even Churchill was impressed, he sent Eaker a message: 'All my compliments to you and your officers and men on your brilliant exploit.' Lord Portal, Chief of the Air Staff, thought it 'the complete answer to criticism of high-altitude, daylight, precision bombing' – praise indeed!

On the next three missions – Wilhelmshaven, Rouen and Rotterdam – over one hundred heavies were dispatched on each occasion but less successfully. In the last raid of the month, on the 31st, to the Rotterdam shipyards, two B-17s of 303rd collided during assembly killing fifteen airmen. In total two thirds of the force was unable to bomb because of the heavy cloud and sadly over three hundred Dutch civilians were killed.

The six Groups that had been 'ploughing a lonely furrow' since late 1942, would soon receive some welcome reinforcements; four B-17 Groups arrived during April, at a stroke doubling its B-17 force, and the fighters would increase threefold.

The Renault motor works at Billancourt near Paris was attacked on April 4th. The formations, which took almost two hours to assemble, were led by the 305th. The journey out went well, clear skies ensured accurate bombing, and it was six months before the factory was back to full production. Early into the return flight enemy fighters attacked in strength and 364th squadron from Chelveston suffered harshly; half of its six B-17s were shot down. *Dry Martini 4th*, piloted by Captain Allen Martini, claimed ten out of twenty-five enemy aircraft destroyed by the Group – a record for a single bomber. The 305th was awarded its first DUC for this successful mission.

Brigadier General Hayward S. Hansell and Colonel Curtis E. LeMay beside B-17, Dry Martini 4th, of 364th squadron of 305th Bomb Group. (National Archives)

The following day the Erla VII aircraft and engine works at Antwerp were bombed by eighty-two crews but not too accurately; the Belgian Ambassador to the US protested at the large number of civilian casualties. The only losses were sustained by the 306th – four; in the previous month it had flown six missions without loss. Brigadier General Frank Armstrong, now heading the 101st Wing, went as an observer; he estimated that at least twenty-five head-on fighter attacks had been made on the leading aircraft. One 306th airman, T/Sgt Michael Roscovitch, known as the 'Mad Russian', became the first to reach the magical total of twenty-five operations. He was commissioned and flew another eight missions before being sent home for publicity purposes. Tragically the aircraft in which he was returning to the States, crashed in Scotland and he was killed.

Two fresh Fighter Groups were ready to join the battle. The 78th had been training at Goxhill on P-38s, such was the shortage of P-47s, and they moved into Duxford on 3rd April. The 56th was training at King's Cliffe, moving early in April to Horsham St Faith. 'The Wolfpack'

P-47s of the 4th Fighter Group before take-off from Debden – May 1943, with 335th squadron in the foreground. (Smithsonian Institution)

commanded by Colonel Hubert Zemke, became one of the most successful Groups in the Eighth. Zemke was not only a fine fighter pilot but became an acknowledged expert in fighter tactics. On 8th April pilots from the two Groups moved to Debden to join the 4th Group in operations over Dunkirk. A week later the Group destroyed three Fw 190s but lost three P-47s; Major Donald J.M. Blakeslee, a brilliant leader and ex-Eagle pilot, opened his score with the Eighth. Not until 4th May would P-47s act as escorts for their 'big brothers'.

On 16th April the crews attacked U-boat pens; B-17s went to Lorient, whilst nineteen B-24s bombed Brest. Both B-24 Groups were experiencing difficulties in maintaining their operational strength – B-24s were in short supply. The 44th had been steadily depleted by operational losses and trained replacement crews were rare. Operating with three squadrons, it was also assisting RAF Coastal Command over Norway. Much to its Commander's relief the 506th squadron finally arrived from the States; Colonel Leon W. Johnson could now plan to make a greater presence. Over Brest the crews were hampered by an effective smokescreen, and the 93rd lost three B-24s with another crash-landing in Cornwall.

The first strike against the German aircraft industry was made on the 17th when a Focke-Wulf plant outside Bremen was the target for one hundred and fifteen B-17s. The Luftwaffe was out in strength – 'The sky was literally swarming with fighters' – and the attacks lasted for about two hours. The 306th and 91st in the leading Wing suffered all the casualties; the former lost ten out of twenty-six with the 91st losing six, all from its 401st squadron. The gunners claimed sixty-three enemy fighters, although the true figure was later disclosed as ten, nevertheless no mean feat. Despite the onslaught, bombing was heavy and accurate and 50% of the factory destroyed; six months earlier the Fw 190 production lines had been dispersed to other factories further inland. It had been a costly exercise for the Eighth with little material effect.

This mission was evidence, if any was necessary, that the Luftwaffe was finally taking the Eighth's daylight offensive seriously. It was building up its day-fighter forces in northern Germany; fighters were transferred from other fronts, and twin-engined night-fighters, Me 110s and Junkers 88, were drafted into the air battle. There was an order that Me 110s should not be used in daylight if they might be exposed to Allied fighters. Reichsmarschall Göring had further complicated matters when he decreed that night-fighter pilots with more than twenty victories should not be used on day operations! Fighter Defensive zones were extended to 480 miles deep and a system of emergency airfields established to enable fighters to re-fuel and re-arm and return to the combat quickly. In May, German fighter production exceeded one thousand for the first time and would further increase. As the fighter pilots had found out to their frustration, enemy fighters could not be tempted up unless heavy bombers were involved. Thus the scene was prepared for the bitter and costly air battles of the late summer.

The second Medal of Honor to be awarded to an Eighth airman came, perhaps not surprisingly, over the notorious St Nazaire. On May Day over seventy B-17s were dispatched but heavy cloud prevented all but twenty-nine crews being able to bomb. The ill-fortune that seemed to dog the 306th manifested itself once again. As the Group turned for home the lead aircraft made a navigational error. Instead of going out over the Bay of Biscay, the crews flew too close and low over the Brest peninsula and heavy flak brought down three aircraft and damaged several others. One, piloted by 1/Lt Lewis P. Johnson of 423rd squadron, received several direct hits starting a number of fires and damaging the oxygen system. It seemed destined for a watery grave.

The ball turret gunner, S/Sgt Maynard 'Snuffy' Smith, on his first mission, emerged from his turret to see three crewmen taking to their parachutes. He decided to remain to fight the fires, as well as administer first aid to the injured tail gunner. For about ninety minutes he put up an amazing bravura performance, fighting the fires, tending to the injured, and when the ammunition boxes started to explode he jettisoned them out through the aircraft's gaping hole. In all this mayhem Smith still managed to find time to man the waist gun when enemy fighters moved in for the kill! As the aircraft neared the English coast he threw out surplus equipment to lessen the strain on the stricken aircraft. Lt Johnson successfully landed at RAF Predannack. A few weeks later Smith was awarded the MOH, which was presented to him at Thurleigh in July.

Three days later (4th) the Ford Motor plant at Antwerp was bombed by sixty-five B-17s escorted for the first time by six squadrons of P-47s. *Eight Ball II* of 303rd carried a celebrated passenger – Captain Clark Gable. The film star had joined the USAAF as a private in 1942. Having passed out of a Gunnery School, he was engaged to appear in a film designed to help train air gunners as well as encourage their recruitment. During 1943 there was a shortage of air gunners, mainly because the size of the turrets imposed a physical limit on the height and girth of prospective candidates! The Eighth took full advantage of the publicity value of the star. One of the many photographs of him is captioned, '[He] wanted to become an aerial gunner because he believed it was the quickest and surest way to strike at the Axis'! The film *Combat America* was not released to the public until October 1944, thirteen months after Gable had flown his last mission.

Antwerp was the last mission that the four 'Pioneer' B-17 Groups would 'go it alone'. They had lost one hundred aircraft in action with a similar number damaged, and the 306th bearing the brunt of the losses – forty-five. Eaker remarked that 13th May was 'a great day for the Eighth'; four new B-17 Bomb Groups (94th, 95th, 96th and 351st) entered the fray. On the following day over two hundred heavies from three Bomb Wings attacked Kiel, Antwerp and Courtrai. The largest force (136) bombed the Germania & Deutschwerke shipyards at Kiel, with the 44th given perhaps the more difficult task. Their B-24s carried incendiaries and followed the B-17s onto the bomb run; because the incendiaries had a lower trajectory, the crews were required to fly a far longer bomb run. Five B-24s fell to either flak or fighters – three from 67th squadron – and a sixth was abandoned close to Shipdham. The Group was awarded a DUC for this mission, in which it lost fifty-two airmen.

Meanwhile B-26s of 322nd Group were to be tested in the ETO for the first time. Twelve crews left to fly low over the North Sea in an attempt to negate the enemy's radar; one crew had to return early. The remaining eleven bombed the power station at Ijmuiden in Holland through severe and accurate flak which damaged nine aircraft. On

Captain Robert K. Morgan and his crew of Memphis Belle before leaving for the USA –

9th June 1943. (Smithsonian Institution)

return one B-26 crashed near the airfield at Bury St Edmunds; five airmen baled out but the pilot was killed. Two days later the Group's CO, Colonel Robert M. Stillman, was informed that most of the bombs had missed the target so they would have to return and try again!

In some four hours the Eighth had mounted 229 bombing sorties to four separate targets for the loss of twelve aircraft, with Kiel being the longest mission to date. Over one hundred and ten P-47s had also been in action and five victories had been claimed, although 78th lost three pilots whilst notching up their first victories. The 92nd Group was also back on operations, so it now could be said that Eaker's 'piddling little force' was a thing of the past.

The day also brought the *official* acknowledgement of the first B-17 to complete twenty-five missions; the honour fell to *Hell's Angels* of the 303rd. However, its glory would be usurped by the *Memphis Belle* of 91st Group, which had completed its twenty-five missions five days later. With due military ceremony *Memphis Belle*, with Captain K. Morgan and his crew, left Bovingdon on 9th June to fly back to the States to undertake a War Bond raising tour and they were feted wherever they went. Wyler's film ensured the aircraft's lasting fame, which was further enhanced by the successful re-make of the film in 1990; the refurbished aircraft is now on permanent display at Memphis.

Three days after the Kiel operation B-24s of 44th and 93rd achieved some remarkable bombing over Bordeaux, whilst the 'Glory boys' were in action further up the coast at Lorient. The B-24 force used RAF Davidstow Moor in Cornwall as a staging post for their long 700 mile flight. The crews flew well out over the Bay of Biscay at a low altitude before turning and climbing to 22,000 feet for their bombing. The lead navigator thought it was 'the finest piece of precision bombing I ever hope to see. The locks collapsed, water gushed out of the basin . . . there were hits on the railroad yards, strikes on the aero-engine factory. It was beautiful!' All but one aircraft returned safely, the damaged aircraft from 44th making an emergency landing at Gijon in Spain – the first to land in a neutral country. By the end of May, B-24 crews had been taken out of operations and found themselves involved on low-level flying practice, roaring across East Anglia just a couple of hundred feet above the ground and in close formation – a frightening and sobering experience for the crews and civilians alike! They were unaware of the reason for this training and were just thankful for some relief from operations.

On the 17th the 322nd prepared for its return to Ijmuiden. Because of damaged aircraft and with only two operational squadrons, Colonel

Stillman could only muster eleven aircraft. He led the Ijmuiden force, with Lt Col Puriton, Group Executive Officer, leading to a generating station at Haarlem. One aborted close to the Dutch coast, the remaining crews took a wrong heading and entered a heavily defended area. Colonel Stillman's B-26 was shot down, another two collided and crashed and the resultant explosion brought down another aircraft. One crew bombed a gas holder in Amsterdam but also crashed. Another was brought down by Me 109s over the North Sea and four crashed into the sea. A total loss of ten – a disaster of some magnitude. Colonel Stillman, badly wounded, was taken prisoner and Lt Col Puriton was later rescued from the sea by a German vessel. The only survivors, two gunners, were rescued from their dinghy two days later. The Group would not return to operations until the end of July.

Eaker did not stray far from the *Pointblank* objectives. U-boat targets at Kiel and Flensburg were attacked on 19th May, followed two days later by Wilhelmshaven and Emden. Then on the 29th St Nazaire was bombed, along with the Naval Storage Depot at Rennes. These operations resulted in the loss of thirty-two B-17s and four salvaged. The Allied *Trident* Conference held in Washington during May, reviewed *Pointblank* and effectively confirmed the original objectives, with submarines, the aircraft industry, ball bearings and oil being specified as primary targets and synthetic rubber and military transport as secondary priorities. It was strictly emphasised – 'second to none' – that the major objective was the destruction of the Luftwaffe. General Arnold noted his opinion on Eaker's copy, 'At all times there is a need for an extensive US fighter force both to protect the bombers and to assist in the reduction of the German fighter strength.' His deep concern can be seen in a direction to Major General Barney M. Giles to find within six months 'a fighter that can protect our bombers. Whether you use an existing type or have to start from scratch is your problem. Get to work on this right away because by January '44, I want fighter escort for all our bombers from UK into Germany.' General Giles later considered that the most important contribution of his military career was 'the development of the long-range fighter'.

During early June poor weather frustrated operations until the 11th when Bremen was the target. Because of heavy cloud the crews attacked the U-boat yards at Wilhelmshaven and the port of Cuxhaven. The Luftwaffe accounted for eight B-17s with the 379th from Kimbolton, on its second mission, taking the brunt of the attacks – 'in next to no time, six aircraft disappeared out of the skies'. Most of its remaining aircraft sustained damage with eighteen crewmen seriously

Colonel Hubert Zemke, the Commander of the 56th Fighter Group. A brilliant fighter pilot and leader. (USAF)

injured. The Group, commanded by the ebullient Colonel Maurice A. Preston known as 'Big Moe', had lost nine aircraft and ninety-one airmen in action – few Groups had such a torrid introduction.

On the following day the 56th finally 'broke its duck' when engaged in a high altitude sweep of the Calais area, along with pilots of the 4th. Captain Walter V. Cook of the 62nd squadron, destroyed a Fw 190, the

Group's first confirmed victory. On the next day (13th) whilst engaged on a sweep over Gravelines they added another three Fw 190s without loss, one to Colonel Zemke. The 78th pilots also downed two Fw 190s but for the loss of two P-47s. On 26th June there was a reversal of fortune with the 56th losing five P-47s and another written-off all for two victories; the 4th's pilots added another two to their growing score without loss.

The Eighth returned to Germany on the 13th when Bremen and Kiel were bombed by over 180 B-17s with losses of twenty-six (13%) – a new high. The newly formed 4th Wing, commanded by Colonel Curtis LeMay, suffered, with the three inexperienced Groups, 94th, 95th and 96th, taking heavy punishment from accurate flak and fighters. As one crewman recalled 'It seemed that most of the Luftwaffe was gathered there. The action was intense and I saw many ships going down in flames or exploding in mid-air.' The 95th lost ten out of twenty-six, including one carrying Brigadier General Nathan B. Forrest as an observer – the first USAAF General lost in action. The 94th lost six crews over the target area but then within sight of the Norfolk coast, they were attacked by a dozen Junkers 88s. Some gunners had stripped down their guns and were cleaning them – a chore that should have been undertaken after landing – and another three were destroyed. Although thirty-nine enemy aircraft were claimed, the Luftwaffe actually lost eight.

Within a week or so both Groups would have new Commanders. Eaker felt a change of leadership would improve performance and raise morale. Colonel Fred W. Castle, an original staff officer, took over the 94th now based at Bury St Edmunds and Colonel John K. Gerhart, assigned to the Eighth back in January 1942, was given command of 95th at Horham. However, Colonel Archie J. Olds Jr would remain with the 96th until early September, at its new base at Snetterton Heath. This move of airfields had been necessitated by the siting of B-26 Groups in Essex to be within closer range of their targets in the Low Countries, and also to centralise the Groups of the 4th Wing around its headquarters at Elveden Hall in Suffolk.

On 22nd June the crews would make their deepest foray into German airspace, to the Chemische Werke synthetic rubber plant at Hüls in the dreaded Ruhr, thought to produce about 30% of Germany's needs. Several ploys were used to keep the Luftwaffe guessing as to the primary target. The formations would fly well out over the North Sea before turning south-east across Holland. At this point a small force of B-17s comprising two new Groups, 381st from Ridgewell and 384th at

Grafton Underwood, would attack transport factories at Antwerp in an attempt to draw the Luftwaffe. Also another new Group, the 100th from Thorpe Abbotts, would make a diversionary flight over the North Sea. But 'the best laid schemes o' mice and men, gang aft a-gley'!

The 'freshmen' crews of 100th were late assembling, which nullified their diversionary flight. The other new Groups experienced assembly difficulties and failed to rendezvous with their fighter escorts. The experienced II./JG 26 had a field day with the novice crews; each Group lost two B-17s and another crash-landed in Kent. The main force were met by over 100 fighters and a fierce battle ensued; sixteen B-17s were shot down, five from the 91st Group. One of the missing aircraft was a YB-40, an experimental B-17 adapted into a virtual flying gun platform or 'fortress', purely for the defence of the bomber formations. It had been modified with the addition of an extra top turret, the first nose 'chin' turret and extra waist guns. YB-40s had been first used by the 327th squadron of the 92nd at Alconbury over St Nazaire on 29th May. As they proved to be slow and cumbersome and just as vulnerable as the normal B-17s, the experiment was not successful and was abandoned in August.

Despite the losses, the Hüls operation was the most effective demonstration of strategic bombing thus far. It was estimated that three months' production had been lost, although the plant was back to full production a month later. Forty-six enemy fighters were claimed, and the gunners of 351st were credited with seventeen. The 4th and 78th were successful over Holland, seven victories without a loss. As Eaker said to his staff at Pinetree the following day, 'Here you are, gentlemen. The accomplishment – Hüls well hit, with bombing concentrated in the target areas. We'll have to wait for the reconnaissance photographs and a complete damage assessment, but it looks to me as if we dealt the plant a crippling blow ... Now, on this next mission ...'

The 'next mission' was to Villacoublay and Bernay St Martin airfields but the aircraft were recalled due to bad weather. Sadly tragedy struck at Ridgewell when a B-17 blew up whilst it was being prepared; twenty-two airmen and one civilian were killed. A similar accident had befallen the 95th less than a month earlier, when they were operating from Alconbury. A bomb detonated during bombing-up. The massive explosion killed eighteen airmen with another twenty-one seriously injured and six B-17s were destroyed – more than had been lost in action.

On 28th June the Eighth returned for a last time to St Nazaire, where so many bombing techniques had been fashioned and honed. Its final attack damaged the lock gates of the U-boat basin, another example of excellent bombing, and mercifully for relatively light losses – eight. The U-boat ports had been reduced to ruins, with many French civilians killed, as a result of the Allied bombing. Most of the local population though, had long since left; a German U-boat commander maintained that 'not a cat or dog remained alive … but our U-boats still were operating from them.' The bombing of these ports was perhaps the most ineffective and sorry chapter in the whole story of the Allied bombing offensive.

During the last week of June over one hundred and twenty B-24s left for North Africa. The original Groups had been joined by the 389th, which had only arrived at Hethel earlier in the month. They would take part, alongside the Ninth Air Force, in Operation *Statesman* – the epic low-level strike at the Ploesti oil refineries in Rumania. The surviving crews would not return to the home airfields for another two months.

One USAAF staff officer described the months of May and June as being 'a period of grim exchanges of blow for blow, savage at times'. Its operations over German targets were increasing but so too were its losses; there was an urgent need to extend the operational range of the P-47s. Colonel Cass H. Hough and his Air Technical Section at Bovingdon had been long wrestling with the problem of drop fuel-tanks. After considerable trials and production delays, the 200 gallon ferry tanks were thought to be the temporary solution. As they were unpressurised they could not be used at higher altitudes but they were brought into use during July and extended the fighters' range to the German frontier and just beyond. The British manufactured 108-gallon pressurised tanks appeared to be the better option, but although ordered in early July there was a three months delay in delivery.

The Eighth had grown into a bombing force of some strength – sixteen B-17, three B-24 and four B-26 Groups – but as yet with only three Fighter Groups. The next four months would be a crucial and costly period for the Force, although many of its operations during this time would enter the annals of USAAF history and ensure the Eighth's enduring fame.

7

'BROUGHT TO THE BRINK OF DISASTER'

On Independence Day 1943 the Eighth Air Force had completed twelve months in the ETO and in celebration it mounted an ambitious operation. Three separate B-17 forces would attack the Gnome & Rhone Aero factory at Le Mans, an aircraft plant at Nantes and the U-boat pens at La Pallice. Eaker would have wished to have marked the day with a strike at Germany, but the weather dictated the selection of targets in occupied France.

The 4th Wing dispatched over eighty of its long-range 'Tokyo' B-17Fs to La Pallice, with Brigadier General Orville Anderson, Chairman of the Combined Operations Planning Committee, flying in *Maggs*, the lead aircraft of the 100th, his first experience of combat in the ETO. The crews made the accepted approach from wide out in the Bay of Biscay. Everything worked smoothly; the bombing was reported to be 'effective', no Luftwaffe, and only one B-17 lost to flak. As the Wing was approaching its target, the other two forces, almost two hundred aircraft flying parallel courses, crossed the French coast to the east of Cherbourg and eighty miles inland, they separated. The smaller Nantes force turned south-west, and came under sustained fighter attacks but survived remarkably with minimal losses – three. They withdrew out to sea making a wide sweep back to England. After successfully bombing Le Mans the main force (105) fought off enemy fighters right to the French coast. Total losses were less than 3%, fifty-two enemy aircraft claimed and 540 tons of bombs dropped – an impressive performance. For once it would appear that the division of forces had caught the Luftwaffe unawares; as an official communiqué stated, 'the hand that guided the high-level daylight bombers could be quicker than the Nazi eye'!

Ten days later – Bastille Day – the Eighth returned to French targets, apparently to raise the morale of the French people. Villacoublay air depot, a major servicing base for Fw 190s and housing a small Junkers 52 plant, was attacked, destroying many aircraft and heavily damaging the factory. Also two airfields were bombed and over sixty fighters were destroyed for relatively light losses – eight; although the 94th lost four over Le Bourget airfield. Eaker could be satisfied by the way the second year had commenced, despite these results having been achieved over French targets; all too soon his crews would be tested again over Germany. Some further heartening news was that two B-17 Groups – 385th at Great Ashfield and 388th at Knettishall – had arrived to strengthen the 4th Wing.

On 16th July B-26s returned to operations but now under the aegis of the Eighth's Air Support Command. After the disastrous low-level mission, crews would now bomb from 11/12,000 feet; their aircraft had been suitably modified and Norden bombsights replaced the D.8 sight. The 323rd Group from Earl's Colne made its debut and would trial the medium-altitude bombing. Colonel Herbert B. Thatcher, its CO, in *Bingo Buster*, led sixteen crews to the marshalling yards at Abbeville. They were escorted by RAF Spitfire squadrons because 'the best fighter units in the German Air Force are based around Abbeville.' Heavy flak damaged ten B-26s but all returned safely. The 'beautiful ladies', as

B-17 of 385th Bomb Group returning to Great Ashfield with wounded on board - a red warning flare has been fired. (USAF)

B-26s of 449th squadron of 322nd Bomb Group. (Smithsonian Institution)

they were called by many crews, were back in business. Towards the end of the month another Group, 386th at Great Dunmow, entered the battle, and on the following day (31st) the 322nd resumed operations. The Eighth's fourth Group, 387th at Chipping Ongar, made its entry in the middle of August. By the end of the month almost 1,500 sorties had been flown for minimal losses thus proving that B-26s could operate effectively and successfully from medium altitudes.

During July plans were finalised for the Eighth to join the RAF in 'round the clock' bombing of German targets, particularly Hamburg; thus achieving the cherished aim expressed by Churchill at the Casablanca conference. The first operation was detailed for the 24th but the weather over northern Germany proved unfavourable, so for the first time the Eighth turned to Norwegian targets – Bergen, Trondheim and Heroya. Heavy cloud prevented the crews bombing Bergen, and rather than risk civilian casualties they returned with their bombs. Just two Groups, 95th and 100th, were sent on the longest haul to Trondheim – a 1,900 mile round trip. It proved to be an effective strike, a U-boat sunk, a destroyer damaged and workshops set on fire. The RAF Photo. Unit sent a telegram: 'please convey heartiest congrats to air crews and all concerned for a wizard bombing . . . Press on, more of it soon please.' Colonel Neil B. 'Chick' Harding of the 100th was awarded a Silver Star for his leadership; he was the Group's third commander in two months.

The attack on the Nordesk Lettmetal magnesium and aluminium factory at Heroya was most destructive. The new plant, south-west of Oslo, had taken two years to build and had recently opened. After the Eighth's successful strike, production ceased for almost four months. The timing of the bombing had been carefully planned to coincide with the changeover of shifts to minimise civilian casualties. Colonel Budd J. Peaslee, the CO of 384th, considered it 'was the most successful, shrewdly planned and executed mission of the entire war.' The only missing aircraft, *Georgia Rebel* of 381st, made an emergency landing at Vännacka in southern Sweden and its crew were interned; the first of over one hundred and thirty aircraft to land in neutral Sweden. The two missions augured well for the next five operations mounted over six days, to be known as 'Blitz Week'.

The next day (25th) the Blohm & Voss shipyards at Hamburg were bombed. A heavy pall of smoke towering some 15,000 feet, the result of the RAF's heavy raid of the previous night, greatly hampered the bombing; one reason why the Eighth would be loath to attack targets directly following RAF night-raids. The Kiel shipyards were also attacked as was an airfield at Wastrow. Heavy flak and enemy fighters accounted for nineteen B-17s, with the 384th flying in the low position of the leading wing, dubbed 'Purple Heart Corner', losing seven. *Happy Daze* of 94th ditched in the North Sea close to the German coast and the crew spent the night and much of the following day in their dinghies reconciled to the idea that they would be picked up by a German vessel. A RAF Hudson of 279 A/S/R squadron sighted them and dropped a lifeboat by parachute, 'landing like a leaf on the water'. The crew arrived safely in England, although the pilot later recalled, '[it] had sleeping bags, food, water, gasoline and directions for running the thing. I had an idea that I might get the boys to head for New York'!

The following day three hundred heavies attacked the Continental Gummiwerke tyre factories at Hannover, along with the Nordhafen synthetic rubber plant and targets in Hamburg. The flak over Hannover was accurate and sixteen B-17s were shot down. One aircraft that survived a frontal attack of Fw 190s on the way out was *Ruthie II* of 92nd. It was heavily damaged, the pilot was mortally wounded and many of the crew rendered unconscious because the oxygen lines had been shattered. The co-pilot, Flight Officer John C. Morgan, fought desperately to keep the aircraft within the formation when many would have turned for home, despite the fact that the pilot's body was heavily slumped over the controls and the windscreen was shattered. Morgan managed to bring the aircraft over the target to bomb and then manfully coaxed it back, finally making a safe emergency landing at RAF Foulsham. For this quite remarkable feat of flying Morgan was awarded the Medal of Honor. Twenty-four B-17s were lost in action and another three salvaged, A/S/R services rescued sixty-five airmen.

The crews were stood down on the 27th, before commencing three successive days of operations when aircraft factories at Kassel, Oschersleben and Warnemünde were targeted and the Kiel shipyards revisited. Over three hundred B-17s took to the air on the 28th, the First Wing to the Fieseler components works at Kassel and the Fourth to the AGO Fw 190 plant at Oschersleben; high cloud formations caused less than one third to bomb. Colonel Castle of the 94th flying *Sugar Puss* led the Oschersleben force, which became the longest penetration of German air space so far. The Colonel's utter determination was shown on this mission; because of adverse weather just twenty-seven crews stayed with him to the target, which was bombed most effectively on the second bombing run. It was estimated that at least one month's production was lost. Castle was awarded a Silver Star for his impressive performance. The cost had been quite heavy – fifteen, seven of them from the 96th. The Luftwaffe used air-launched rockets; one hit a 385th aircraft causing it to crash into two B-17s and all three were lost.

'Blitz Week' proved that the Eighth could sustain a concentrated bombing offensive for at least a limited period, but eighty-eight aircraft were missing in action with another fifteen salvaged – perhaps a third of its effective bomber force. As a comparison, during the same period the RAF mounted over three thousand sorties on four nights, mainly directed at Hamburg, dropping 78% more bombs for the loss of eighty-one bombers (2.6%). It was of some interest that Brigadier General Fred Anderson, the Eighth's Bomber Commander, flew as an observer in a Lancaster on two of the RAF night-raids; perhaps night-bombing was the way forward for the Eighth?

Losses would have been heavier but for the fact that on two days, the 28th and 30th July, P-47s were provided with belly drop fuel-tanks (known as 'babies') enabling them to provide support and withdrawal cover. On the 28th the 4th Group came to the aid of the bombers returning from Kassel, claiming nine victories for the loss of a P-47. Then on the 30th, the three Groups were in action and twenty-five enemy fighters were shot down for the loss of seven P-47s. The 78th, the most successful Group, claimed sixteen, but lost its Commander, Lt Col Melvin F. McNickle. He had only recently replaced Colonel Arman Peterson, who had been killed in action on 1st July. Major Roberts in *Spokane Queen* shot down three Fw 190s, the highest individual score on a single mission, and Captain London in *El Jeppo*, added two to his total, making five in all; thus becoming the Eighth's first fighter 'ace'. Another pilot, Lieutenant Quince L. Brown, Jr in *Okie* suffered engine problems, lost altitude and whilst 'hedge-hopping' back across Holland, shot up a locomotive and a gun battery to the west of Rotterdam – the first recorded strafing by an Eighth pilot. 'Strafing' was a German term adopted by the Allies to describe the destruction of ground targets by fighters; it originated from the First World War – *'Gott strafen England'* literally meaning 'God punish England'.

The crews had twelve days to recover from the hectic and traumatic week of operations. This breathing space was sorely needed to repair the many battle-damaged aircraft, to process replacement aircraft and train new crews; it also allowed a new B-17 Group, 390th at Framlingham, to prepare for its operational debut. It acquired the name of 'Wittan's Wallopers' from its first Commander, Colonel Edgar M. Wittan, and was the first to pass through the School of Applied Tactics in Florida; the Group's subsequent performances showed the value of this advanced training. Whilst the B-17 crews were basking in this blessed relief from operations, their B-24 colleagues were far away in Libya operating with the Ninth Air Force.

On 1st August the 44th, 93rd and 389th took part in the epic low-level attack on the oil refineries at Ploesti in Romania. Over half the force came from these Groups and of the fifty-two B-24s lost, thirty came from the Eighth including six crews interned in Turkey. This memorable but costly operation brought the award of four Medals of Honor to Eighth airmen – Colonel Leon W. Johnson, CO of 44th, Lt Col Addison E. Baker, CO of 93rd, Major L. Jerstad of 201st PC Bomb Wing and 2/Lt Lloyd H. Hughes of 389th – the latter three were posthumously awarded. All three Groups received a most deserved DUC for this historic mission. Before they returned to East Anglia at the end of the month, they were engaged over a large Messerschmitt factory at Weiner Neustadt in Austria as well as several Italian targets.

For the Eighth's units in England, it was back to business on 12th August when three hundred and thirty crews were detailed for targets in the Ruhr valley – Bochum, Gelsenkirchen and Recklinghausen. Heavy cloud posed difficulties and the formations became straggled and strung out and the Luftwaffe took full advantage; twenty-five B-17s (12.5%) were lost and another three salvaged. Four days later the Eighth was engaged in Operation *Starkey*, the Allied attempt to convince the enemy that a full-scale invasion was imminent on the Pas de Calais coast, thus releasing pressure on its Russian ally battling on the Eastern Front.

A concentrated air offensive against airfields, marshalling yards, coastal defences, gun emplacements and troop concentrations in the area, *Starkey* had another objective – that of trying to entice the Luftwaffe into the air. The Eighth's heavies were mainly engaged in bombing airfields, with its P-47s making fighter sweeps, but the B-26s made the largest contribution, their crews often flying two missions a day. Although weather impeded several operations *Starkey* continued until 9th September, but the enemy showed scant reaction to the subterfuge and no major air battles materialised; as a staff officer ruefully commented, 'the enemy did not want to take part in the dress rehearsal.'

By early August plans were in hand for an operation to attack the three major ball-bearings factories (KGF and VKF 1 and 2) at Schweinfurt, thought to produce almost 50% of the German war requirements and a target high on the list of *Pointblank* objectives. A combined operation by the Eighth's Fourth Wing and the Ninth Air Force to attack two Messerschmitt factories at Regensburg in southern Germany and Weiner Neustadt in Austria respectively, was also drawn up, which would require the Wing to withdraw to North Africa. In the event both operations were postponed because of adverse weather, although the Ninth attacked Weiner Neustadt on the 13th. The Eighth quickly produced a revised plan, a combined operation with the Fourth Wing going to Regensburg, followed fifteen minutes later by the First's Wing's larger force to Schweinfurt. The two forces would have fighter escorts as far as the German border, and it was hoped that they would effectively split the Luftwaffe opposition and swamp the enemy's flak defences; or at least that was the theory!

This bold plan was finally agreed by General Eaker although not until considerable pressure had been applied by the Air Staff in Washington. He later remarked, 'there was always someone who wanted to do something facile to get a quick result. We were pushed into it before we were ready. I protested it bitterly.' Thus Schweinfurt and Regensburg were 'writ large in the history of the Eighth Air Force' and permanently etched on the memories of those crews who took part in what has been described as 'the most intensive air battle of the

Second World War'. On 16th August the weather over Germany was forecast to be good and the operation was activated for the following day – the anniversary of the Eighth's heavy bombing offensive.

On the morning of the 17th after the briefings, the crews were aware that they were in for a 'hot mission', summed up by one as, 'too deep, so many miles without fighter protection. It was sheer fear that gripped us all.' True to form the British weather again intervened, as low cloud and heavy ground mist shrouded the airfields and postponed the departure. After a delay of $1\frac{1}{2}$ hours the Regensburg force could not be detained any longer if the crews were to land at unfamiliar bases in North Africa before dusk. It was now that the critical decision was made wherein was sown the seeds of disaster. The departure of the Schweinfurt force was postponed for $3\frac{1}{2}$ hours to allow the skies to clear for safer assembly of the formations and to provide time for the P-47s to return and refuel. Thus the bomber forces would, each in turn, face the full fury of the German air defences.

The Regensburg force, led by Colonel LeMay, comprised one hundred and forty-six B-17s from the Wing's seven Groups. RAF Spitfires acted as escorts to Brussels, then were replaced by P-47s to give protection as far as Eupen, about ten miles from the German border. By the time the formations had reached Eupen, the 95th and 100th, at the rear of the formation, stretching some twenty miles, had been under constant fighter attack. The 353rd Fighter Group, new-comers to the war, could only cover the leading formations. They were then relieved by the experienced pilots of the 56th, who downed six enemy fighters.

Once the P-47s had reached their operational limit, the mayhem continued well into southern Germany with another eight B-17s destroyed; the 100th lost six crews and the 95th three. Lieutenant Colonel Beirne J. Lay Jr, a staff officer flying as an observer with the 100th, wrote a dramatic account of the mission: 'the sight was fantastic and surpassed fiction ... Our airplane was greatly endangered by flying debris. Emergency hatches, exit doors, prematurely opened parachutes, bodies and assorted fragments of B-17s and Hun fighters breezed past ... after we had been under constant attack for a solid hour, it appeared certain that the 100th Group was faced with annihilation ... I knew that I had long since mentally accepted the fact of death and that it was simply a question of the next second or the next minute.'

The Messerschmitt factory was bombed accurately from a height of 17/19,000 feet and although the flak was said to be 'negligible' three

Devil's Daughter – B-17 of 390th Bomb Group showing damage from a fighter attack – of the fourteen that survived the Regensburg mission, 17th August 1943.

aircraft were damaged and did not reach North Africa. After leaving the target the crews continued south over the Alps; two crews crash-landed in Switzerland (the first to land there), two came down in Italy, one in France and five ditched in the Mediterranean. After eleven hours or so 'of sheer and utter hell' twenty-four aircraft had been lost in action (16.4%). Colonel Lay expressed the feelings of the surviving airmen, 'We all felt the reaction of men who had not expected to see another sunset.' His article, 'I saw Regensburg Fall', was published in the *Saturday Evening Post*, ensuring the lasting fame of this mission and that of the 100th Group, which had lost nine crews. The inexperienced 390th (its third mission) lost six aircraft, the 95th four and the leading Group, 96th, miraculously survived unscathed. All Groups were awarded a DUC and probably none was more deserved.

The two hundred and thirty crews of the First Wing, formed into two task forces and led by Brigadier General Robert B. Williams, were about to face an even more horrendous and traumatic onslaught with perhaps three times the number of enemy fighters in action – estimated at 260/300 single-engined and about sixty twin-engined. Just one B-17 fell before the formations crossed into Germany, but at least six enemy fighters had been shot down by the escorts. The Luftwaffe bided its time until the P-47 escorts departed before really attacking in strength. As one crew member recalled: 'when the P-47s left and we went on to suffer all those casualties, was the major turning point when the Air Force had it proved to them that their idea of sending B-17s unescorted on a deep penetration just wasn't valid'. In some thirty minutes crews faced the full fury of 'the greatest massing of enemy aircraft that I ever saw' and, 'Never before or after did I ever see such incessant action – it was the most terrible experience of my life.'

Unlike the Regensburg mission it was the leading Groups that suffered most heavily in the early massed and ferocious attacks, and as their formations became depleted so the attacks became more intense. The 91st, led by Lieutenant Colonel Clemens L. Wurzbach, lost nine aircraft before reaching the target, with the 381st flying in the low position, losing seven. Colonel Wurzbach, one of many airmen with German ancestry, later maintained that he was convinced that he would not survive the mission and his sole objective now was to make as accurate a bombing run as possible. Before Schweinfurt was reached another twenty-three had fallen to fighters, all but one from the leading Groups. Because the flak was heavier at Schweinfurt, the bombing altitude was about 3,000 feet higher than over Regensburg. The three targets were more difficult to identify as they were located in residential areas of the town. Despite everything that had happened 80% of the crews dropped 420 tons of bombs, but the heavy clouds of smoke made it almost impossible for many to bomb accurately.

Three B-17s fell victim to the flak near Schweinfurt and the surviving crews now faced a two hundred mile ordeal before they met up with the P-47 escorts on the German side of Eupen; another two B-17s were destroyed by Me 110s. *M'Honey* of 384th, in a vain attempt to make it back to England, finally crash-landed at Rheims after a hair-raising low-level flight across Germany and France; four crewmen escaped and ultimately returned to England. Indeed no fewer than thirty-eight airmen successfully evaded capture.

The 56th came to the aid of the battered formations, claiming seventeen victories for the loss of three pilots. It proved to be the turning point in the Group's fortunes; Lt Glenn Shiltz, on his first mission, claimed three, with two of its successful pilots, Captains Gerald Johnson and Walter Mahurin each getting two. Nevertheless another four B-17s crashed in Belgium and two ditched in the North Sea. This 'brutal, heroic and bloody mission in the extreme', which had lasted for about eight hours, resulted in the loss of thirty-six aircraft. The 381st lost eleven crews and the 91st ten. Colonel Wurzbach later maintained that his Group was 'so sadly crippled that it took several months to build up again into a first class fighting organisation.' Sixty B-17s lost in action with another eleven written-off, more in a single day than in the first six months of operations over Europe; over five hundred and fifty airmen were killed/missing. Although over three hundred enemy aircraft were claimed, it is now thought that the Luftwaffe lost forty-seven on the day. The USAAF tried to put on a brave face: 'the price was no higher than expected and was more than justified by the results achieved ... the battle for air superiority is becoming a slugging match between offense and defense. The side with the most stamina will win by a knockout.' Ominous thoughts for the bomber crews?

The bombing over Regensburg had been excellent and perhaps six weeks' production halted; unbeknown to the Eighth, fuselage jigs for the projected jet-fighter, Me 262, were destroyed, delaying its development. However, the harsh reality was that despite accurate bombing, the total tonnage and the 500lb high-explosive bombs were not sufficiently heavy enough to inflict substantial damage. The operation did have an effect on local morale, as it was felt that if enemy bombers could come so far in broad daylight then 'Germany had as good as lost the war'! The bombing at Schweinfurt was far less precise and effective, and although heavier bombs (1,000lb) were used, they were also largely ineffectual in causing serious damage. It had been expected that the RAF would follow up with a night-raid on Schweinfurt; but it had the opportunity to attack a more vital target on the 17/18th – the experimental rocket establishment at Peenemünde. Thus the Eighth was compelled to return to Schweinfurt just two months later with catastrophic results.

In one of those strange quirks of fate that would befall most Groups, the 303rd that had survived Schweinfurt somehow without loss, went out two days later on what in theory was a 'milk run' and lost two crews. Their target was Gilze-Rijen airfield in Holland, only thirty minutes over enemy territory – 'just a short haul before supper'. Unfortunately the Group was forced to make a second bombing run and thus became isolated. They were attacked by Fw 190s which 'struck like devils from Hell. Yellow-nosed Goering's elite crew [JG 26]. Them people lived to fight.' The battle lasted right up the Dutch coast;

one aircraft, *G for George*, crashed and another, *Stric Nine*, ditched near the coast. Twenty-one airmen killed/missing in action, six more wounded, fourteen damaged aircraft and all before supper! The 56th had another good day, nine victories for one P-47 missing.

On 24th August only 70% of the B-17s in North Africa were considered sufficiently airworthy to fly back to England. Eaker maintained that the crews had earned the right to fly home direct, but LeMay said that his men would prefer to attack a target *en route*. Merignac airfield at Bordeaux was bombed and three aircraft failed to return to England. Two came from the 385th Group. *Lulu Belle* piloted by Major Preston Piper, the Group leader over Regensburg, ditched near to Land's End; he and seven of his crew were rescued.

Three days later the Wing was still able to provide sixty-five B-17s for a maximum effort to a target in the Pas de Calais that was shrouded in great secrecy. All sixteen Groups were detailed for the operation and the crews were briefed that their target was 'special aeronautical facilities of major importance'. There was more concern when they were told that the bombing altitude would be 16,000 feet to ensure maximum accuracy. All were aware that at this height the 88mm flak batteries could be deadly accurate. Each aircraft would carry two 2,000lb HE bombs on external wing racks. Their destination was Watten near St Omer, and unbeknown to the crews they would be bombing the concrete launching sites for the German's secret V1 weapons. This was the first of countless attacks, code-named *Crossbow*, made by the Allied air forces against V1 weapon sites. Although most crews would dub them 'Noball' targets.

In August there was a change of Fighter Commander, when on the 29th Frank Hunter was replaced by Major General William E. Kepner, hitherto commander of the stateside Fourth Air Force. General Arnold had been harbouring doubts about Hunter's leadership; he viewed the low loss rate of his fighters as evidence of Hunter's 'lack of urgency'. Earlier in the month Hunter had been clearly directed to use his *full* resources on escort duties rather than mainly on fighter sweeps. He had countered with the argument that he had insufficient numbers, that P-47s lacked the operational range, and he also felt that they were not effective close-escort fighters. Hunter was loath to send them to the limit of their range, at least until his Command could outnumber the Luftwaffe. Really he saw the battle for air superiority as more akin to that of the Battle of Britain – fighters against fighters in 'dog fights' – in which aspect he considered the P-47 to be superior. After the bomber losses suffered during August, Arnold demanded that the Command's

General H.H. 'Hap' Arnold visited Eighth's bases during September 1943. (USAF)

primary duty be the protection of the bombers. Clearly Hunter had to go, despite the fact that Eaker supported him.

In early September General Arnold made his first visit to the Eighth and toured a number of operational airfields, meeting many crews. Whether his presence provided a boost to flagging morale is debatable. Eaker felt that he needed to demonstrate to Arnold that the Eighth could still strike a heavy blow at German targets despite the Schweinfurt/Regensburg disaster. On the 6th the SKF instruments bearings plant at Stuttgart and a nearby diesel engine factory were selected as the targets. Stuttgart was almost 100 miles further south than Schweinfurt, another deep penetration mission with only limited

Polly Ann of 366th squadron of 305th Bomb Group over Stuttgart – 6th September 1943. Seventeen days later it crash-landed at Chelveston, killing ten airmen. (National Archives)

fighter escort, with the added complication, at least in respect of the First Wing's B-17s, of critical fuel consumption, as Stuttgart was nearing their operational range.

For the first time Eaker was able to despatch over four hundred bombers albeit that almost seventy B-24s, on their first mission since returning from North Africa, merely flew a diversion over the North Sea. Heavy cloud hampered the assembly of the B-17s and as the formations crossed over enemy territory, the conditions worsened considerably; perhaps but for the presence of General Arnold the mission would have surely been aborted. It proved almost impossible to locate the primary targets, indeed Brigadier General Robert Travis, Commander of the 1st Wing, circled Stuttgart for some thirty minutes in a vain attempt to sight the target. The adverse weather had caused the formations to become scattered with Groups seeking optional targets over a wide area.

The Luftwaffe waited patiently for the B-17s to be beyond the range of their escorts before it struck with a vengeance at the scattered

B-24s of 389th Bomb Group prepare to take-off from Hethel. The 'Sky Scorpions' were operational from the UK on 7th September 1943. (USAF)

formations. The 388th bore the brunt of the frenzied attacks; it was later estimated that enemy fighters attacked every thirty seconds. Out of seventeen B-17s destroyed, eleven came from the 388th with one squadron (563rd) disappearing from the skies. The 92nd also had a hard time, losing seven. In total forty-five B-17s (13%) were lost in action with at least another ten written-off; many losses were due to battle-damage and fuel shortage. Five came down in Switzerland, twelve ditched in the Channel and eight crash-landed in southern England. It was a disaster of some magnitude, although the press releases highlighted the crews' heroism and claimed that 'a vital blow had been struck against Nazi Germany'. General Arnold thought it a total failure, and the mission is now considered as the Eighth's most costly fiasco of the war.

On the night of the 8/9th, five crews of the 422nd squadron of 305th Group at Chelveston joined RAF Lancasters attacking a long-range gun battery at Boulogne. Another seven night-operations were mounted by the squadron in the coming weeks with two B-17s lost in action. Selected crews of 95th, 96th and 385th also began night-training with some taking part in the RAF's practice night-bombing exercises. However, it was decided that the necessary B-17 modifications and the enormous task of training its crews in night-flying made it an unpractical proposition. The salvation of its daylight offensive rested firmly on the provision of long-range fighter escorts, and as yet that was still a while away.

For the next few weeks it was a matter of returning to airfields as part of Operation *Starkey*, and also revisiting a number of familiar French targets. On the 9th of the month two new Groups entered the fray. The fourth B-24 Group, 392nd based at Wendling, attacked Drucat airfield at Abbeville. It would remain in England flying mainly diversionary missions whilst the three vastly experienced B-24 Groups returned again to North Africa. Amongst the fighter escorts were pilots of 352nd at Bodney, destined to become one of the most successful fighter Groups. Five days later another new P-47 Group, 355th at Steeple Morden, became operational; Fighter Command was gaining in strength.

On 13th September changes were made in the structure of Bomber Command. The First Bomb Wing was redesignated Bombardment Division comprising three Combat Bomb Wings (1st, 40th, and 41st), the Second Division (B-24s) would have three Wings (2nd, 14th and 20th), and Fourth Wing became the Third Division also with three Wings (4th, 13th and 45th). Each Wing would control two or three Bomb Groups. Fighter Command had already introduced the Wing structure to control its Groups, it ultimately comprised three – 65th to 67th. This operational structure would remain in place for the rest of the war, except for extra Wings as new Groups arrived, and in 1945 the Bombardment Divisions would be renamed 'Air'.

In August a new Bomb Group, 482nd, had been formed at Alconbury; the only one to be activated in the UK. It was commanded by Colonel Baskin R. Lawrence, Jr and the nucleus of its original aircraft and crews came from the 92nd. Its specific function was to provide a Pathfinder Force (PFF) of radar-equipped aircraft to precede the main force, to locate and mark targets obscured by cloud. It was almost a year to the day since the RAF had formed its own Pathfinder Force. The Group comprised three squadrons, 812nd, 813rd and 814th, and operated B-17s and B-24s. The aircraft were equipped with H2S, the RAF's airborne radar scanner, and some with *Oboe* Mk 1, a blind bombing device, although difficulties were experienced fitting *Oboe* into B-17s. The B-17s with H2S were most distinctive, having the appearance, or so it was said, of 'a bath tub slung under the nose' – the scanner had to extend clear beneath the aircraft. The Americans called their H2S sets 'stinky' and when their own version, H2X, was developed, it was dubbed *Mickey* – short for Mickey Mouse sets! The Group's ultimate objective was to train a sufficient number of PFF crews to provide a nucleus for each Bomb Group.

After several trials, the first PFF-led mission was mounted on 27th September to the small port of Emden, just across the border with

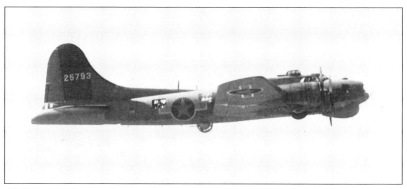

Stinky – PFF B-17 of 482nd Bomb Group at Alconbury. It crash-landed on 10th November 1943 and was salvaged. (Smithsonian Institution)

Holland, thought to be handling considerable shipping due to the severe damage inflicted by the RAF on Hamburg. Emden was also selected as it provided a strong contrast of land and sea to show more clearly on the airborne cathode ray screens. Four PFF aircraft were detailed, but only two were effective because of malfunctioning radar sets. Nevertheless there was some improvement in the bombing accuracy, 'our bombardiers dropped their bombs through 9/10 cloud' and the operation was considered 'a moderate success'.

The mission had the advantage of fighter escorts for the whole trip, some using US 108-gallon drop tanks and the rest US 75-gallon tanks to enable them to make the four hundred mile round trip. The Luftwaffe's pilots were perhaps more shocked than the bomber crews to see so many fighters – over two hundred and sixty – supporting the formations. The six Groups claimed twenty-one victories with the 78th in the forefront with ten, followed closely by 353rd with eight – all Me 110s – proving that these rather out-dated twin-engined fighters were no match for P-47s.

In the first week of October Eaker and his staff at Pinetree could view the future with, at the very least, a certain guarded optimism. Since the disastrous Stuttgart operation, losses had been relatively light – forty-eight in ten missions. For the first time two heavy bomber missions had been mounted on the same day (23rd September) and the full B-24 force would be back in action after an absence of some months. H2S had been trialled on two missions and although it was acknowledged that greater expertise was required of its PFF crews, the new technology offered a welcome bonus in cloudy conditions. The British device

120

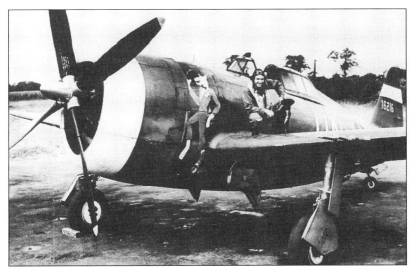

Lt Wayne O'Connor of 63rd squadron, 56th Fighter Group with his dog Slipstream. O'Connor was lost on escort to Münster – 11th November 1943. (USAF)

Carpet, an airborne radio transmitter to jam the enemy's *Wurtzburg* gun-laying radar, was being installed in a number of B-17s; there was evidence that *Carpet* did reduce casualties from flak. Furthermore the first B-17Gs, with their greatly improved armament, had begun to arrive as replacement aircraft.

General Kepner could also consider that the fighter situation appeared more favourable. In the last few missions his pilots had claimed over fifty victories for the loss of a handful of aircraft, and their presence in strength had certainly reduced bomber losses. American drop-tanks were arriving in greater numbers, thus extending the range of his burgeoning force. Two new Groups, 356th and 55th, were in training and would shortly become operational; more significantly the 55th was equipped with the long-range P-38s, and General Arnold had assured Eaker that the Eighth would be afforded priority in the supply of this scarce fighter.

Therefore it would appear that the Eighth had managed to survive and surmount the heavy losses of the summer, and could now enter the Fall with a measure of optimism and confidence that their sternest tests had passed. Yet, within a week these hopes would have been dashed and the Eighth Air Force found itself, as one US historian wrote, 'brought to the brink of disaster'.

8

FROM 'BLACK WEEK' TO BEYOND

A crisis point for the Eighth was reached when in just seven days, one hundred and fifty-four aircraft were lost in action and fifteen hundred airmen were killed or missing in action. This traumatic time became known as 'Black Week' when its fortunes sank to their lowest point, and its future, and that of the daylight bombing offensive, once more hung perilously in the balance. But any air force that could sustain and survive such harrowing losses and still come back fighting with even greater strength, deserves to be called 'Mighty'.

The first operation in 'Black Week' was mounted on 8th October 1943 to the shipbuilding and industrial town of Bremen and the U-boat yards at Vegesack. The First Division made the more direct flight across Holland, whereas the Third's Groups approached Bremen from the North Sea, followed by the Second Division's B-24s to Vegesack with 93rd and 389th Groups making their operational return after North Africa. The 381st, led by Major Bill Ingehutt, flying in the low group position of the leading Wing, encountered severe Luftwaffe opposition, losing seven aircraft, over half of the First Division's losses; its gunners claimed nineteen enemy aircraft and for its crews' courage and determination the Group was awarded its first DUC.

One that miraculously survived was *Tinker Toy*, which had quickly acquired the reputation of a 'jinx ship', several times returning with dead and wounded on board. It was attacked head-on by several fighters and one of the many 20 mm cannon shells shattered the windscreen and beheaded the pilot, Lt William Minerich. The co-pilot, Lt Thomas Sellars, although wounded and in a severe state of shock, managed to bring the aircraft back to a safe landing at Ridgewell assisted by T/Sgt Henry T. Miller, the top gunner, who operated the throttles. For their outstanding courage and determination Sellars was awarded the DSC and Miller the DFC. Sellars did not return to operational flying for another three months.

The Third Division also suffered, especially the unlucky 100th. A tailgunner tersely reported the Group's demise: 'Three-eight-six got it. A Fw rammed it and both blew up ... *Phartsac* gone to the worst flak I have seen [300 guns] ... *Salvo Sal* ... *War Eagle* ... *Piccadilly Lilly* ... *Marie Helena* ... all gone ... the 100th doesn't exist any more.' Seven aircraft, seventy airmen lost, including the 'indestructible' Major Gale 'Bucky' Cleven, the 351st Squadron Commander and 'hero' of Regensburg, who had been nominated for a Medal of Honor but was awarded the DSC; he and his crew survived as POWs. Another, *Just-a-Snapping*, flown by Captain Everett Blakeley with Major John Kidd as co-pilot, crash-landed at RAF Ludham with five injured crewmen; the B-17 had 800 separate flak holes and was a write-off. The mission had

B-17s of the 94th Bomb Group return from Marienburg – 9th October 1943 - 'A classic example of American precision bombing.' (Imperial War Museum)

Miss Noralee II: B-17 of 548th squadron of 385th Bomb Group. MIA Anklam – 9th October 1943, force-landed in Denmark – 1 evaded, 10 POWs. (via G. Hammond)

cost the Eighth thirty heavy bombers (7.5%) and three P-47s; its crews were firmly back on the operational treadmill. As one commented, 'losses just came to be a way of life in the ETO'.

The next day four targets were detailed for three hundred and seventy-eight heavies – the Focke-Wulf plant at Marienburg, U-boat yards at Danzig, the port of Gdynia in Poland and the Arado aircraft components factory at Anklam near the Baltic coast. This was the shortest mission and Brigadier General Travis of the First Division led his six Groups. They faced the stiffest and heaviest Luftwaffe opposition on the day; over two hundred fighters employing rockets, air-to-air bombing and heavy cannons. The three Groups, 91st, 351st and 381st, lost thirteen out of eighteen aircraft destroyed. Despite the fierce onslaught and heavy flak, accurate bombing was achieved causing considerable production delays. The 351st returned to Polebrook with twenty-six claims and was awarded its first DUC.

The bombing of Danzig and Gdynia was less impressive. Effective smokescreens hampered the crews, although some direct hits were made on several vessels. In direct contrast the bombing of Marienburg, led by Colonel Russell Wilson of the 4th Wing, was of the highest standard. Because minimum flak had been expected ninety-six crews bombed from 11/13,000 feet, 60% were within 1,000 feet of the target and 83% within 2,000 feet. A new type of incendiary was used – M.47A2, jellied napalm – and extensive damage was inflicted. One crewman described how 'the whole building complex seemed to leap about 50 feet into the air and then began to disintegrate ... very satisfying type of warfare ... and very rare'. Eaker described it as 'a classic example of American precision bombing' and it was considered the best bombing of the year, if not of the entire war. In total twenty-eight bombers failed to return, three landed in Sweden, and one in Denmark; but losses were slowly and ominously mounting.

For the third day in succession, the Eighth was out in force on the 10th, this time over Münster, a vital rail centre for the industrial Ruhr and the nearby Dortmund-Ems Canal, as well as a major garrison city for the German Army. For the first time the crews were briefed to bomb the city centre; '[You] will hit the homes of the working population of these marshalling yards. You will disrupt their lives so completely that their morale will be seriously affected and their will to work and to fight will be substantially reduced'.

It was a disastrous day for the Third Division and its leading Wing, the 13th. Colonel John K. Gerhart of the 95th led the Force and the two Divisions would fly about fifteen minutes apart, creating a bomber stream some seventy-five miles long. The 13th Wing suffered thirteen crews aborting for various mechanical defects thus weakening the formations. The B-24 diversionary flight over the North Sea was abortive when the lead aircraft lost all electrical systems and radio contact with its formations, which then turned back. Additionally the 355th detailed to give escort cover over the target area, was fogged in at Steeple Morden and failed to make the rendezvous.

The Wing, comprising the 95th, 390th and 100th, was attacked by over two hundred and fifty fighters of all types firing cannons and rockets, as well as Dornier 217 bombers firing projectiles from a safe distance. For some forty minutes they endured probably the most intensive and concentrated Luftwaffe onslaught of the war. As one survivor recalled, '[They] came at us in endless waves ... again ... again and again ...' The 95th lost five, the 390th eight crews, including *Tech Supply* piloted by Lt John Winant, the son of the US Ambassador to Britain (he survived as a POW in Colditz Castle). Its gunners claimed sixty enemy aircraft – the highest total on a single mission – such was the ferocity of the air battle, which has been likened to 'the Charge of the Light Brigade or General Picket's charge at Gettysburg in the Civil War.'

The luckless 100th Group, which had already lost seventeen aircraft in four weeks, was virtually decimated losing twelve out of fourteen. Only the badly damaged *Royal Flush*, piloted by Lt Robert Rosenthal on his third mission, returned to Thorpe Abbotts, landing on two engines. Rosenthal became a living legend in the 100th, rising to the rank of Major, completing fifty-two missions, shot down twice and success-fully evading. The only other survivor, *Little Mike*, made an emergency landing at RAF Wattisham; it was salvaged a couple of days later. From this disastrous mission the 100th became known as 'The Jinx outfit' and acquired the macabre name of 'The Bloody Hundredth'. As one member said, 'When we lost, we lost big ... we lost with panache'!

For its leadership and excellent bombing the 95th was awarded its second DUC; the citation recorded 'extraordinary valor, audacity and courage under fire'. The Division lost twenty-nine aircraft (21%), whereas the First escaped virtually intact, losing only a solitary B-17 *Argonaut III* from 351st; six Groups had been forced to seek 'targets of opportunity' at Coesfeld and Enschede airfields in Holland, and they had been well escorted by the 4th Group. Their 'rivals', the 56th led by Major David Schilling, had provided excellent withdrawal support, claiming ten enemy aircraft with the Major destroying a Fw 190 to become an ace. Captain Walter Beckham of 353rd Group shot down three, also giving him ace status. Despite the high claims, post-war records revealed that the Luftwaffe had lost twenty-six in action and another seven salvaged. The city centre had been severely damaged and over 760 civilian and army personnel were killed.

Mercifully, for the crews, the following day (11th) their airfields were shrouded in fog, time to digest the harrowing and sobering facts that in just three days eighty-eight bombers had been lost and eight salvaged. Eaker received a congratulatory cable from General Arnold: '[You] are putting an increasing proportion of your bombers where they will hurt the enemy. Good work. As you turn your effort towards crippling the sources of the still-growing German fighter forces the air war is clearly moving toward our supremacy in the air. Carry on.' Air Chief Marshal Sir Charles Portal sent a message: '[My] deep admiration of your splendid achievements over Germany during the last few days ... and expressing our full confidence in ever-growing success for your command in the future.' The scene was now set for one of the most bloody and costly battles in the Eighth's short history – a return to Schweinfurt.

On Thursday 14th October hundreds of bomber crews waited at their bases for the take-off flares. They all knew they 'were in for a bad day'; memories of their previous Schweinfurt mission just two months earlier were still all too fresh and real. Intelligence sources had revealed that ball bearing production had returned to maybe 65%; so this return operation was necessary to strike a serious blow at the industry, which, if successful, would 'shorten the war by at least six months', or at least that was what the crews were told at their briefings. It would be a round trip of some nine hundred miles or about seven hours flying time, mostly without fighter escort.

The Eighth planned to send three hundred and sixty B-17s and sixty B-24s in three task forces. However, weather and mechanical defects considerably reduced this figure. Two hundred and ninety-one B-17s ultimately left and just twenty-nine B-24s made the assembly. This depleted force was sent on a diversionary feint towards Emden. The First Division's Wings (40th, 1st and 41st) would be in the vanguard, taking the direct route to the north of Aachen. The Third's Wings (4th, 13th and 45th) would follow after an interval of ten minutes, flying a parallel course some thirty miles to the south along the Luxembourg border before swinging east to Schweinfurt. Heavy cloud formations caused problems for the escorting fighters, only 56th and 353rd managed to make it to Aachen; the latter Group claimed ten enemy aircraft.

Unbeknown to the Eighth the number of flak batteries at Schweinfurt had been doubled since August making it now 'the best defended town in Western Germany'; the Luftwaffe was also far stronger than believed, its losses over the previous week having been relatively light. The crews were approaching what was described as 'sheer utter merciless hell'! The First Division, and in particular its 40th and 41st Wings, mainly suffered from the concentrated and severe aerial onslaught. The 40th lost twenty-nine out of fifty-three (55%!), the 305th thirteen, the 306th ten (the second time that it had lost one hundred airmen on a single day) and the 92nd six crews. The 41st Wing had thirteen aircraft missing (25%); in total the Division lost forty-five aircraft (30%). By comparison the Third fared better, fifteen aircraft lost (10.5%), of which the 96th lost seven crews and 94th six. All fifteen crews of 390th managed to make it to the target and they placed 50% of their bombs within 1,000 feet of the target, with fourteen returning safely to Framlingham. Their performance earned the Group its second DUC. Only one Group, the 100th, survived intact; it could only provide eight aircraft such was the severity of its recent losses.

The air battle was intense in the extreme, with the Luftwaffe flying over five hundred and sixty sorties. One crewman recalled 'as many as ten to fifteen B-17s going down at one time'; it was also said that on the route home, 'we could see the smoking, flaming wreckage of ships that had gone down ... For awhile one could actually follow the path of the battle, by looking at the wreckage on the ground.' Wing Commander J.E. 'Johnnie' Johnson, leading a Spitfire formation to escort the B-17s across Holland and the North Sea, recalled that 'the Fortresses had taken a terrible mauling, there were gaping holes in their precise formations. Some were gradually losing height ... what a fight it must have been ... more than half the bombers we escorted were shot up. One or two ditched in the sea, and many others, carrying dead and badly injured crew members, had to make crash landings.'

'Black Thursday', as it became known, resulted in sixty B-17s lost in action, another seven salvaged and over one hundred and thirty damaged to some extent. Although almost two hundred enemy aircraft were claimed, the Luftwaffe actually lost thirty-eight – still a formidable total. It lost a leading ace, Oberleutnant Wilhelm-Ferdinard Galland of JG 26, the brother of the famous Adolf. He had been shot down by a P-47 over Holland. The bombing had been accurate and considerable damage inflicted, causing a 50% fall in production. As a result the ball bearing industry was dispersed, thus making it less vulnerable to attack and in that sense the costly operation could be considered counter-productive.

The operation was hailed as a great success. General Arnold commented, '[The] opposition isn't nearly what it was and we are wearing them down'! Air Chief Marshal Portal thought, 'The Schweinfurt raid may well go down in history as one of the most decisive air actions of this war.' But nothing could really disguise the fact that it was a serious body blow to the Eighth, especially considering its recent heavy losses. It proved conclusively that unescorted bombers, however heavily armed, could not operate against determined fighter opposition without incurring heavy and unacceptable losses, and that long-range fighter escorts were desperately needed if the Eighth was to survive. Certainly it had lost the capability to compete for air superiority; it was now time to lick the wounds, wait for replacement aircraft and crews and moreover the arrival of long-range fighters. In fact poor weather over the following months dictated that operations would be restricted, and the Eighth's bombers would not venture to any German targets beyond fighter range.

During this time of unremitting gloom when morale in the Eighth sank to a low ebb, there was the faintest glimmer of hope. On the day after Schweinfurt, P-38s of 55th Group at Nuthampstead carried out a sweep of the Dutch Islands. Would they now prove to be the Eighth's saviours? Another P-38 Group, the 20th, was busy training at King's Cliffe but due to shortage of aircraft it would not become fully operational for another two months. The P-47 force had also increased now that the 356th at Martlesham Heath had entered the fray.

The Eighth was now joined in the UK by another US Air Force – the

P-38s returned to the Eighth in October 1943. (via J. Adams)

Ninth – which had been operating in North Africa since November 1942. It became a major tactical force preparing the way for the invasion of Europe, along with the RAF's 2nd Tactical Air Force. The most immediate effect on the Eighth was that its B-26 Groups were transferred to the Ninth; the last B-26 mission had been flown on 9th October. General Eaker viewed this as a 'blessing in disguise', as he had always felt that B-26s 'did not sit easily' in his Command. The arrival of the Ninth also meant that for the next few months the Eighth could call upon its fighters to provide additional escort support.

The losses sustained during 'Black Week' reduced the operational status of Bomb Groups; there were many empty hard standings and empty beds in the billets. The First Division had only one hundred and thirty-five operational B-17s compared with over three hundred and twenty just a week earlier, and the number of operational combat crews numbered one hundred and two, a reduction of 50%. Nevertheless, on the 17th and 18th October missions to Düren were dispatched, only to be recalled whilst over the North Sea because of bad weather.

The Düren operation was finally made on the 20th, although cloud formations upwards to 28,000 feet caused considerable problems for the crews. Düren was considered 'an important factory-railroad-centre'; it was situated to the east of Aachen well within fighter escort range. The 41st Wing led the B-17 force with *Oboe*, the blind-bombing

129

device, being used for the first time. Whether by mechanical fault or human error, the apparatus failed and all but one of the First Division's Groups returned with their bombs. The Third bombed from 30,000 feet, nine aircraft were lost, and it was not a successful operation.

Weather conditions ensured that there would be no further heavy bomber operations during October. But on 3rd November the Eighth proceeded to demonstrate it was far from a spent force. Over five hundred and sixty heavies and three hundred and seventy-eight fighters were dispatched to the port of Wilhelmshaven. The 96th Group was able to send fifty B-17s in three formations – a record; as was the one hundred and seventeen strong B-24 force. The 482nd (PFF) would use H2X for the first time; this American version used a new and shorter microwavelength, claimed to produce a sharper picture of the ground below. Some Groups were armed with incendiaries; as one crewman remarked, 'we intended to burn up the city'. The feature of the mission was the strong fighter support with P-38s going all the way to the target, which was greatly appreciated by the bomber crews – 'Those Lightnings were beautiful that day. It sure felt good having them there.' The pilots downed four enemy fighters without loss and P-47s chalked up another eleven. Just seven B-17s were lost; two from the 306th collided outwards over the North Sea. The American press described it as a '1,000 airplane raid', factually correct if the Ninth's B-26s were included. The mission did much to restore the American public's confidence in the Eighth's ability to bomb Germany without suffering high losses.

Two days later (5th) three hundred and seventy-four B-17s bombed marshalling yards at Gelsenkirchen and they were outnumbered by

Jerk's Natural: B-24 of the 93rd Bomb Group at Hardwick on return from North Africa. (USAF)

over three hundred and eighty fighters; P-38s claimed five victories with the 56th downing one more. Bomber losses were again light – eight. B-24s attacking marshalling yards at the dreaded Münster were not afforded fighter escort and three were lost, all from the 392nd. Obviously the P-38s were making a difference and the 55th's Commanding Officer, Lt Col Frank B. James, reported that, 'Morale is sky high'. Sadly these initial successes were a false dawn. The Group would suffer a hard time during the winter, mainly due to the unreliability of their aircraft especially at high-altitudes, and also once the enemy pilots had gained the measure of the new fighter.

For days British weather successfully hindered the Eighth's operational schedules. For much of the time its airfields were shrouded in fog; several missions that did start were recalled and most were hampered by heavy cloud. On 13th November the first of six missions to Bremen was mounted, the start of what could be called the 'Battle of Bremen'. It was a prime *Pointblank* target. Not only a major port with important shipyards, it also housed a Focke-Wulf plant as well as several synthetic oil plants. As the Eighth knew from previous visits, it was well protected with upwards of six hundred flak guns and the Luftwaffe usually defended the city and port in strength. On this occasion the bombers had strong fighter support, although severe winds limited their range. During the assembly heavy turbulence and icing caused problems; four B-17s of the First crashed killing thirty airmen and the Division was recalled before the assembly was completed. The Second Division bore the brunt of the losses – thirteen out of sixteen missing in action, and the 55th Group returned somewhat battered, losing seven out of forty-five pilots (15%) with two P-38s crashing on return, for seven victories.

Three days later the Eighth returned to Norwegian targets. The First Division was allocated a molybdenum mine at Kraben, believed to produce 85% of this vital steel hardening metal. The bombing was successful with almost half the buildings destroyed. *Knock Out Dropper*, from the 303rd, became the first B-17 to complete fifty missions. It would soldier on to seventy-five in March 1944 before returning to the States to act a crew trainer. The target for the Second and Third Divisions was a generating plant at Rjükan, set deep in the mountains of the Telemark province, which produced 'heavy water' for the German nuclear programme. The crews were informed that it created material essential to the enemy's secret weapons, which added a certain spice to the mission. Because of the distance involved bomb loads were reduced and precise and accurate bombing runs were

B-17s of 95th Bomb Group (334th Squadron top and 412th below) to Rjükan, Norway – 16th November 1943. (USAF)

needed to hit the small target. It was a most successful strike, intelligence later revealed the progress of the programme had been delayed for several months. B-24s returned to Norway on the 18th when a Junkers 88 assembly plant at Kjeller near Oslo was targeted; again the bombing would be made at 12,000 feet. On the return flight a dozen Junkers 88s attacked with rockets and cannons; nine B-24s were lost, including three forced to land in Sweden with another three salvaged. The experienced 'Flying Eightballs' (44th) lost six.

Since late 1942 the Eighth's Fighter Command had considered using fighters in a fighter/bomber role. Now blessed with a stronger P-47 force, the project was revived and one squadron (351st) of the 353rd at Metfield had undertaken dive-bombing training in North Wales. On 25th November the squadron led by the Group's Commanding Officer, Lt Col Loren G. McCollom (late of 56th Group) bombed Ft Rouge airfield near Omer. Each P-47 carried a single 500 lb bomb. Heavy flak was encountered and *Cookie*, flown by the Colonel, received a direct hit; he survived as a POW. The experiment was not a great success but the Group, under Colonel Glenn E. Duncan, persevered during December, developing dive-bombing and ground attack tactics that became

22nd November 1943 – Presentation of the MOH to Colonel Leon W. Johnson at Shipdham. 'Flying Eightball' symbol of 44th Bomb Group painted out. (USAF)

standard procedure. Another method was trialled by the 56th at the nearby Longuenesse airfield; its pilots bombed on a signal from a lone B-24. Sadly a failure in the release mechanism delayed the bombing and most missed the airfield. Early in 1944 several other Groups would try their skill at this new type of fighter warfare.

The following day the fighter pilots were back at their normal duties – escorting over five hundred heavies bound for Bremen. It was a hard and physically demanding mission, heavy clouds forced the formations above 28,000 feet, temperatures fell to -50°C, thick ice covered the screens and windows and guns froze. The bombers' heavy contrails gave cover for the strong and persistent enemy fighters, and the crews reported every known type of German fighter in action including some Junkers 87s (Stuka dive-bombers). The target was obscured by cloud and smokescreens and the flak was 'as thick and heavy as usual'. The fighters made their presence felt, downing thirty-six for the loss of four P-47s, the best performance on a single mission. Most successful was the 56th, no fewer than twenty-three claimed – then a record. The 'Wolfpack' had scored its 100th victory earlier in November, double that of its closest rival – the Fourth. Nevertheless twenty-five bombers

B-24 of 392nd Bomb Group on the way to Bremen – 29th November 1943.

were lost. Bremen was proving to be a hard and costly nut to crack.

A new B-17 Group, the 401st from Deenethorpe, made its debut over Bremen. It was commanded by Colonel Harold W. Bowman, whose firm and positive leadership ensured that it became one of the most efficient and effective Groups in the Eighth with a high standard of bombing accuracy. New combat units allocated to the Eighth had fallen well behind the planned figures considered necessary to achieve its *Pointblank* objectives – as low as 40% in October. Several Groups destined for the Eighth were diverted to the new strategic bombing Air Force – the 15th – activated in Italy on 1st November, and Eaker formally protested to Washington but to no avail. During December three fresh B-24 Groups, 445th, 446th and 448th and one B-17 Group, 447th, along with two P-47 Groups, 358th and 359th became operational. Nevertheless, with twenty-five operational Bomb Groups the Eighth was still far short of the planned thirty-eight by the end of 1943, although its eleven Fighter Groups were as projected.

Bremen was again the target on the 29th. As one Group's crews were told at their briefing, 'We destroyed Bremen three days ago, today we are returning to destroy it again', which raised a few smiles! Heavy cloud and effective smokescreens resulted in less than 50% of the crews bombing, thirteen were lost with the Luftwaffe gaining some revenge for the previous mission, accounting for sixteen fighters (including seven P-38s). The following day when an aircraft engine castings plant at Solingen in the Ruhr was the target, the weather prevented the First and Second Divisions from continuing. Eaker's diktat to his commanders had always been clear and unequivocal: '[If] a target has not been bombed effectively, you will return again and again until the job is done properly.' Thus the two Divisions returned to Solingen on 1st December and 8% of the force (twenty-four) failed to return.

With the benefit of hindsight this day can be seen as a critical turning point for the Eighth in its long and bitter battle for air superiority – with the arrival of P-51Bs of the 354th Group based at Boxted. Considering the Eighth's need for long-range fighters, it is perhaps surprising to find the Group allocated to the Ninth Air Force. However, Eaker in his wisdom had agreed with Major General Lewis Bretherton, the Ninth's Commander, that P-51s should go to his Force to simplify maintenance and repair; although there was an agreement that *all* of the Ninth's fighters would be used to support and escort the Eighth's heavy bombers until further notice, and on these operations they would be under the direction of the Eighth's Fighter Command.

The production of P-51s had fallen well behind schedule and they would be relatively rare aircraft in the coming months, with the 354th being the sole operational P-51 Group until February – hence it acquired the name 'The Pioneer Mustang Group'. Its pilots and ground crews experienced problems with their new aircraft; coolant leaks, plug failures and jammed guns reduced the Group's operational efficiency and caused several fatalities. Lt Col Donald Blakeslee, Group Executive Officer of the 4th, had been seconded to the 354th to help during their early operations. He was one of the Eighth's most experienced fighter leaders and an ex-RAF 'Eagle' pilot. Blakeslee led twenty-three P-51s, with Colonel Kenneth Martin, the Group's CO as his wingman, on a fighter sweep of the Belgian coast near Knocke. All the aircraft returned safely, as they did four days later after their first fighter escort mission to Amiens. The weather had again ensured that this bombing operation to a number of French airfields and air depots was nullified with only three out of over five hundred and forty crews bombing.

The atrocious weather persisted for several days and it was not until

11th December that another bombing mission could be flown – to Emden. On this day it was the experienced P-47 pilots of the 56th that returned to Halesworth with seventeen victories – mostly Me 110s. Two days later some First Division Groups were back over Bremen whilst the majority of the Eighth attacked Kiel and Hamburg. Just over one thousand aircraft were in action, for the loss of five bombers and two fighters. The Second Division was able to dispatch over one hundred and ten B-24s due to the entry of 445th Group at Tibenham, and the newcomers returned from Kiel without loss. James Stewart, the famous film star, was the Commander of its 703rd squadron. He would reach the rank of Colonel before returning to his pre-war career in Hollywood.

At long last the Second Division was really beginning to burgeon. On the mission to Bremen on the 16th, another new Group, 446th from Bungay, mounted its first operation. Although all the B-24s returned safely, two from 446th crashed on return but with no loss of life. The Group adopted the name 'Bungay Buckeroos' and two of its squadrons, 706th and 707th, gained a high standard of operational safety. Ten B-17s failed to return with the 96th losing four as a result of collisions and seven in total. The 354th opened its score – a Fw 190 claimed by Lieutenant Charles F. Gumm, the first of literally hundreds of enemy fighters that would fall to P-51s. The Group's day was rather marred with the loss of Major Owen M. Seaman, CO of 353rd squadron, over the North Sea due to mechanical failure.

The final operation in the 'Battle of Bremen' was mounted on the 20th. Over five hundred and forty crews were dispatched on the sixth mission to this target in five weeks; the fighter force almost numbered five hundred, helped by the entry of the 358th Group from Leiston. This P-47 Group would only operate with the Eighth for about six weeks before being transferred to the Ninth.

For the first time 'Window' or 'Chaff' was dropped – metal foil strips designed to confuse the enemy's gun-laying radar. The crews again faced fierce fighter opposition, which lasted for almost an hour, and the flak was also said to be 'very concentrated and deadly accurate ... it seemed to follow us wherever we went'. The 303rd's operational records noted it 'as one of the roughest our crews have been on.' Twenty-seven bombers failed to return, along with six fighters, including four P-51s. Although a total of forty enemy aircraft were claimed, three to P-51s, it is now thought that the Luftwaffe might have lost twenty-seven. The 381st Group suffered four losses, including their 'jinx ship', *Tinker Toy*; a Fw 190 collided with its rear fuselage and the aircraft disintegrated, only four parachutes were seen to open. The 303rd lost three B-17s, one of which resulted in the second Medal of Honor to be awarded to one of its airmen.

Jersey Bounce Jr was struck by flak and the radio/gunner, T/Sergeant Forrest L. Vosler, was wounded in the legs but still continued to fire his gun. A second direct hit resulted in shell splinters injuring his face and chest and he lost his sight. Vosler declined first aid and between bouts of consciousness he attempted to repair his damaged radio by touch, which later enabled him to radio the A/S/R services. The heavily damaged aircraft finally ditched in the North Sea off the Norfolk coast and Vosler, despite his severe injuries, managed to drag another injured crewman out onto the wing of the aircraft, where they were both pulled onto the life-raft. The crew were picked up by a trawler before being transferred to an A/S/R launch. Vosler, only twenty years old, was later awarded the Medal of Honor. After long hospital treatment in the States his sight was eventually restored.

Two missions were mounted before Christmas. The largest, on Christmas Eve, was directed at various V1 sites in the Pas de Calais. Over seven hundred and twenty bombers were engaged on the Eighth's second 'No Ball' or *Crossbow* operation. A new B-17 Group, 447th from Rattlesden, joined the Third Division for the first time. The only casualties from this large force were two B-24s of 448th, which crash-landed on their return to Seething. The Group had only started operations two days previously, when two crews failed to return from Osnabrück.

The Eighth's second Christmas in the ETO was a quiet affair, as far as operations were concerned, and the crews enjoyed their five days break; two planned missions were scrubbed due to bad weather. On the 30th another large force (710) were sent to Ludwigshafen, described as 'an important inland port with major oil and chemical plants'. It would be a long and arduous mission some eighty miles to the south-west of Schweinfurt. The targets were obscured by 10/10 clouds giving difficult bombing conditions and no substantial damage was inflicted. Twenty-three aircraft were lost, including three B-24s from the inexperienced 448th, also thirteen fighters failed to return, several as a result of fuel shortage.

Yet more long and exhausting missions were planned for New Year's Eve. Airfields at Merignac, Chateaubernard and St Jean D'Angely near Bordeaux were targeted. Five of the Third's Groups would have a shorter trip to airfields around Paris, and just fifty-seven crews of the First were detailed to attack a special target – the blockade runner,

P-51B of 353rd squadron of 354th Fighter Group creates great interest at Deenethorpe – 27th December 1943. (National Archives)

Orsono, in the Gironde estuary, known to have a cargo of crude rubber. Assembly procedures were hampered by darkness and the numbers involved, and the weather conditions over south-west France were quite unfavourable for bombing. The three Groups, 303rd, 379th and 384th, were unable to locate the *Orsono*, and Lannion, an alternative target was covered by cloud so they returned with their bombs.

The 351st suffered its worst day so far. In some six months of operations thirty-four crews had been lost in action, a moderate figure compared with the losses sustained by other Groups; indeed one of its squadrons, 509th, had not lost a single aircraft since 13th June – an amazing record. The thirty-one crews led by their CO, Colonel William A. Hatcher Jr, found Bordeaux completely obscured and as they turned away to bomb an airfield at Cognac, the Colonel's B-17 received a direct hit; he and his crew baled out and were taken prisoner. Another six aircraft were lost in action and two more crash-landed on their return. In total twenty-five bombers were lost in action; several ditched in the sea. The returning crews experienced difficult conditions – fuel shortages, poor weather and the gathering darkness – resulting in fifteen crash-landings throughout southern and eastern England;

additionally seven fighters came to grief, mainly in Kent. A costly operation to end the year, forty bombers and eleven fighters destroyed and over two hundred and sixty airmen killed/missing in action.

Despite the poor weather during December, ten bombing missions had been completed but at a high cost – one hundred and sixty-two bombers lost in action, not far short of the October total. The loss rate had fallen to 2.7% because of the record number of sorties flown – 5,895 – well below the tolerable level. The increased fighter force had not only reduced bomber losses but had claimed sixty-nine victories for the loss of twenty-eight aircraft.

Although the last three months of 1943 had been costly for the Eighth there were signs that the Luftwaffe was beginning to feel the strain. Its fighter force was slowly and steadily being depleted, although not at quite the rate that the Eighth believed. It had lost twelve most experienced fighter *experten* and its training schools were unable to replace such expertise. Also in December fighter production had fallen by 30%, though this would increase remarkably in 1944. However, the USAAF could provide far more aircraft, crews and pilots than the enemy and the Luftwaffe was beginning to lose the bitter war of attrition.

Since the dark days of 'Black Week', the Eighth had somehow managed to survive. Now with increased strength it was poised to enter 1944 with a modicum of confidence, tempered by the realisation that it would soon be severely tested on deep penetration missions into Germany, which had previously proved so costly.

9

A NEW YEAR
AND A NEW
COMMANDER

General Arnold's New Year message to the Eighth effectively set the tone for the early months of 1944. He exhorted its airmen to, 'Destroy the enemy air force wherever you find them, in the air, on the ground and in the factories.' Without doubt they proceeded to do just that with a vengeance, helped in no small measure by new orders and direction from their new Commander, Lieutenant General James H. 'Jimmy' Doolittle.

On 1st January 1944 a new Air Command was created, the United States Strategic Air Forces (USSTAF), which in February had 'in Europe' tacked on. It comprised the Eighth and Fifteenth Air Forces and its headquarters was established at Bushey Hall, Teddington. General Carl A. Spaatz returned to the UK to become its Air Commander. The Eighth's Bomber Command – 'Pinetree' – ceased to exist and its Commander, since July, Major General Frederick L. Anderson became Spaatz's Chief of Operations. Perhaps the most contentious command change was the replacement of General Eaker as the Eighth's Commander by General Doolittle, then in charge of the 15th Air Force in Italy.

The various changes had been finalised in December and possibly stemmed from the appointment, on the 6th, of General Dwight D. Eisenhower as the Supreme Commander of the Allied Expeditionary Force for *Overlord*. He wanted Spaatz as his Air Chief, as they had worked closely in the Mediterranean. Although it must be admitted

Three USAAF Generals in early 1944 – Carl A. Spaatz, James Doolittle and William Kepner. (USAF)

that General Arnold in Washington had, for several months, been harbouring misgivings of Eaker's direction of his Air Force, and the new Command offered him an opportunity of replacing Eaker. Arnold was notoriously impatient and ever eager for results, quite unwilling to accept any excuses for delay or failure, however solid or valid they were. He maintained that Eaker was only using 50% of his bomber resources, whereas Commanders in other theaters of war were closer to 70%. On 3rd December Eaker was personally directed 'to expand his operations to the greatest extent possible with aircraft and crews available'; it was rare for a senior Commander to be specifically named. Arnold was also unhappy with Eaker's rather belated acceptance of the importance of fighter escorts; he had, after all, removed Hunter despite Eaker's support for him. It was fairly clear that General Arnold had decided that he wanted a new Commander for the Eighth.

Eaker was notified of his new command by telegram on 18th December and protested most vigorously. He wanted to remain with the Eighth now that it appeared to be 'coming of age'. However, all his protests were in vain and he moved in January to command the newly formed Mediterranean Allied Air Forces. Eisenhower's view on the matter was that 'it is something of a waste to have both Spaatz and Eaker in England ... We do not have enough top men to concentrate them in one place'. It was also considered that Doolittle's previous

141

experience of providing air support for an invasion would be most beneficial for *Overlord*. The general view in the Eighth was that Eaker 'deserved and needed a rest'. Many felt that 'it mattered little as the Eighth was so well established that any Commander could run it'. One B-17 pilot spoke no doubt for many: 'all I wanted to do was to complete my twenty-five missions, whoever the hell was running the joint'!

There were just two missions flown under the 'old management' before 'Jimmy' Doolittle took charge on 6th January. Fog and heavy rain grounded the crews until the 4th when some 560 heavies left before dawn to bomb the Kiel shipyards; 10/10 clouds and an effective smokescreen resulted in mainly inconclusive bombing. The following day, Mission No 176 was mounted – the last under its Bomber Command; a force of B-17s and B-24s, two hundred and forty-five, was bound for Kiel. The crews had an even earlier take-off time, 0715 hours, due to a forecast that their airfields might possibly be closed in by mid-afternoon. The assembly in darkness caused many problems. Two B-17s collided and four crashed after take-off, resulting in thirty-six airmen killed. The First and Second Divisions each lost five aircraft, the 448th lost four B-24s to sustained Fw 190 attacks. P-51s of 354th Group had a field day bagging sixteen without loss.

Five Groups of the Third Division faced a long flight to Merignac airfield at Bordeaux and came under fighter attack for almost three hours, losing eleven B-17s with the 94th and 96th suffering the loss of four and five crews respectively. A small B-17 force attacked Tours airfield, including the 91st making its 100th mission, the first Group to reach that milestone. Since its first mission, on 7th November 1942, it had lost more aircraft and airmen than any other Group. The day's operations cost the Eighth twenty-four bombers and twelve fighters (including seven P-38s), not a particularly favourable end to its Bomber Command.

In their operational reports several Group Commanders made pertinent comments concerning the various problems associated with pre-dawn assemblies. It was generally felt that the numbers of accidents and aborts weakened a Group's defensive formations and placed added stress on the pilots and navigators. It was considered that the time saved in night-assembly (perhaps 30/40 minutes) did not warrant the loss of security of the formations or indeed the confidence of the crews. The Eighth's planners tried to avoid such pre-dawn assemblies in the future.

The first operation conducted under the new Commander was dispatched on 7th January to Ludwigshafen with moderate losses –

eighteen including six fighters. Four days later General Doolittle's mettle would be tested to the full. It was his first call for a 'maximum effort' with aircraft factories and assembly plants in the Brunswick area selected as primary targets for over six hundred and sixty bombers from the three Divisions. The First would lead to a major Fw 190 plant at Oschersleben, some thirty miles south-east of Brunswick previously visited in July 1943, whilst a smaller force was bound for a Junkers factory at Halberstadt nearby. The other Divisions were allocated aircraft plants at Brunswick.

The weather on the outward flight deteriorated quite dramatically with formidable rain clouds, sometimes towering over 28,000 feet, causing some of the fighter escorts to miss their rendezvous with the bombers. After two hours in the air the Second and Third Divisions were recalled, but as the leading Wing of the Third, under the command of Lt Col Louis E. Thorup of 94th, was nearing its target – the Me 110 assembly plant at Waggum – there was a fair chance of visual bombing so he carried on. The small formation came under almost continuous attention from the Luftwaffe but nevertheless the crews bombed with some accuracy. The 94th lost eight crews but Lt Col Thorup made it back to Bury St Edmunds and was awarded the Silver Star; the Group's brave and determined battle and its high standard of bombing brought its second DUC.

The main force, led by Brigadier General Robert Travis flying with the 303rd in *The Eight Ball*, pressed on regardless. He later maintained he had not heard any recall message! The formations encountered severe fighter opposition, said to be the strongest since the Schweinfurt mission back in October; it was estimated that three hundred fighter attacks were made in some three hours. One survivor remembers, 'they were queuing up about fifteen at a time to attack ... that day we took an all-time whipping'. The 303rd lost ten B-17s, the 381st eight and the 351st six. The 401st Group, led by Lt Col Allison C. Brooks, became isolated after the bombing run and found itself under sustained attack from thirty rocket-firing Me 110s. Then 'suddenly out of the blue' a solitary P-51 appeared and the situation miraculously changed.

The P-51, *Ding Hao*, was flown by Major James H. Howard of the 354th. Without waiting for any assistance Major Howard went into the attack and proceeded to put in a brilliant and bravura performance. For about thirty minutes he attacked the Me 110s until only one of his four machine guns was operating. He accounted for at least four and probably six with several others damaged. Colonel Brooks said, 'It was a case of one lone American against what seemed to be the entire

Bad Check – B-17 of 359th squadron, 303rd Bomb Group at Molesworth. Lost over Oschersleben – 11th January 1944. (Smithsonian Institution)

Luftwaffe . . . a one-man air force . . . it was really like something out of a Hollywood movie.' As a result of the Group's reports Major Howard was awarded the Medal of Honor for 'his skill, courage and intrepidity, which set an example of heroism, which will be an inspiration to the Armed Forces of the United States'. Howard, who had served in the Pacific and had $6\frac{1}{2}$ Japanese victories to his name, became the only fighter pilot in the ETO to receive the highest award. But for his actions the 401st could have been decimated, as it was they lost four B-17s, their highest total so far. Another crash-landed at RAF Ludham and seven made emergency landings at RAF Matlaske.

When the dust finally settled it emerged the Eighth had lost sixty bombers, for the third time in its short history, forty-two from the First Division. The gunners claimed an unrealistic number of victories (228!) and the fighters thirty-one, sixteen falling to the 354th and ten to the 56th. The Luftwaffe admitted losing forty-six. The operation again highlighted just how costly a deep penetration mission could be without adequate fighter support. General Josef Schmid, the Commander of the Jagdkorps I, stated after the war that it was 'the last victory of the German Air Force over the American Air Forces.' In August the eleven First Division Groups engaged in this mission were each awarded a DUC.

Doolittle now found the weather conditions that had so frustrated

Eaker during late 1943 also hampered his operational plans. On the 14th a number of V1 sites were attacked. These missions were no longer the easy 'milk runs' of yesteryear, the flak batteries around them had been greatly strengthened thus forcing the attacks to be made from higher bombing altitudes – closer to 20,000 than 12,000 feet. A week passed before the Eighth was again out in force, almost eight hundred heavies striking thirty-six V1 sites, some of which required up to ten bombing runs before the small targets could be located. The experienced 44th Group lost five B-24s. One ditched in the Channel as a result of fighter attacks and another three crash-landed in Kent. All were salvaged; the Group's heaviest loss since the Ploesti raid back in August.

The operation saw the entrance of a new Fighter Group, the 361st from Bottisham; the last P-47 unit to enter the Eighth. The decision had been made in Washington that P-51s would equip the Eighth in future, or at least when adequate supplies became available. This would involve the Eighth in a large retraining programme.

On 24th January General Spaatz received an urgent plea from Arnold in Washington: 'Can't we, some day, and not too far distant, send out a big number – and *I mean a big number* – of bombers to hit something in the nature of an aircraft factory and lay it flat?' A week devoid of operations had already tested Spaatz's patience and he had expressed his impatience at the Eighth's lack of action. He told Doolittle in no uncertain terms that he didn't want him using the excuse of bad weather for cancelling operations. Doolittle would later reveal that Spaatz had said to him, 'It looks like you don't have the guts to command a large air force. If you haven't I'll get someone else who has.' Spaatz thought that Doolittle had excessive concern for his airmen and too little concern for completing missions; certainly 'Jimmy' Doolittle was a very popular Commander, gaining a high respect from his airmen. But realistically he had not been given much time to settle into his new command.

Although an operation planned for the 26th was cancelled because of heavy rain and high winds, three days later the Eighth, perhaps in a direct response to Spaatz's criticism, sent out their largest force of bombers to date – eight hundred and sixty-three to Frankfurt with over six hundred and thirty fighters in attendance. The American press proudly reported 'The Greatest Armada of American airplanes ever.' One of the most famous of the Eighth's bomber pilots and leaders was flying his thirty-second mission; Lt Col Lewis E. Lyle of 303rd in *Vicious Virgin*. He had been a mere 2/Lieutenant in January 1942, having

Splendid formation of B-17s of 379th Bomb Group returning to Kimbolton. (USAF)

previously served several years in the infantry. Lyle completed his first tour in June 1943 and ultimately commanded the 379th Group with over eighty missions to his name. Twenty-nine bombers were lost but the fighter pilots had a good day, forty-seven victories for the loss of fourteen. P-38 pilots claimed thirteen and the 352nd at Bodney six; since December it had seen scant air combat. Both Captain George Preddy and Lieutenant William 'Whizz' Whisner were successful on the day and each became leading aces, with $26\frac{1}{2}$ and $15\frac{1}{2}$ victories respectively.

The next day (30th) a slightly smaller force of seven hundred and seventy-seven heavies attacked aircraft plants at Brunswick and Hannover for the loss of twenty. It was another good day for Fighter Command, forty-five enemy aircraft destroyed, with 'The Wolfpack' to the fore with sixteen to add to the six over Frankfurt; it had now passed the 200th mark. The 352nd notched up another seven; it would appear the Group's fortunes had changed for the better. All Groups were beginning to benefit from being given a certain freedom to seek out enemy fighters wherever they could be found.

This new 'free-lance' policy authorised by Doolittle on the 21st of the month at a meeting with his fighter commanders, may have originated from his first visit to Fighter Command's headquarters where he saw a large notice stating that 'The First Duty of the Eighth Air Force fighters is to bring back the bombers alive.' Kepner said that the notice dated from General Hunter's days. Doolittle ordered 'that Damned Sign' be removed and replaced with one emphasising 'The First Duty ... is to destroy German fighters'. Kepner was delighted at this new-found freedom and asked whether he now had authority to take the offensive. Doolittle replied, 'No, I am *directing* you to take the offensive.' He made it clear that a reasonable fighter escort must still be maintained but the *first priority* of Fighter Command was the destruction of the Luftwaffe's fighter force.

On the 24th a new system of escort protection was introduced whereby each Group was allocated a designated area along the bombers' route, and its pilots would provide protection as the formations passed through. Additionally Kepner authorised his Commanders to allocate a 'bouncing squadron', allowing its pilots to attack and follow any enemy fighters, as well as undertaking wide-ranging sweeps, attacking enemy aircraft either on the ground or when they were forming up. The decision to free the large fighter force would have far-reaching effects on the battle against the Luftwaffe, indeed *General der Flieger* Adolf Galland considered that from this time the Luftwaffe began to lose the air war. It is somewhat ironic that this 'free-lance' policy was really the kind of air war Hunter had envisaged back in the summer of 1943. Of course the bomber crews saw it all a little differently: 'we started to feel that the fighters are not for us ... we were feeling that we were expendable ... we were just the bait.'

The 358th at Leiston flew its last mission with the Eighth on 30th January, bowing out with two victories. It became a pawn in some 'horse trading' between the Eighth and the Ninth; the objective was for the Eighth to get their 'own' P-51 unit. By mutual consent the 358th was exchanged for the 357th Group at Raydon, then in the process of working up to operational readiness on P-51s. The 357th moved into Leiston, some forty miles away, and as one pilot remarked they just exchanged 'one mudhole for another'! The Group, led on this occasion by Major James Howard, went out on 11th February on its first mission – a fighter sweep of Rouen. The exchange proved beneficial as the 357th became the most successful P-51 unit in the Eighth, ultimately with a total of 609 victories in air combat, second to the 56th.

There was a quiet start to February. On the 2nd, ninety-five B-24s attacked V-1 sites and only two failed to return. The following day Wilhelmshaven was the primary target for some six hundred bombers and it was described as 'a fairly routine mission with little trouble at any stage.' Certainly losses were slight and unusually Fighter Command lost more fighters – nine compared to four bombers. Strong head winds had caused fuel shortages and several P-47s were abandoned near the coast and a number crash-landed. Next day

Frankfurt's marshalling yards were attacked by the three Divisions and although heavy flak was encountered, the Luftwaffe were absent from the skies; nevertheless twenty bombers were lost with another three salvaged.

For the third day in succession over five hundred bombers were dispatched, this time to French airfields. The operation was notable for the debut of two new Bomb Groups; the 452nd at Deopham Green with B-17s and the 453rd out of Old Buckenham with B-24s. The 453rd achieved the lowest loss rate in the Second Division and one squadron, 733rd, completed eighty-two missions without loss. By contrast the 452nd had a costly introduction and gained the unenviable record of having the highest number of Commanding Officers, nine in under eighteen months!

French airfields were again the targets on the 6th, although due to heavy cloud less than one third of the crews were effective. This was the day when the first official credits were given for enemy aircraft destroyed on the ground; they had to be seen to blow up or burst into flames. The Eighth recognised such ground victories as equally, if not more, dangerous as those achieved in air combat due to the concentrated flak encountered around airfields. Nevertheless, many pilots still considered that victories achieved in the air were the truest measure of a fighter pilot. However, ground strafing of airfields and other targets became increasingly important but could be expensive in men and machines, as many Groups found out to their cost.

Another day of operations was lost to bad weather, but on the 8th B-24 crews attacked V1 sites at Siracourt and Watten. The former, in the Pas de Calais, was one of a number of fixed concrete V1 sites. It would receive more than 2,000 tons of Allied bombs in over five months! The crews of the Third Division returned to Frankfurt, and whilst on its second mission the 452nd lost a crew when one aircraft crashed on take-off. Another three failed to return, including their CO, Lt Col Herbert O. Wangeman. No operations were mounted on the following day and General Spaatz recorded in his diary, 'Today is to go on record as completely wasted. Good weather at the bases, good weather over the target. But Doolittle sent NO bombers.'

The next day (10th) was not much better with only one hundred and forty-three B-17s in action over Brunswick. The weather created havoc with the fighter escorts, two Groups failed to get off and another two arrived late and were virtually ineffectual. However, those Groups that were in action had a good day – fifty-six victories – with the 356th claiming ten for the loss of one P-47. Two weeks earlier it had claimed

Flight of P-47s of 353rd Fighter Group over Metfield. First Group operation 9th August 1943.

double figures over Frankfurt, although these would be rare occasions for a Group that acquired the title of the 'hard luck' unit. The Brunswick operation was costly – twenty-nine missing in action (17%) – the 95th lost seven and the 452nd Group, five.

On the 11th, General Spaatz made it quite clear to Doolittle that once the heavy bombers had crossed the enemy coast, he should *not* recall them on account of weather, only the Air Commander had that authority. Also some rather disturbing news for the Eighth's airmen arrived from Washington. General Arnold had informed Doolittle that if the Eighth was to win air superiority, its crews would have to complete more missions, twenty-five were considered insufficient to achieve this objective. Arnold also stated that he was in favour of not imposing a minimum number but rather to leave it to the needs of the Eighth to determine when a combat tour was completed. Early in March Doolittle increased the number of missions to thirty, and in the case of fighter pilots two hundred hours of combat flying would no longer automatically constitute a completed tour.

During the following nine days just four bombing operations were mounted, mainly to V1 sites for the loss of only ten bombers. It was almost as if the Eighth was biding its time and bracing itself for Operation *Argument*, the combined Allied bombing offensive against the German aircraft industry, the plans for which had been finalised back in early November. Since then the weather had not been favourable for such an offensive. *Argument* had been first mooted in April 1943 by the Combined Operational Planning Committee headed by Brigadier General O.A. Anderson, but its broad objectives had been scaled and narrowed down to fighter airframes and components production along with ball bearings – in reality the German aircraft industry had taken centre stage.

The crew of Carol Dawn of 379th Bomb Group arrive home tired but safe after a tyre burst on landing – 11th February 1944. (USAF)

On 19th February the meteorologists forecast a spell of several days of clear skies, which would allow the visual bombing so necessary to ensure accuracy. This forecast had been confirmed by *Ultra* intercepts of German weather forecasts for Poland and eastern Germany. The massive Allied bombing offensive was activated, with the Fifteenth Air Force in Italy also being involved. RAF Bomber Command started *Argument*, later popularly called 'Big Week', on the night of 19/20th February with a heavy raid to Leipzig, which proved very costly – seventy-eight bombers lost (9.5%). The Eighth made their first contribution to 'Big Week' on the following day (20th).

On Sunday morning one thousand and three crews in sixteen Combat Wings were detailed for an ambitious strike at twelve targets, all vital to the German aircraft industry, and no less than eight hundred and thirty-five fighters would give escort support. One crewman recalled that 'the weather people had called the shot right, the weather was not a factor that morning.' Nevertheless General Doolittle, supported by Kepner, requested Spaatz to cancel the operation because of the high risk of wing and windscreen icing. But Spaatz, after seeking the advice of his right-hand man, General Anderson, and an up-dated weather forecast, gave the order to go.

Three hundred and fourteen B-17s of the Third Division were the first to leave on their long flight via Denmark, the Baltic and then south to the factories at Tutow to the north of Berlin. Three Wings found their targets at Poznan and Kreising in Poland covered by cloud, so they turned back to bomb the Marienke Heinkel plant and shipyards at Rostock with some effect. Despite encountering the heaviest fighter opposition on the day, the Division survived the ordeal with minimal losses, six, of which two were incurred by 'The Bloody Hundredth' – one landed in Sweden.

The other two Divisions crossed Holland into Germany with the 401st leading the six Combat Wings; considering it was the junior Group in the First Division, this was recognition of its growing reputation. Despite adverse weather conditions, which also hindered the Luftwaffe, the Erla Me 109 factories at Leipzig were accurately bombed causing substantial damage. For its leadership and bombing, the 401st was awarded its second DUC. Only one of its B-17s was lost in action – *Doolittle's Doughboys* – it had not taken long to acquire such an apt name!

The B-24 force also had to contend with heavy cloud. The Junkers 88 components plant at Halberstadt was obscured and the PFF equipment failed, so Helmstedt and Oschersleben were bombed with 'good results'. Over half the crews attacked the Me 110 factories near Brunswick and at Gotha with 'reasonable accuracy'. The two Divisions escaped with relatively light losses – fifteen – with no individual Group suffering unduly, although the 445th lost three crews. The fighter escort had proved to be most effective, sixty-one victories for the loss of four pilots. Once again the 354th and the 56th were to the fore, sixteen and fourteen enemy aircraft respectively. The Eighth's 'own' P-51s opened their score with Captain Calvert L. Williams downing a Me 109.

It was a promising start to 'Big Week' and the mission did create a record, the first and only time that three Medals of Honor would be awarded to Eighth airmen flying from England. The first was awarded to I/Lieutenant William R. Lawley Jr of the 305th, who was flying his fourteenth mission. His aircraft was heavily damaged before the bombing run, his co-pilot and seven of his crew were wounded and Lawley received facial injuries. With great courage and determination Lawley, despite loss of blood and suffering from shock, brought his aircraft back to make a safe emergency landing at RAF Redhill on its one sound engine. After a spell in hospital Lawley returned to the States and remained in the Service after the war.

A B-17 of the 351st, *Ten Horsepower*, took a direct hit in the cockpit whilst in action to Leipzig. The co-pilot was killed and the pilot, 2/Lieutenant Clarence R. Nelson was severely injured, losing consciousness. The bombardier considered the aircraft to be doomed and ordered the crew to bale out, which he did. However, the navigator, I/Lieutenant Walter E. Truemper and the engineer/ball-turret gunner, Staff/Sergeant Archibald Mathies, on only his second mission, had other ideas, and managed to fly the aircraft back despite intense cold because of the shattered windscreen. When they contacted their home base, Polebrook, they were advised to abandon the aircraft but refused on account of the injured pilot. They made an unsuccessful landing attempt at nearby Molesworth. Colonel Eugene A. Romig, their CO, went up to fly alongside them to try to guide them down safely. Two attempts failed and on the third attempt the B-17 finally crashed near to the airfield killing both men. The injured pilot survived the crash but later died in hospital. Truemper and Mathies, both aged twenty-six years, were posthumously awarded Medals of Honor.

On the following day (21st) the weather grounded the Fifteenth in Italy but on the previous night the RAF had bombed Stuttgart for light losses. The Eighth targeted a number of Luftwaffe air parks and airfields. Over eight hundred crews were involved but thick cloud obscured most of the primary targets. So much for the long-range weather forecast! Sixteen were lost, including one B-17 from the 457th Group at Glatton making its debut. Its crews had been ready to go the previous day but it was decided that Leipzig was far too distant and daunting a task for novice crews. The fighters accounted for thirty-three enemy fighters, with the 56th claiming twelve, all single-engined aircraft. P-51s of the 354th returned to Boxted with nine victories.

RAF Bomber Command had the following night off but the Fifteenth Air Force attacked the Messerschmitt factories at Regensburg, whilst

Colonel Donald Blakeslee leading P-51Ds of 335th and 336th squadrons of 4th Fighter Group: in combat with P-51s – 24th February 1944.

152

the Eighth planned to attack aircraft factories at Oschersleben, Bernburg, Halberstadt and Gotha, as well as returning to Schweinfurt and its ball bearing factories. Bad weather once again intervened to virtually nullify all the careful and precise planning. The Third Division's force experienced problems during assembly and before the crews reached the enemy coast Brigadier General LeMay recalled them. B-24 crews bound for Gotha were recalled whilst over Holland, and some Groups bombed airfields in that country. Only about one third of the First's crews bombed their three primary targets and it proved a costly mission – thirty-eight lost (13%) – with every Group suffering losses. The 306th engaged over the Junkers plant at Bernburg and despite the weather and strong fighter opposition, its crews bombed with great accuracy. Seven failed to return to Thurleigh and the surviving twenty-three aircraft were all damaged to some extent; the Group was awarded its second DUC. The experienced 91st lost five as did the 379th at Kimbolton, which was leading the Division. Fighter pilots were taking a steady toll of the Luftwaffe, returning with a total of fifty-nine victories, P-51s making their mark again with nineteen, four more than fell to 'the red-nosed Thunderbolts' of the 56th, as they were known to the Luftwaffe's pilots. Sadly the Eighth's leading fighter ace, Major Walter C. 'Turk' Beckham of 353rd with eighteen victories, was shot down in his P-47D *Little Demon* whilst strafing an airfield near Cologne; he was taken prisoner.

The weather forecast for Germany on the 23rd was said to be 'unsettled', sufficiently so for the Eighth to ground its crews, thus giving them a short but welcome break. The ground crews were afforded no such luxury as they strove to repair damaged aircraft and prepare their 'ships' for the next day. The Fifteenth from bases in Italy sent its B-24s to bomb the Daimler-Puch aircraft factory at Steyr in Austria. The next day the Eighth was out in force; eight hundred and nine bombers in thirteen Combat Wings, escorted by over seven hundred and sixty fighters. The Fifteenth Air Force would also be in action attacking the Messerschmitt assembly plant at Weiner Neustadt in Austria.

The Third's Groups returned to those targets detailed four days earlier – Tutow, Poznan and Kreising. This time all were obscured by heavy clouds, so alternative targets at Rostock were bombed. Only light fighter opposition was encountered and five B-17s were lost; one from the 388th landed in Sweden. The Luftwaffe had concentrated its forces over western Germany to counter the Eighth's twin major strikes against Schweinfurt and Gotha.

*Formation of B-24s of 706th squadron, 446th Bomb Group en route to Gotha –
25th February 1944. (via D. Lewis)*

The First Division escaped relatively lightly over the infamous
target – eleven lost – a marked change from the losses of 'Black
Thursday'; although the 306th that had suffered so harshly on that
day, still lost two crews. The B-24 crews bound for Messerschmitt 110
factories at Gotha faced the full fury of the Luftwaffe. Gotha was
described as 'the most valuable single target in the enemy's twin-
engined fighter complex.' From bitter experience it was known to be
heavily defended with a formidable array of 88 and 110 mm flak
batteries. The Division's leading Wing, the 2nd, sustained by far the
heaviest casualties. The experienced 'Sky Scorpions' (389th) led, along
with two relatively new Groups, the 445th and 453rd. Heavy flak was
encountered over Holland and from the German border the Luftwaffe
made strong and persistent attacks on the leading formations, despite
the presence of P-47s.

In a matter of minutes five B-24s from 445th were shot down, quickly
followed by another three. Close to Eisenach the lead bombardier of
389th suffered oxygen failure and collapsed, triggering the bomb
release lever, and other crews followed suit, releasing their bombs well
short of the target. However, the tattered remains of the 445th, only
half of the original twenty-eight crews, continued on to bomb the
primary target. Just twelve returned to Tibenham; the grim reckoning –
thirteen aircraft missing, nine heavily damaged. The 389th had lost
seven aircraft, more than it had lost in the epic Ploesti raid back in
August. The 392nd from Wendling, in the following 14th Wing, also

lost seven aircraft, but achieved a high standard of bombing, 98% falling within 2,000 feet of the aiming point; Colonel Irving A. Rendle could be proud of 'his boys'. In total thirty-three B-24s were lost (13.8%) with another three abandoned over England. The damage to the complex was not as severe as first thought, probably two to three weeks of production lost. The 445th and 392nd were each awarded a DUC for this operation.

On the following night RAF Bomber Command sent out its first major operation to Schweinfurt and lost thirty-three bombers. The Eighth mounted its fifth major operation in six days on the 25th. The First Division was dispatched to the Messerschmitt assembly plant at Augsburg and the VFK ball bearing factory at Stuttgart. The Second was detailed to attack a large air park at Fürth near Nurnberg and the Third's crews had the long haul to Me 109 plants in Regensburg. Almost clear conditions over the targets ensured that the majority of the bombing was of a high standard, especially at Regensburg where production was restricted for several months. Thirty-one were lost – twenty-five B-17s and six B-24s – the 96th lost four crews over Regensburg. Several Fighter Groups flew two escort missions and the three P-51 units – the 363rd of the Ninth flew its first mission – claimed twelve of the twenty-six victories, although two pilots were lost.

It was RAF Bomber Command that brought Operation *Argument* to a close, with a heavy and destructive night-raid on Augsburg, which the German press described as 'an extreme example of terror bombing.' Both Spaatz and Doolittle were convinced that the Eighth had administered a severe blow to the German aircraft industry, although photographic evidence proved that the damage inflicted was far less than was estimated. In fact single-engined fighter production would increase considerably over the next four months.

In a most intensive series of operations 3,328 effective bomber sorties had been mounted and 8,310 tons of bombs dropped for the loss of one hundred and fifty-eight heavies in action (4.7%) and twenty-one salvaged. A total of four hundred and forty enemy aircraft were claimed to have been destroyed, over two hundred and ten by fighter pilots; Luftwaffe sources revealed losses between two hundred and seventeen and two hundred and forty-eight, possibly 20% of its force, compared with thirty-three fighters lost by the Eighth. This was certainly a serious blow to the Luftwaffe, if not purely in terms of aircraft, which could be replaced, but in the loss of 18% of its combat pilots. As far as the Eighth's crews were concerned, their feelings about 'Big Week' might be summed up by a pilot of the 452nd at Glatton. 'We

Pistol Packing Mama – B-24D of 44th Bomb Group Shipdham. Landed in Sweden 9th April 1944. (via M. Harris)

went into it like boys and four days later we were men.'

With the weather closing in again, the Eighth was not in action until 28th February when its crews were engaged over V1 sites; it mounted thirteen *Crossbow* operations in January and February. Since it had commenced, the Eighth, the Ninth and the RAF had bombed ninety-seven sites; in two months over 12,000 tons of bombs had been dropped. Fifty sites were considered sufficiently damaged to be removed from the target list, but intelligence revealed that another twelve new sites had been completed and many others previously bombed had been repaired. There was no cause for complacency. Even in April over 17% of the Eighth's bomber sorties would be directed to V1 sites.

Without doubt the Eighth had come of age during 'Big Week'. It demonstrated that it could maintain a heavy and intensive bombing offensive over six days with comparatively low losses overall. With thirty heavy Bomb Groups now in operations, the Eighth was able to call on a greater number of aircraft and crews than RAF Bomber Command, and yet it had still not attained its full strength. It had been a harsh two months of operations, five hundred and ten bombers and one hundred and eighty-three fighters lost in action or salvaged and over 5,560 airmen killed or missing. The month ended with the Eighth acquiring its second P-51 unit; the 4th Group, the famed 'Eagles', had been equipped with P-51s during February. Despite such progress its new Commander, along with General Spaatz, realised that the ultimate German target now beckoned – Berlin – and the Reich capital would provide the true test of the Eighth Air Force.

10
BATTLING TO
'BIG B'

Early in November Air Chief Marshal Sir Arthur Harris wrote to Churchill, 'We can wreck Berlin from end to end if the USAAF will come in on it. It will cost us between 400-500 aircraft. It will cost Germany the war.' The Eighth was then hardly ready to tackle this major target. Berlin was some five hundred and fifty miles distant and without adequate long-range fighters, its losses were likely to have been prohibitive. It would have also needed clear skies for visual bombing, a rarity during the winter of 1943/4. Nevertheless the crews were first briefed for Berlin on 23rd November, but the mission was cancelled before take-off. Thus the RAF went it alone on their bitter and costly 'Battle of Berlin'; in fifteen major raids over four hundred and twenty aircraft were lost.

Some three months later it was a completely different matter. Doolittle had at his command eleven hundred heavy bombers available with combat crews, along with six hundred and fifty fighters, of which over one third were long-range P-38s and P-51s. Now the attrition of the enemy's fighter force had become the Eighth's main priority, as the planned date for

Colonel Jack S. Jenkins, CO of 55th Fighter Group; first USAAF airman over Berlin. (USAF)

Operation *Overlord* was nearing. Furthermore it was cogently argued that by attacking Berlin in strength, the Luftwaffe would 'certainly come up in great numbers to defend it.'

The first attempt was made on 3rd March 1944 but adverse weather forced the mission to be abandoned. However, the recall signals failed to reach Colonel Jack S. Jenkins and his P-38 pilots of 55th; when they finally arrived over Berlin, they flew around and could not understand where the bombers were! Thus Colonel Jenkins in his *Texas Ranger IV* could claim the honour of being the first USAAF airman over the German capital.

The following day another Berlin mission was planned for the three Divisions. It was suggested to Spaatz that B-24s should not go to Berlin because of their lower operational altitude. General Anderson at USSTAFE pointed out that the RAF went into Berlin at even lower altitudes. His namesake, Brigadier General Orville A. Anderson, the Eighth's Chief of Operations, replied, 'God, they'll just get killed in them', to which Fred Anderson is reputed to have answered, 'Well?' Heavy clouds caused assembly problems, and the Second Division was recalled; its crews' date with the Berlin flak was postponed for two days.

The extremely severe weather also hampered the B-17s. Some turned back at the enemy coast and others sought targets of opportunity in and around the Ruhr. Just three squadrons, two from 95th and one from 100th, of the 13th Wing carried on to Berlin. They were led by Lt Col Harry J. Mumford, Group Executive Officer of 95th. He later recalled, 'Going in wasn't tough, the weather was pretty bad but the clouds were broken. And it was cold – damn cold – down to 55° below zero ... the bombing was done through clouds. I'm sure we hit the place ...'

In fact thirty crews bombed by radar. They were supported by P-51s of 4th Group, led by Colonel Don Blakeslee, and later joined by 354th and 357th Groups. Despite their presence the 95th lost four crews and the 100th one. The Eighth's first mission to Berlin received maximum publicity, more so as it was completed by a 'lone formation'. Fighter Command fared badly on the day, losing twenty-four for eight victories; Flight Officer Charles E. 'Chuck' Yeager of 357th claimed his first. The following day he was shot down over France but evaded capture. Yeager finally returned to England and became a famous 'ace' with $17\frac{1}{2}$ victories. He would have a distinguished post-war career as a test pilot, the first to break the sound barrier. Eleven P-51s of the Ninth's 363rd Group were lost; they 'disappeared into heavy cloud off the French coast and were never seen again'. The 95th was awarded its

Pre-dawn briefing for crews at Polebrook before the Berlin mission of 6th March 1944. (Imperial War Museum)

third DUC, the only Group to be so honoured.

On 6th March the Eighth finally made it to Berlin in strength – its 250th mission, and the most costly operation of the war. A force of seven hundred and thirty bombers in fourteen Wings set out to bomb three primary targets. The First Division, in the lead, was bound for the VKF ball bearing factory at Erkner to the south-east of Berlin. Next came the Third with its target the Bosch electrical works at Klien Macknow in the south-west of the city. At the rear was the Second destined for the large Daimler Benz aero-engine plant at Genshagen south of Berlin. Should the targets be cloud-covered then the Friedrichstrasse railway station in the city centre was briefed as the alternative. Once assembled the bomber force extended some ninety miles long and a mile wide. Seventeen Fighter Groups with three RAF Mustang squadrons – well over eight hundred – provided escort support from the Zuider Zee to Berlin and back.

The Luftwaffe made its first assault near Hasseluerre some twenty miles inside Germany, with the 13th Wing victim of a fierce strike by Me 109s and Fw 190s; in less than thirty minutes twenty B-17s were shot down and a number seriously damaged. The 100th lost thirteen and the 95th six. Ten minutes later the leading 1st Wing suffered a sustained attack by over one hundred single and twin-engined fighters in *gruppens* of thirty to forty strong – 'it looked as if they were throwing the entire Luftwaffe at us.' Thirteen B-17s were destroyed – six came from the leading Group, 91st – two collided and several were

Tremblin' Gremlin of 384th Bomb Group following two 303rd B-17s through flak – 6th March 1944. This B-17 was lost over Hamm in September. (Imperial War Museum)

damaged.

The embattled crews now had to face the city's formidable flak defences – seventy-eight heavy batteries (over four hundred guns from the feared 88 mm to the 128 mm 'master guns') besides fourteen light batteries. The intensity of flak was such that 'it didn't seem possible that anything could fly through it.' Two B-17s and three B-24s fell, including a PFF B-17 of 482nd with Brigadier General Russell Wilson, the Force Commander on board. One of the four survivors was its co-pilot 1/Lt John 'Red' Morgan, a Medal of Honor winner, who was taken prisoner. Several other aircraft were so severely damaged that they could not make it back. The B-17s' targets were covered in cloud and it was too late to change course for the city centre so the crews dropped their bombs in and around greater Berlin and elsewhere. Only three Groups of the Second Division were able to bomb their primary target.

On the long journey home the Luftwaffe struck again. This time the 45th 'A' Wing suffered with the 388th losing six B-17s. General

Doolittle chose Kimbolton to witness the return of the bombers. He must have been heartened, if only briefly, to watch all but one of the 379th's aircraft return safely. The final figures were horrendous, sixty-nine bombers lost in action along with eleven fighters. The 100th lost fifteen, adding more credence to its 'jinx' reputation, and the 95th lost eight. The Second's heaviest loss was borne by the 458th from Horsham St Faith on only its third operation, four fell to flak and one to fighters.

One hundred and seventy-eight enemy aircraft claimed destroyed far exceeded the Luftwaffe's true loss of sixty-six, although over forty pilots were either killed or seriously wounded including two leading *experten* or aces – Oberleutnants Hugo Frey and Gerhard Loos. Frey, the Kapitän of 7./JG 11, had claimed twenty-six heavy bombers out of his thirty-two victories, including four B-17s on a single mission. Both sides claimed a great victory, the *New York Times* reported it as 'Air War At Peak ... Three-Hour Combat Over the Reich Gives Major Victory Against Luftwaffe'; the German newspaper *Berliner Lokal-Anzeiger* headlined 'The Victorious Air Battle Around Berlin ... Blow against US Terror ... 140 shot down.' Little did the Luftwaffe expect that during the next four days it would be called upon twice to defend the Reich capital.

Six hundred and twenty bombers left on the 8th for the same targets and by the same route, clearly a deliberate 'baiting' operation to tempt the Luftwaffe into the air again. It is quite remarkable that the Eighth could dispatch this number considering over three hundred bombers had been damaged two days earlier. The ball bearing works at Erkner were heavily damaged but another thirty-seven bombers were lost although the opposition was lighter because 'some of the aircraft put out of operation on 6th had not been repaired.' The Third Division again fared the worst, bearing over 60% of the losses, although this time the 95th and 100th Groups survived with just a single loss; the 100th was awarded its second DUC for its three Berlin operations. Although eighteen fighters were missing against seventy-nine victories, the 'veteran' Groups, 4th and 56th, claimed sixteen and twenty-eight respectively; the Luftwaffe's actual losses were fifty-five.

General Doolittle wanted to cancel the Berlin mission planned for the following day (9th) partly on account of an unfavourable weather forecast but mainly because of his deep concern for the continual stress on his crews. However, General Fred Anderson was adamant that it should go ahead and Spaatz agreed. This day the Luftwaffe was absent. Adverse weather conditions had grounded its fighters, but it was attempting to conserve its fighter pilots; bomber and transport

B-24 of 467th Bomb Group: operational 10th April 1944. (via D. Hastings)

pilots were being transferred and hastily retrained for fighter duties. Only eight bombers were lost and not a single victory was claimed.

During the next six days the Eighth was in action over Münster, Brunswick and V1 sites, incurring light losses. The next testing mission came on 16th March when the B-17s attacked Augsburg, noted for its flak, whilst B-24s went to Friedrichshafen on the shores of Lake Constance. Twenty-three bombers failed to return, four from the 94th. Seven crews landed in nearby Switzerland, where the number of interned crews would steadily increase as the Eighth made more forays into southern Germany.

Two days later (18th) airfields and aircraft plants in the Munich area were targeted. The First Division had been allocated the Dornier factory at Oberpfaffenhofen along with the Luftwaffe's experimental base at Lechfeld. The B-24s would attack airfields around Friedrich-shafen, whereas the Third's primary target was the city of Munich, described as 'the cradle of Nazism' by the Eighth headquarters. Many airmen felt a little apprehensive about returning to the same target quite so quickly, it was as if they were tempting providence, and in the case of two Groups, 44th and 392nd, their fears were fully justified.

Virtually every Bomb Group would suffer heavy losses on a single mission at some time. Mostly these tragic occurrences could be explained by sheer ill-fortune, a moment when either the weather conditions, or the position in a formation and maybe the odd human error all conspired to exact a terrible toll on aircraft and men. On this day the 392nd suffered its worst disaster of the war. On the flight out

162

B-24s of 392nd Bomb Group: lost 14 B-24s on mission to Friedrichshafen – 18th March 1944. (USAF)

two aircraft collided over France, then over the target area the crews encountered 'the biggest mass of flak, I was ever to see', followed by a massed attack of enemy fighters. Some B-24s strayed into Swiss airspace and were fired upon by Swiss fighters as well! The 392nd lost fourteen; three found sanctuary in Switzerland to join another thirteen bombers also landing there.

The 44th, also in the 14th Wing, fared only a little better. Eight crews failed to return to Shipdham, six landed in Switzerland. Colonel Joseph A. Miller, CO of 453rd, flying his fourth mission, was leading the 2nd Wing; his B-24 was hit by flak and he baled out over France, managing to evade capture until within sight of Spain. It had been a costly operation – fifty-six aircraft; the Luftwaffe admitted the loss of thirty-six, the same as claimed by the escorts, and the 4th Group was credited with ten victories.

'Big B', as Berlin was universally called by the crews, was attacked for the fourth time on the 22nd. Aircraft factories at Oranienburg and Basdorf were the main targets for almost seven hundred bombers. The 466th at Attlebridge, 'The Flying Deck', joined the 96th Wing for the first time and it was not a particularly auspicious debut. Two B-24s collided in thick cloud over Holland and a third was heavily damaged and its crew landed in Sweden. In five days the Group lost six aircraft in collisions, such accidents becoming more prevalent as the Eighth's numbers increased and assembly procedures became even more complicated.

For the second time the enemy fighters were almost non-existent, and casualties were light – twelve. One B-17 of 96th went down over the target, struck by incendiaries from another B-17. This mission marked the final operation for the 482nd PFF Group. Henceforth a PFF squadron would operate within each Division, later in each Combat Wing and ultimately in each Bomb Group. The first PFF squadrons were based at Chelveston, Hethel and Snetterton Heath for each Division.

On the next day (23rd) the Luftwaffe managed to mount strong opposition to the Third's Groups over Brunswick. The 45th Wing found itself lacking fighter escort near the Dümmer Lake and in a matter of minutes eleven B-17s were shot down. Once again the 4th's pilots were successful, claiming thirteen out of twenty. The 'Eagles' claimed one hundred victories up to the end of March; one victim over Brunswick was Oberst Wolf-Dietrich Wilcke, Geschwaderkommodore of JG 23, who had sixty-two air victories to his name.

The weakened state of the Luftwaffe was all too apparent the following day when Schweinfurt and Frankfurt were attacked for the loss of three aircraft, two of which had collided near the target. It was evident that the Luftwaffe was trying to conserve its force, although five days later (29th) it was still able to mount over two hundred and fifty sorties despite stormy weather. It lost thirty-three fighters and twenty-seven pilots whilst destroying nine B-17s over Brunswick. One of its historians has maintained that 'by the end of March the daylight bombing offensive had put the Luftwaffe on the ropes ... with little hope of recovery for its daylight fighter force.' Nevertheless it would still be able to inflict some heavy losses on the Eighth in the months ahead.

In March 1944 the Eighth had been in action over Germany on twenty-three days for the loss of five hundred and seventy aircraft in action and salvaged and over 3,290 airmen killed/missing. Such losses could now be sustained as new aircraft and replacement crews and pilots were arriving in the UK almost daily. The American war machine had gathered a tremendous momentum, it was producing aircraft at a prodigious rate. Although German fighter production was still on the increase, the steady depletion of its fighter pilots was taking a toll on its operational efficiency and effectiveness. The coming month would only exacerbate its problems.

At the end of March General Doolittle made a broadcast to the States: 'Our immediate goal is the destruction or neutralisation of the German

Air Force ... In our most recent operations the German fighters have shown little inclination to come up and fight, an indication that their losses are now exceeding their replacements and that they are conserving their forces.' With this thought uppermost the Eighth authorised an increase in strafing airfields, aircraft depots and parks.

Colonel Glenn E. Duncan, CO of 353rd, had already proposed the establishment of an 'elite' squadron manned by experienced pilots drawn from four Groups, to develop and perfect the techniques and tactics of ground-attack. The unit – 353rdC – placed under Duncan's control at Metfield, acquired the name of 'Bill's Buzz Boys' from General 'Bill' Kepner, the Fighter Commander. From late March until mid-April six missions were flown, in all fourteen enemy aircraft and thirty-six locomotives were destroyed for the loss of three aircraft. The unit was then disbanded as sufficient evidence had been gathered to draw up plans for ground-strafing on a large scale.

Perhaps the most successful strafing Group was the 355th at Steeple Morden. On 5th April its pilots attacked six airfields in the Munich area, claiming forty-three aircraft destroyed and over eighty damaged; they also claimed another eight in air combat. The Group was awarded a DUC and became known as 'The Steeple Morden Strafers'. It was ultimately credited with over five hundred aircraft destroyed on the ground, the highest in the Eighth. On the same day the 4th was engaged in strafing several airfields near Berlin and its pilots also claimed forty-three on the ground. Three days later the 20th Group would be awarded a DUC for its strafing exploits over several airfields to the west of Berlin. The P-38 pilots also claimed eighteen locomotives and fifty rail wagons destroyed, and gained the reputation of a 'train busting outfit' and the nickname 'The Loco Group'! Colonel Harold J. Rau, its Commander, was unique in that he had once served as a private with the 20th Group.

During April the Group, along with the 55th, would use their P-38s as fighter/bombers. During the previous winter Colonels Cass Hough and Dan Ostrander, an Armaments expert, had been conducting experiments at Langford Lodge into modifying the P-38 by installing a plexiglas nose section to house a bombardier and a Norden bomb-sight. The modified P-38s became known as 'Droop Snoots' and it was planned to use them as sighting aircraft for other P-38s operating as bombers. Both Groups went out on their first 'Droop Snoot' operation on 10th April. Colonel Jenkins, CO of 55th, was shot down on this day whilst strafing, he made a forced-landing and was taken prisoner. The two Groups would mount more 'Droop Snoot' operations during the

P-47s of 62nd squadron, 56th Fighter Group.

month. On the 20th, the 357th, under its new Commander, Colonel Donald W. Graham, would for the first time use its P-51s as fighter/ bombers.

The loss of Colonel Jenkins was evidence of the inherent dangers of strafing. In the previous two weeks another two leading aces – Majors Duane 'Bee' Beeson of 4th and Gerald W. Johnson of 56th – had been shot down by ground fire whilst strafing airfields. The first full scale strafing operation was mounted on 15th April code-named *Jackpot*. Each Group was allocated an airfield or airfields in Germany, over six hundred pilots were in action and forty enemy aircraft were destroyed on the ground and another eighteen in the air. It proved to be a costly exercise, thirty-three fighters were lost. The weather probably caused many of the losses, the cloud bank was over 28,000 feet and three Groups were forced to abandon the mission. A third of the losses were P-38s with the unfortunate 364th losing eight pilots.

On 1st April control of the Allied Strategic Bomber Forces was passed over to General Eisenhower's headquarters to provide support for *Overlord*, although the effective date of the change would be 14th April; from then the control of the air campaign was vested with Eisenhower's deputy, Air Chief Marshal Sir Arthur Tedder, who would retain the overall command until 18th September. It was Tedder who strongly supported the planned Allied heavy bombing campaign in preparation for *Overlord*, known as the 'Transportation Plan'.

The Plan, aimed at neutralising the Wehrmacht's known dependence on rail transport, was the brain-child of Professor Solly Zuckermann,

Tedder's scientific adviser. The objective was to create 'a railway desert' between western Germany and the French coast, by bombing marshalling yards, stations, rail centres and junctions, tunnels and bridges. Both Harris and Spaatz strongly opposed the Plan; Harris wanted to continue his bombing of German cities, whereas Spaatz considered that the German aircraft industry and the Luftwaffe remained the main priorities. Churchill had reservations because of the high risk of heavy civilian casualties.

On 25th March there was a high-powered meeting of Allied Chiefs when the Plan was discussed in detail. Spaatz, with Washington's agreement, argued strongly in favour of an Allied bombing offensive against the German oil industry, which he considered would cripple the Luftwaffe and also its armoured forces. Harris had already mounted some trial missions against rail targets, as he had been instructed, and their success made him more enthusiastic. The Plan was approved at this meeting; eighty-three rail targets were specifically identified and the Eighth was allocated twenty-six. Two objectives were issued to the Allied Bomber Forces on 17th April. The first was 'to deplete the German fighter force and to destroy the forces supporting the Luftwaffe.' The second related to the enemy's rail communications and particularly 'those affecting the enemy movement to the *Overlord* lodgement area'. Spaatz was somewhat tardy in bringing the Eighth into the Transportation Plan, he still continued to order strikes against German strategic targets and would even send the Eighth out on its first attack on the German oil industry.

April did not start well; the attack on a large chemical works at Ludwigshafen on the 1st was hampered by heavy cloud. The First Division was grounded and the Third's Groups were recalled over France, leaving the Second Division's B-24s to plough on alone. Cloud cover extended over central Germany and most crews sought other targets, mainly Pforzheim, some miles to the north-west of Stuttgart. The leading B-24 of the 14th Wing suffered a malfunction and as the formation flew southwards the navigational error increased. Thirty-eight B-24s of 44th and 392nd Groups bombed the Swiss town of Schaffhausen in error, ten miles inside the border with Germany and about 120 miles further south than Ludwigshafen. Twelve B-24s failed to return from this unfortunate operation, four from the 448th including its Commander, Colonel James McK. Thompson.

The two Group Commanders, Colonels Irvine A. 'Bull' Rendle of 392nd and John H. Gibson of 44th, had to face some difficult questions from the official inquiry. It was particularly hard for Gibson as he had only taken command of the Group a couple of days earlier. There was an intense amount of American diplomatic activity at the highest level, which finally resulted in the Swiss Government being paid $1 million in compensation – a rather expensive operation.

Seven days later when the Eighth was out in strength again, Colonel Gibson at Shipdham had another traumatic day. The familiar target of Brunswick brought the downfall of thirty B-24s (8.5%) with the 44th losing eleven. The relative newcomers, the 466th, lost six, which would be their worst single mission; one pilot recalled, 'They don't come any harder than the one we flew that day.' The Division had fallen prey to a Fw 190 unit that had been nick-named 'The Battling Bastards of Brunswick'. However, despite the losses the escorts took a heavy toll – eighty-eight in the air and forty-nine on the ground, for the loss of twenty-three pilots. The 4th Group was credited with thirty-one and the 354th twenty.

The following day (9th) – Easter Sunday – saw five hundred and forty bombers attack aircraft industry targets at Tutow, Marienburg, Rahmel and Warnemünde, with the Third Division sent on the longest haul to the Fw 190 components factory at Poznan in Poland, which had so far avoided the Eighth's attention. One Wing abandoned the mission due to adverse weather, but the 96th flying its 100th mission, along with aircraft from 388th and 452nd, continued eastwards. The crews successfully and accurately bombed causing considerable damage. On the return flight they were directed to divert to give some added protection to B-17s returning from Marienburg. Before they met up with this formation, the crews had to stave off some determined fighter attacks. All told twelve B-17s were lost from the Poznan mission, one of the more successful operations of late, and the 96th was awarded its second DUC.

The Eighth's offensive against the German aircraft industry continued two days later with a major strike at assembly plants in eastern Germany; over nine hundred bombers and eight hundred fighters were engaged. The Third Division returned to Poznan, although cloud cover saved the Focke-Wulf factory from further damage, and the crews turned to Rostock. Now without fighter cover and close to Hannover, two Wings, 13th and 45th, encountered fierce opposition from rocket-firing Ju 88s and Me 410s. Twenty-seven were shot down with the 96th losing eleven and the 95th seven.

The First Division's attack on Cottbus and Sorau was most successful, but its 40th Wing engaged over Stettin faced fierce and sustained attacks from Me 110s. Twelve B-17s were destroyed and

Pattie IV – P-51D of 328th squadron, 352nd Fighter Group – P-51s from 8th April 1944. (via R. Smart)

many more damaged. *Bertie Lee* of the 305th was riddled with cannon fire and went spinning down chased by fighters. Both the pilot and co-pilot were injured and the instruments were wrecked. The pilot, 1/Lt Edward Michael managed to control the aircraft, only to find that some of its incendiaries were on fire. The B-17 seemed doomed and the crew was ordered to bale out. The co-pilot, 2/Lt Westberg decided to remain along with the injured bombardier. Despite his loss of blood and spells of unconsciousness, Lt Michael managed to summon enough strength to make an amazing belly-landing at RAF Redhill. The aircraft had no hydraulics, the bomb bay doors were jammed open and the ball turret guns were also jammed downwards! He was awarded the Medal of Honor.

The day's operations proved most costly, sixty-four bombers and sixteen fighters, which equalled in total the epic Berlin mission of 6th March. Nine bombers landed in Sweden to add to the ten from the previous two days. Over fifty enemy aircraft were claimed in the air, the same number admitted by the Luftwaffe, with the 357th achieving twenty-three for the loss of three pilots. The 352nd flew two missions, outward with their new P-51s and later withdrawal cover with their 'old' P-47s.

Two days later (13th) another long and exhausting mission was mounted to targets in southern Germany. The Third's Groups attacked the Messerschmitt complex at Augsburg with the First's Groups revisiting Schweinfurt. The expected heavy flak was encountered at both targets, but also the Luftwaffe was encountered in greater force than for many weeks. Colonel Maurice A. Preston leading the 41st Wing over Schweinfurt described the frontal attacks as 'the most severe ... I have ever witnessed', and he had been flying operations since May 1943. Thirty-two B-17s were lost in total with the 384th losing nine. The B-24 crews in action over Oberpfaffenhofen and Lechfeld, escaped with lighter losses – six – of which three landed in Switzerland.

There was scant planned respite for the crews in this frenetic period of operations but some unfavourable weather did allow a break of four days before targets in the Berlin area were detailed for the 18th. The Luftwaffe carefully bided their time as the bomber formations passed over Germany and indeed many Groups hardly saw an enemy fighter. However, the 94th and 385th became separated from their Wing formation, and Fw 190s of JG 3 struck with a vengeance. The 94th proceeded to lose eight aircraft in a matter of minutes. It was a harsh introduction for Colonel Charles B. Dougher, who had only taken command of the Group the previous day; its previous popular CO, Colonel Fred Castle, had been elevated to the 4th Wing, which also had its headquarters at Bury St Edmunds.

Four days later (22nd) the Eighth turned its attention to the major marshalling yards at Hamm, which had been its first Ruhr target back in March 1943. The crews awaited clearance as unfavourable weather delayed the start of the operation. When the all clear was finally given, the rescheduled timing meant they would be returning to their bases during the hours of darkness. The complicated exercise of landing several hundred aircraft, many probably damaged, on different airfields in a relatively small area, was difficult enough in daylight let alone at night.

Although heavy flak and some moderate fighter opposition was encountered, the eight hundred strong force escaped with fifteen lost – almost half from the Second Division. As the B-24 Groups commenced their landing patterns off the Norfolk coast, the Luftwaffe struck with some severity. A force of Junkers 88s and Me 410s had followed the bomber streams back from the Dutch coast, and had come in low to avoid radar detection. As one pilot from 448th recalled, 'they were waiting like vultures for us to come in ... we were being shot at like sitting ducks ... it was like as if all hell had broke loose ... there were ships everywhere ... some going down in flames ... it doesn't bear thinking about.'

In about five minutes, five B-24s were shot down and a number of airfields were strafed with Seething the worst hit. One of the 448th's B-24s was shot down and crash-landed on the runway, two aircraft following collided with it and all three were destroyed. The fires at Seething were not finally extinguished until the early hours of the morning. A B-24 from 448th at Horsham St Faith was brought down by 'friendly fire' over Norwich. In total thirteen B-24s crashed or crash-landed and another couple were heavily damaged; thirty-eight airmen had been killed and another twenty-three injured. It was a tragic evening for the Second Division.

There was no let-up in the relentless schedule of operations. Two days later aircraft factories, air depots and airfields in southern Germany were the targets for the three Divisions. The First was bound for Oberpfaffenhofen, Landsberg and Erding, the Third to Friedrich-shafen and the B-24s to Gablingen and Leipham airfields. The 384th had just cause to think that Oberpfaffenhofen had become its *bete noire*. On 18th March two crews had failed to return from the mission but on this day it experienced a more torrid time. The 41st Wing came under severe attack from Me 109s and Fw 190s for well over an hour, 'they repeatedly came in waves head-on into the formations in elements of ten abreast'. Seven were lost by the 384th and one damaged B-17 made for Switzerland but it was shot down by Swiss fighters, crashing into a lake and killing five of its crew. Another member of the Wing, 303rd, had three crews missing, all landed in Switzerland; but the 379th survived unscathed. Amazingly this Group, although in the same Wing, would go through April without a single loss in action, whereas the 384th lost twenty. It was some consolation for the 384th that it was awarded a DUC for this mission.

Another of the Division's Wings, 40th, also suffered heavily; the 306th lost ten and the 92nd five. Hitherto the 306th had survived the month's operations with just two losses. No fewer than thirteen B-17s and a solitary B-24 landed in Switzerland; the American *terrorfliegers*, as they were described by German propaganda, were creating considerable local interest! Total losses amounted to forty and although one hundred and forty-four enemy aircraft were claimed, the Luftwaffe admitted losing fifty-six; although three Groups, 4th, 357th and 355th, between them claimed fifty-nine. By the end of May the 355th, under Colonel W.J. 'Bill' Cummings, had made quite an impact with their new P-51s – sixty-two victories in the air and almost one hundred on the ground.

Three days later (27th) the Eighth mounted two bombing missions. In the morning a number of V1 sites were bombed by almost six

Formation of B-17s of 306th Bomb Group bound for Berlin. The aircraft in the foreground, 10Point, crash-landed in Switzerland – 24th April 1944. (USAF)

hundred heavies, and then on their second mission the crews attacked their first targets in accordance with the Transportation Plan. Marshalling yards at Chalons and Blainville to the east of Paris were bombed as well as a number of airfields; 'Droop Snoot' P-38s along with P-51s acting as fighter/bombers were also engaged over airfields. Two operations were also mounted on the 28th. A B-17 force attacked airfields near Metz and a V1 weapon site at Sottevast to the south of Cherbourg was the target for five Groups of the Third Division. Over the latter target heavy clouds prevented most of the crews from bombing, but the leading B-17 of the 100th Group was shot down on its second bombing run. The Group's Commander, Colonel Robert H. Kelly and his crew were missing in action; he had been in charge of the Group for only a week. A second crew also failed to return to Thorpe Abbotts.

If the main object of the Berlin operation mounted on the 29th, was to tempt the Luftwaffe into the skies, then it proved most successful; over three hundred enemy fighters were estimated to be in action. The cost to the Eighth was high – sixty-three bombers destroyed – the second time in the month over sixty had been lost in action. The Friedrichstrasse Bahnhof, the railway centre of the capital, was the primary target for the three Divisions.

The mission was beset with problems from the outset. Difficulties were experienced at assembly, resulting in poor and ragged formations, and heavy and overcast skies all the way over Germany impeded the accompanying escorts. The lead PFF aircraft of 4th Wing made a slight but critical navigational error taking the Wing some forty miles south of the main force and away from its escorts. Near Magdeburg a strong force of Fw 190s struck with speed and venom; in barely twenty minutes seventeen B-17s were shot down, ten from 447th, and seven from 385th. It was the latter Group's 100th mission, not the best way to celebrate. Another B-17 from the 447th ditched in the North Sea, making it the Group's most costly operation of the war. April had been a harsh month for the Rattlesden outfit, twenty-one aircraft lost in action and another three destroyed in a tragic accident on the 21st, when an exploding bomb killed several ground crew.

The Second Division also experienced assembly difficulties and its Wings were some thirty minutes behind the planned schedule. Shortly after the crews had completed their bombing runs enemy fighters struck as they were bereft of escorts; in total twenty-five B-24s were lost. Considering the losses inflicted on the Second and Third Divisions, the First escaped relatively lightly – ten – of which the 401st lost three crews, the same number as had gone missing in *total* on the five previous Berlin missions.

The Eighth suffered its heaviest losses of the whole war in April – over five hundred and fifty aircraft lost in action and over four thousand airmen killed/missing. But such were the number of effective sorties flown that the loss rate (3.8%) was well below the tolerance. One serious matter of concern was the number of aircraft known to have been destroyed by flak – one hundred and thirty-one – double that of the previous month. The flak defences had undoubtedly been strengthened, especially at the major cities and important strategic targets. The feared and lethal 88 mm batteries, had been grouped into *Grossbatteries*, which produced a 'fearsome wall of flak'. These guns had been improved and were now effective at 30,000 feet; the enemy's gun-laying radar had also been further developed bringing about greater accuracy. Damage and destruction by flak would become a major hazard for the Eighth's future bombing operations.

The Eighth claimed over twelve hundred enemy aircraft destroyed and although this figure was greatly exaggerated, the Luftwaffe had nevertheless suffered serious inroads into its fighter force, over four hundred destroyed and perhaps another two hundred damaged. P-51s were proving their worth, the lion's share of the victories were falling to their pilots. Early in May the Eighth would have six P-51 Groups in action and still be able to call upon the Ninth's Groups. Indeed, General Bill Kepner wrote to James Kindelberger, President of North American Aviation, to compliment him 'on the very fine work your Mustangs are doing. They are roaming around all of France and Germany like the proverbial Devil's Ghost'!

11
'CHARGED WITH A MOST SOLEMN OBLIGATION'

On 6th June 1944, almost two years after its first operation, the Eighth Air Force attained its full strength. It comprised forty combat Bombardment and fifteen Fighter Groups – a truly massive and awesome phalanx of B-17s, B-24s, P-38s, P-47s and P-51s. The months of May and June were its most active period of the war. Sixty-eight heavy bombing operations were mounted, over 45,700 sorties for the loss of 540 aircraft in action (1.2%), and its fighter pilots were fully engaged in escort, bombing and strafing missions flying some 37,700 sorties for the loss of over 370 aircraft; in the process they destroyed over 1,000 enemy aircraft in the air and on the ground.

For such a sustained period of operational activity May opened on a low-key due to unfavourable and unseasonable weather. When such conditions prevailed the planners always had 'Noball' targets just across the Channel to fall back on; indeed, during the first week of the month V1 sites were attacked on five days. Although targets under the Transportation Plan were given priority, General Spaatz lost no opportunity to direct the Eighth to other strategic targets in Germany, on the premise that they broadly came under the Allies' First Directive – the reduction of the German Air Force.

Thus, on the 7th, B-17 crews were sent to Berlin whilst the Second's B-24s were in action over Münster and Osnabrück. No enemy opposition was encountered and losses were slight. The twelfth and final Group to join the First Division, the 398th flew its second mission,

All three of the Eighth's fighters can be seen in this unique photograph. (Smithsonian Institution)

and the 'freshmen' crews returned to Nuthampstead intact. Two other new Groups, 486th and 487th, went out on their first missions in the afternoon to marshalling yards at Liege in Belgium. Both were equipped with B-24Hs but were placed in the 92nd Wing of the Third Division, making it a mixed force. Another three B-24 Groups would join the Division over the next month and General LeMay would use his B-24s as a separate force. Considerable operational problems were experienced using both types of heavy bombers and quite early it was decided that the five Groups would ultimately convert to B-17s.

The 486th operated from Sudbury and the aircraft of one squadron, 834th, carried the signs of the Zodiac, all expertly painted by an ex-commercial artist, Corporal Brinkman. The 487th was based at Lavenham and was commanded by Lt Col Beirne J. Lay Jr, one of

Eaker's original staff officers. Both Groups were considered to be 'too green' to go out on the Berlin and Brunswick missions mounted on 8th May, instead they were sent to marshalling yards in Brussels.

For the second day running the Eighth sent out over 900 bombers. Berlin was particularly costly for the Third Division, it lost eighteen B-17s mainly in its 45th Wing with the 96th losing ten crews. But it was the 453rd from Old Buckenham that suffered under an intense fighter assault at Brunswick; it lost seven B-24s and another two later crashed.

The loss of eleven B-24s would have been greater but for the spirited defence by the 352nd Group with their newly acquired P-51s. They returned to Bodney with claims of twenty-seven victories for a single casualty. 1/Lt Carl J. Luksic shot down five to become the Eighth's first 'ace in a day'. Two other pilots, Lt Col John C. Meyer and 1/Lt John Thornell, each claimed three. John 'Whips' Meyer was awarded his first DSC and in February 1945 when his tour expired he had twenty-six confirmed air victories along with thirteen ground. The Group was awarded its first DUC.

Notwithstanding the successes of P-51 pilots, the 56th still had the Eighth's leading 'aces'; Major Robert S. Johnson flying his last and ninety-first sortie claimed two victories to bring his total to twenty-seven. He returned to the States to undertake a War Bonds tour and remained there, commanding a P-47 operational training unit. Another 56th pilot, Lt Col Francis S. 'Gabby' Gabreski took over the mantle of the Eighth's leading pilot with nineteen victories. In total fifty-five enemy aircraft were claimed on the day, the Luftwaffe is thought to have lost forty-five.

On the 9th and 11th May a number of marshalling yards in France and Belgium were bombed along with several of the almost one hundred airfields in France within 350 miles of Normandy, which had to be put out of action before the invasion. On the 11th, three hundred and sixty-four B-24s were in action, the largest B-24 force so far, achieved by the first operation of the 492nd at North Pickenham under Colonel Eugene H. Snavely, late of the 44th. Unfortunately it would suffer the heaviest losses of any B-24 unit over a three-month period. On this mission the 92nd Wing of the Third Division flew over a heavy flak area in error whilst *en route* to Chaumont marshalling yards. The 487th had three B-24s shot down, including the lead and deputy lead aircraft, and the mission was abandoned. Lt Col Beirne J. Lay Jr, managed to bale out, evade capture and ultimately return to England. Shortly after the war he and another Eighth airman, Sy Bartlett, wrote a book about a 'fictional' Bomb Group (but closely based on the 306th),

B-17s of 91st Bomb Group: Ack-Ack Annie (232095) of 322nd squadron completed 143 Missions. (USAF)

entitled *Twelve O'Clock High*; in 1949 it was made into a classic film starring Gregory Peck.

General Spaatz now turned his attention to the German oil industry and his alternative 'Oil Plan'. He was utterly convinced that the Luftwaffe would defend such targets to the utmost. Spaatz now initiated the Eighth's long and bitter oil offensive, which proved so costly in aircraft and airmen. No other single strategic target resulted in such high losses and perhaps none was so critical in the ultimate demise of the German Air Force. Already on three occasions in April Spaatz had sent the Fifteenth Air Force to the Ploesti oil fields. The enemy's reliance on the production of synthetic oil had long been recognised, it was estimated that 75% of its oil was produced by fifty-eight refineries and twenty-three large plants. However, because Air Chief Marshal Harris had an aversion to attacking individual strategic or 'panacea' targets as he called them, the German synthetic oil industry had largely escaped heavy bombardment; now this was about to radically change.

The mission mounted on 12th May was directed at major oil targets in the Leipzig area, especially the Leuna plant at Merseburg, considered one of the most important in Germany. Other oil plants at Lützkendorf, Brüx, Böhlen, Zeitz and Zwickau were attacked and all would figure large in the crews' minds over the next six months or so, none more so than Leuna, which would be bombed on eighteen occasions. Certainly the Eighth's planners were proved correct in their assumption that the Luftwaffe would defend in strength. The Third Division bore the weight of severe and sustained fighter attacks, 'it was the roughest trip of the war ... they [enemy fighters] were everywhere you looked ... the sky seemed black with them.' The Third Division lost forty-one aircraft (14%) with its 45th Wing losing twenty-seven crews – fourteen from 452nd and twelve from 96th. The 4th Wing also suffered, especially the 447th with seven missing in action. The Wing was led by Colonel Vandevanter of the 385th Group, and whilst over Belgium, enemy fighters struck and the brutal onslaught continued unabated for almost half an hour. Then the Colonel ordered a reduction in speed to allow the tattered Wing to reform. His crews achieved a high standard of bombing accuracy over Zwickau, almost 100% of their bombs falling within 2,000 feet of the aiming point. All but two of the Group returned to Great Ashfield and the 385th was awarded its second DUC.

Only another five aircraft were lost by the other two Divisions and considerable damage had been inflicted. The Leuna plant lost 18% of its production but by the end of the month it was fully operational. Albert Speer, the German Minister for War Production warned, 'the enemy has struck at one of our weakest points. If they persist this time, we will no longer have any fuel production worth mentioning'. Two days later many flak batteries were reassigned to oil plants and refineries and Merseburg would become one of the heaviest defended targets in Germany, one which 'sent shivers down your spine'. The Germans employed every means available to protect its vital oil industry – decoy plants (the one at Leuna was bombed almost as much as the real one!), camouflage, smokescreens, anti-aircraft balloons and blast walls.

On the following day (13th) oil targets in Poland were briefed but weather conditions precluded their bombing and the crews turned to alternative targets along the Baltic coast – Stettin and Stralsand. It was the turn of the First Division's Groups to be punished – ten lost – three from the 379th. The escorts had a successful day with forty-seven victories including twelve Me 410s of 11./ZG 26. The losses of night-fighters had become so serious that their crews were ordered to attack only unescorted bombers. Once again the 352nd – the self-styled 'Blue-nosed Bastards from Bodney' – was to the fore with sixteen victories.

The P-51s had made their longest escort mission so far, 1,470 miles – a long time to remain confined in a small cockpit.

A period of inclement weather curtailed operations for six days, but then on 19th May B-17s were bound for Berlin again, whilst B-24s made their now familar way to Brunswick. Both forces were compelled to bomb by radar (H2X) and each faced heavy Luftwaffe opposition. Almost by rote the Second Division returned with the heaviest losses – twelve; the 'new boys' (492nd) experienced their first costly mission with eight B-24s missing. One, *Lucky Lass*, collided with an enemy fighter, which removed a large part of its starboard wing; quite remarkably 2/Lt Wyman Bridges brought his stricken aircraft back home on two engines, resulting in an immediate award of a DFC.

On 21st May Fighter Command released over 600 fighters in a strafing mission of railways, canals and river traffic in Germany, under the code-name *Chattanooga*, taken from Glenn Miller's popular song. Some two hundred locomotives were attacked and ninety-one were considered destroyed. The P-38s of 55th were particularly active wrecking twenty-three engines and damaging another fifteen, as well as canal and river barges; it lost six pilots.

Two days later 1,045 bombers attacked marshalling yards and airfields in France with the 34th Group at Mendlesham in action with B-24s for the first time. It was the oldest Bomb Group to serve in the Eighth and since 1941 had been engaged on anti-submarine duties off the east coast of America, although latterly used as a replacement crew training unit. It was placed in the new 93rd Wing of the Third Division, shortly to be joined by another two Groups.

Berlin was targeted on the 24th for the tenth time in a matter of months. The USAAF was trying to make up for lost time! Over 200 enemy fighters were in action and two Groups, 100th and 381st, which had already suffered harshly over the Reich capital, were again the victims; the former lost nine crews and the latter six. In total thirty-three B-17s were shot down, by coincidence the same number claimed by the escorts. The 339th from Fowlmere accounted for ten for the loss of a pilot. The 'greenhorns to the game', as the CO, Colonel John B. Henry Jr, called 'his boys' were making quite an impact; by the end of the month they had forty-five victories for the loss of fourteen P-51s.

During the last week of May the Eighth devoted considerable resources against rail targets and airfields in western Germany, Belgium and France, mounting over 3,100 sorties and dropping almost 5,000 tons of bombs. Perhaps the most successful strikes were to the marshalling yards at Brussels, Saarbrücken, Rheims and Troyes where

B-24s of 486th Bomb Group over Lützkendorf – 28th May 1944. (Imperial War Museum)

substantial damage was inflicted. Despite this concentration on Transportation targets, General Spaatz was determined that his cherished oil offensive should not be put on hold until after *Overlord*. On the 28th and 29th bombers totalling 2,334 were dispatched to oil and aircraft industry targets, and not surprisingly these two missions brought heavy losses – sixty-six.

The mission on the 28th to Leuna, Zeitz, Lützkendorf, Ruhland and Magdeburg created a record – 1,341 heavies – the largest number dispatched so far. The next day when Pölitz, a synthetic plant to the north-east of Berlin, and a Fw 190 plant at Tutow, were the primary targets for B-24 crews, the B-17 Groups were in action over a number of aircraft factories at Leipzig, Poznan, Sorau, Cottbus and Krzesinki. On both days the Luftwaffe mounted strong and determined opposition. Its standard assault formation now appeared to be concentrated attacks of 50 to 100 fighters and as General 'Bill' Kepner explained, '[They] have decided to throw a big moving mass through the bomber formations ... what we have choosen to call "a flying wedge" ... we put up a heavy barrage on them and let them fly through it'. Some

Bomb Groups lost quite heavily. On the 28th the 401st had seven missing in action with another salvaged on return, its heaviest loss of the war. The 390th and 351st lost seven and six crews respectively over the two days. Half of the losses on the 29th were B-24s – seventeen – of which six landed in Sweden.

Luftwaffe records reveal that it had also sustained heavy losses – almost one hundred fighters in the two days with some sixty pilots killed and another thirty injured. During the month it lost 50% of its single-engined fighter strength and 25% of its pilots. They included two very experienced leaders, Oberst Walter Oseau, the Kommodore of JG 1, a most successful 'bomber specialist' with a quarter of his hundred victories being American heavy bombers, and Major Freidrich K. Muller. There was a deep concern in the Luftwaffe that their young and inexperienced pilots were exhibiting *Jagerschreck* ('fighter fear') by avoiding direct combat with the fighter escorts. Certainly the American pilots were far better trained with at least 225 hours on operational aircraft before entering the fray, compared with some 60/80 hours by the Luftwaffe pilots. Although one veteran Eighth fighter pilot later recalled, 'The German pilots were well-disciplined, aggressive and very brave.'

As a result of these operations, it was thought that oil production had fallen by 50%, although it would quickly recover whilst the Eighth was fully engaged with *Overlord*. However, in early June intelligence sources did reveal that 'flying training and production aircraft testing was severely curtailed by the reduced quantities of aircraft fuel available'. The Eighth's oil offensive, which had barely started, seemed to be already bearing fruit.

On 30th May seven hundred and twenty-eight bombers were bound for aircraft industry targets in Germany, whilst a smaller force of B-17s (two hundred and fifty) attacked marshalling yards and airfields in France and Belgium. What was impressive on the day were the number of fighters in action, over 1,300 of which almost 50% were from the Ninth Air Force. One of the B-17 crews recalled, 'It was the greatest display of fighter strength, I've seen in thirty missions, a regular parade over Europe with Thunderbolts, Mustangs and Lightnings massed around us ... The sky was full of planes, all ours. There wasn't room for any Germans'! There were however some around because fifty-eight were accounted for, with the 357th claiming eighteen.

The operation heralded the arrival of the 489th at Halesworth under Colonel Ezekiel Napier. One of its B-24s ditched in the North Sea on return because of fuel shortage, but eight of the crew were saved. In early June the Group would be joined in the new 95th Wing by the last B-24 Group to join the Second Division – the 491st operating from Metfield. The Third's last Groups, 490th based at Eye and 493rd at Debach, also entered the action. The latter, known as 'Helton Hellcats' from its CO, Colonel Elbert Helton, flew its first mission on D-Day. Fighter Command was already up to full strength, its fourth and last P-38 Group – 479th – had flown its first patrols on the 26th, and had acquired their name, 'Riddle's Raiders' from their CO, Lt Col Kyle L. Riddle. The Eighth was now at its peak strength just in time for *Overlord*, only days away.

On the morning of 2nd June eight hundred and five bombers attacked over one hundred and thirteen V1 sites in the Pas de Calais; almost half bombed with the aid of Gee-H (G-H). Gee was a British radio device for navigation and in conjunction with airborne transmitter screens and beacons from two ground stations was employed as a blind bombing device. It had an effective range of 200 miles at 25,000 feet and was more accurate than H2X, suitable for small and precise targets such as V1 sites and road/rail bridges. G-H had been first used operationally by B-24s in late January, but in May a number of B-17s of 41st Wing had been equipped with the device. It was perhaps most effectively used by the 379th Group.

In the afternoon airfields and rail targets around Paris were attacked along with other airfields. The new 95th Wing encountered quite severe flak and five B-24s were shot down, four from the 489th, with another two crashing; the 491st on its first mission lost one crew in action. The following day some twenty tactical targets, mainly coastal defences, in the Pas de Calais were bombed, all part of the Allied grand deception plan; it was said that for every bomb dropped over Normandy, two were dropped in the Pas de Calais and on other stretches of coastline.

Three bombing missions were flown on the 4th and on the day before D-Day coastal defences at Le Havre, Caen, Boulogne and Cherbourg were bombed. Lt Col Leon R. Vance Jr, the Deputy Commander of the 489th, led the Group in a PFF B-24 of the 44th, *Missouri Sal*. Close to the target, Wimereaux north of Boulogne, the aircraft was hit by flak, killing the pilot and wounding the co-pilot. Vance, who was standing in the cockpit, was severely wounded in the foot. Three of the aircraft's engines were put out of action and the crew were ordered to bale out. Vance took control of the aircraft and managed to ditch in the sea. The explosion as it hit the water, blew him clear of the aircraft, severing his injured foot. He clung to the wreckage and attempted to locate an injured rear-gunner. Only when he realised

P-47D of 78th Fighter Group resplendent in D-Day markings at Duxford. (Smithsonian Institution)

that nobody was left did he begin swimming away from the wreckage and fifty minutes later he was picked up by an A/S/R launch. Whilst in hospital Vance was awarded the Medal of Honor. During late July he was being transported back to the States for further treatment when the aircraft was lost over the North Atlantic.

With Operation *Overlord* only hours away, all leave was cancelled and everybody confined to their bases. P-38s were the first of the Allied fighters to be painted with their 'Invasion Stripes' – easily identifiable broad black and white bands across the wings and fuselages. Many ground crews maintained that for security reasons the paint tins had been labelled 'For the Cake Walk'. P-38 Groups had been given the task of escorting the vast armada of Allied vessels sailing across the Channel under Operation *Neptune*. A rota system was set up to ensure that at least two squadrons would be on patrol from dawn to dusk.

Briefings for D-Day were lengthy affairs because of the number of aircraft that would be airborne over southern England. The orders were most exact, and it was stressed that the operating altitudes and precise flying corridors had to be strictly observed. The sheer logistics in mounting such an operation were quite staggering as waves of heavy bombers (nearly 2,400) would leave their bases at various times during the early morning. General Doolittle's message was read out to all the crews: '. . . the 8th Air Force is currently charged with a most solemn obligation in support of the most vital operation ever taken by our armed forces.' Most briefing officers and COs added their own words to capture the great moment of the occasion. At Deenethorpe Colonel Bowman said, 'Gentlemen remember this day – June 6th 1944. Remember it because your grandchildren will ask you about it. This is D-Day.' At Horham the crews of 95th were told that 'this is the day that you have been waiting for ... Good luck gentlemen and give 'em Hell.'

The Eighth had been given the initial task of suppressing beach defences as the landing craft were moving into the assault. There was a high risk of bombing the landing craft but crews had express instructions not to bomb unless they were completely certain as to their target. The 2nd Division force would be the first over the beaches with their targets at the American 'Omaha' beach-head, whereas the other two Divisions had the British landing areas at 'Gold', 'Juno' and 'Sword'. Each Fighter Group was given a particular area to patrol.

The 446th at Bungay was given the honour of leading the whole of the Eighth on this momentous operation. The Group's CO, Colonel Jacob 'Joe' Brogger in *Red Ass* (renamed *Buckaroo* for publicity purposes!) of 704th squadron, would lead the Division. The crews recalled 'hundreds of ships in the Channel ... more ships than you could count ... and more heavy bombers in the air than thought possible to put up in one area.' The first aircraft over the beach-heads was a PFF B-24 *Liberty Run* of the 389th and the first bombs were dropped at 0600 hours – thirty minutes before H-Hour. One war correspondent reported, '[The] air power that we have seen most forcibly was the final attack by the American Eighth Air Force. Immediately before H-Hour they dropped a vast weight of bombs on

Tar Hell Baby of 446th Bomb Group over Portland Harbour on D-Day – 6th June 1944. (USAF)

the beaches. The beaches shook and seemed to rise into the air and ships well out to sea quivered and shook.'

During D-Day 1,622 effective bomber sorties were flown for the loss of four aircraft; only one (from the 487th) due to enemy action, two collided and the other crashed. Fighter Command flew 1,719 sorties of continuous escorts and patrols as well as four hundred and sixty-six fighter/bomber sorties for the loss of twenty-five aircraft, the highest number, ten, being lost by the 4th. The 56th flew eleven missions on the day with the other Groups flying between six and ten. Even General Doolittle was in on the act, he flew over the beach-heads for about $1\frac{1}{2}$ hours in a P-38, and General Eisenhower's proud boast to his troops that 'If you see fighting aircraft over you, they will be ours', proved to be accurate. The Luftwaffe was virtually non-existent; fewer than one hundred sorties flown, only seventy single-seat fighters in action. It was admitted by the Luftwaffe that from 'the very first moment of the invasion, the Allies had absolute air supremacy.'

From the 7th to 13th, with a blank day on the 9th due to unfavourable weather, the Eighth bombed a variety of tactical targets in support of the invasion. Over 4,400 effective sorties were flown for the loss of twenty-four bombers; four belonged to the 34th and were shot down by intruders (Me 410s) over their airfield at Mendlesham on the evening of the 7th. This proved to be the Group's highest single loss of the war. It would gain a remarkable record, these were the only aircraft lost to enemy fighters, the other thirty losses were due to flak.

On 11th June B-24s of the 96th Wing were given the task of bombing an important bridge at Blois-Saint-Denis over the Loire between Tours and Orleans, which was being used to supply troops to the Normandy bridgehead. It had to be 'destroyed at all costs.' This called for low-level bombing from a height of about 4,000 to 5,500 feet, the first time the Eighth's heavies undertook this form of bombing. The 458th from Horsham St Faith led the operation. One of its squadrons, 753rd, had been experimenting with the use of Azon bombs. These were 'normal' 1,000 pound bombs equipped with special radio tail attachments and moveable fins, which enabled them to be steered after release. The bombing was highly successful. General Doolittle considered the operation, 'an outstanding performance with extraordinary heroism.'

The fighter pilots were equally active during the same period, with over 7,100 sorties mounted to bridges, road junctions, airfields, and defence installations besides the normal escort duties. Over one hundred fighters had been lost whilst claiming one hundred and fifty enemy aircraft. Within 36 hours of the invasion the Luftwaffe had

Dry Run of 615th squadron, 401st Bomb Group at Deenethorpe. M/I/A 14th June 1944. (USAF)

moved over two hundred fighters from Germany, followed by another hundred on the 10th. They needed to hastily prepare emergency landing grounds for these aircraft and were unable to mount any serious opposition until the 12th. On that day they claimed twenty-four aircraft for the loss of twenty-six. But it was all too clear that the Luftwaffe was fighting a losing battle, overwhelmed by the massive Allied fighter force continually in action over Normandy. In the two weeks from D-Day it lost 75% of its fighter force based in France.

On 14th June the Eighth moved away from tactical targets in Normandy and attacked airfields in France and Holland, and an oil refinery at Emmerich just across the Dutch border. It lost fourteen bombers, the highest so far in the month. The following day airfields and rail targets in north-west France were bombed as well as an oil refinery at Misburg. Then on the 18th the Eighth mounted its first major mission to German oil targets since D-Day, refineries at Hamburg and Misburg were bombed for relatively light losses – eleven. The other important targets demanding attention were the V1 sites because on the night of 12/13th the first V1 (flying-bomb) landed on southern England. From now until the end of August the Eighth would mount over 4,000 sorties to 'Noball' sites dropping over 10,600 tons of bombs.

It was on 20th June that the Eighth returned in earnest to its oil offensive; refineries at Magdeburg, Hamburg, Harburg and Pölitz were bombed in a costly operation. B-24s of the Second Division on a $9\frac{1}{4}$ hour round trip to Pölitz and Ostermoor faced strong opposition from rocket-firing Me 110s and 410s at a time when the Division had just one

Fighter Group, 339th, to protect the whole of its formations. The 14th Wing was severely dealt with, the 492nd lost fourteen aircraft, 392nd four and the 44th one. Although the plants at Pölitz and Misburg were heavily damaged forty-nine crews failed to return; the destruction of the German oil industry was taking its toll. Twenty of the missing aircraft landed in Sweden, including five from the 492nd.

Crews landing in neutral Sweden had become a deep concern for the Eighth's chiefs. Without doubt the majority were genuine forced landings, the aircraft so damaged that the chances of surviving a North Sea crossing were very slim. Some of the landings, however, were thought to be more an opportunity for the crews to opt out of combat flying, as they were interned and aircraft impounded by the Swedish government. Since the Eighth's Berlin operations in March the number of aircraft landing in Sweden had greatly increased, so much so that an appreciable 'American colony' had sprung up, and subsequently a special Air Attache was appointed to look after their interests. The airmen still received flying pay during internment and they were housed in quite comfortable camps. Towards the end of the year American ground personnel were allowed into Sweden to repair the aircraft, and ultimately an agreement was reached, allowing the aircraft and crews to be released provided neither were used again in any European operations.

An ambitious operation was planned for the 21st – a joint RAF/ USAAF strike at Berlin – in retaliation for the V1 offensive; however, the RAF had to reluctantly pull out because of insufficient fighter support for its slower and less heavily armed bombers. The Eighth decided to mount their own mission. The majority of the force (1,070) would attack targets in and around Berlin. Two Wings of the Third, the 13th and 45th, were given the Schwarzheide synthetic oil plant at Ruhland, about ninety miles south-east of Berlin, as their target. After bombing the six Groups would swing eastwards to land at three Russian airfields – Poltava, Mirgorod and Piryatin – all to the east of Kiev. This was the first of the Eighth's so-called *Frantic* missions, largely mounted to placate Stalin but also to enable the Eighth to attack targets in Poland and Hungary. The Fifteenth Air Force had completed the first such mission on 11th June. Pilots of the 4th Group and the 486th squadron of the 352nd would escort the bombers to Russia. This shuttle mission would be the first under the control of the Third Division's new Commander, Major General Earle Partridge; General LeMay having been moved to the Pacific to introduce the B-29s into operations.

Intense flak and strong fighter opposition took a heavy toll of the Berlin force – forty-four – with the First Division losing sixteen B-17s and the Second nineteen B-24s; the heaviest losses were sustained by the 389th – six crews missing in action. One hundred and sixty-three B-17 crews left for the twelve hour flight to Russia, their aircraft having been adapted to carry a long-range bomb fuel tank. On the outward flight four from the 452nd collided near Cuxhaven and one of the 390th ditched. The target was bombed quite accurately and no fighter opposition was encountered until they were over Poland. A number of Fw 190s struck and shot down one aircraft (452nd) but the 4th's P-51s destroyed at least six. Finally the 13th Wing landed at Mirgorod, the 45th at Poltava and the P-51s put down at Piryatin after a $7\frac{1}{2}$ hour flight.

Unbeknown to the Eighth the 45th Wing had been tracked by an enemy reconnaissance aircraft and about five hours after the Wing had landed at Poltava the Luftwaffe launched its attack. A force of Ju 88s and He 111s bombed the airfield inflicting terrible damage. Forty-four of the seventy-two B-17s were destroyed, another twenty-six damaged and twenty-five Russian airmen were killed but miraculously there were no American casualties. The aircraft at the other two airfields were moved as a precaution but the Luftwaffe did not return. In some 24 hours the Eighth had lost eighty-eight bombers and twenty-two fighters, a most costly operation, probably the worst in its history. General Spaatz admitted, 'it was the best attack the Luftwaffe ever made on the AAF.'

On the 26th the remaining B-17s, escorted by P-51s, bombed targets in Hungary *en route* to Italy and their ultimate return to England; only fifty-two out of sixty-seven P-51s successfully returned. The entire mission covered 6,000 miles, ten countries and over 29 hours of operational flying. Nevertheless, despite the heavy casualties the USAAF doggedly persevered with *Frantic* missions in the coming months. One of the Groups, the 388th, was awarded a DUC for this mission along with two earlier ones in June 1943 and May 1944.

Back home in England it was a return to airfields, bridges and rail targets in France in support of the land battle. However, on the 25th of the month, the 4th Wing of the Third Division was engaged in Operation *Zebra*. It entailed dropping small arms, ammunition and other supplies to the French Maquis, Resistance and OSS (Office of Strategic Services), and some OSS agents; the five dropping-zones were in the Ain and Haute Savoie regions of south-east France. Each B-17 carried 420 canisters and the crews came down to less than 1,000 feet over the dropping-zones. One crewman recollects, 'seeing people on

Colonel M. M. Elliott of 379th Bomb Group made a perfect belly-landing at Kimbolton – all the crew survived. (Smithsonian Institution)

the ground waving at our airplanes as we flew over them ... after the drop Fw 190s came in to strafe the Maquis as they were collecting the supplies.' Only two B-17s were lost on the mission, one to flak and the other to fighters. Another three operations were dispatched over the next three months, providing assistance to the hard-pressed 801st Group at Harrington, which will be detailed in the following chapter.

V1 sites were still a major priority. On the 27th the 379th Group was in action over a V1 storage site at St Martin L'Hortier. Brigadier General A.W. Vanaman, recently appointed Head of Intelligence at the Eighth's HQ, went along on this mission as an observer in a B-17, *Nightjar N-Nan*. Unfortunately it received a direct hit from flak and was set on fire, and the General, along with four of the crew, baled out and were taken prisoner. Shortly afterwards the fire went out and the pilot, 1/Lt Clarence Jamieson, successfully brought the damaged aircraft back to Kimbolton. I imagine there was a lot of explaining to do about how he managed to 'lose' a General *en route*!

A major mission was launched on the 29th to Leipzig, Bernburg and Oschersleben as well as to a synthetic oil plant at Böhlen. Some 1,150 crews were involved and as the targets were several hundreds of miles apart, the bomber formations were rather extended, a nightmare for the fighter escorts and ideal conditions for the Luftwaffe. Near Leipzig the leading wing of the First Division was attacked by Me 109s and 410s but they were speedily countered by P-51s of 357th and 361st Groups.

189

P-51s of 375th squadron, 361st Fighter Group. (USAF)

The 357th claimed twenty-one for the loss of a pilot and 361st shot down three Me 109s; the Division lost only two B-17s. Shortly afterwards the 361st, led by Lt Col Roy A. Webb, made no fewer than eight separate strafing attacks on an airfield at Oschersleben, where at least sixteen aircraft were destroyed and many more damaged; all the pilots returned safely to Bottisham. The two Groups received fulsome praise from General 'Bill' Kepner for their exploits and the 357th was awarded its first DUC for this and an earlier Berlin mission.

The Group had been testing and trialling a new gyroscopic gunsight, a British design for use in heavy bombers. The sight, quickly dubbed 'No miss 'um', allowed successful firing at nearly twice the previous maximum range, as well as offering deflection shooting. The ground crews at Leiston had managed, with some difficulty, to fit the sights into P-51Cs but ultimately an American version, K-14, was produced and it was later fitted into all P-51Ds.

June ended with the Eighth engaged in attacks on airfields in France and Belgium, whilst its fighters made a number of fighter/bomber strikes on rail targets and bridges in France; only one aircraft failed to return. It had been a long and exhausting month, over 28,500 bomber and some 55,000 fighter sorties flown, totals that would not be exceeded until March 1945. Although the Eighth would still be engaged in giving air-support to the land battle waging in France in the coming months, it would be increasingly involved in its oil offensive and would have to contend with the new and potent jet-fighters, Me 163s and Me 262s – and more especially the latter.

12
FOCUS CATS, CARPETBAGGERS, NIGHT OWLS...

Although the Eighth was an independent Air Force, it initially had to rely heavily on the RAF to provide a number of ancillary but essential services including photographic intelligence, meteorological information and air/sea/rescue. In time the Eighth would establish units for these vital duties, but in the latter two their role would be to supplement and assist the various RAF squadrons engaged on these tasks. However, the question of photographic reconnaissance demanded fairly immediate attention.

The value of photographic intelligence had been fully recognised in the First World War with the widespread use of aerial cameras, so it was not surprising that the initial complement of the Eighth Air Force should include a photographic group – the 3rd. It had arrived in the UK in early September 1942 but was then assigned to the Twelfth Air Force. One of its Squadron Commanders, Major Elliott Roosevelt, son of the US President, would command the Group in North Africa. Two of its squadrons, 13th and 14th, remained in the UK and formed the nucleus of the Eighth's own Photographic Group – 7th.

The RAF's Photographic Reconnaissance Unit's permanent base was at Benson in Oxfordshire and quite naturally the Eighth's PR unit would gravitate to the area to operate under RAF guidance. Benson's satellite airfield at Mount Farm was first occupied in January 1943 by the USAAF and in the following month the 13th squadron moved in

A Spitfire XI and F-5 of the 7th Photo. Group. (USAF)

with F-5As – photographic versions of P-38Gs. The machine guns in the large nose section were removed and replaced by two or three heavy K-24 cameras. The squadron was commanded by Major James G. Hall, a First World War flyer, who at the age of 45 years might be considered a 'veteran' pilot; nevertheless he made the Eighth's first PR sortie on 28th March. In the early days the PR pilots, who acquired the name of 'Focus Cats', made regular flights over Northern France taking mapping photographs and six aircraft were lost either to enemy action or engine failure.

The Group was formally established in early July 1943 under Colonel Hall, although he would return to Washington to become the USAAF's PR 'expert'. Ultimately it comprised four squadrons, 13th, 14th, 22nd and 27th, and in August its F-5s began to photograph targets that had been bombed by the Eighth. The pilots of 14th squadron had been trained on Spitfire Vs and in October they were provided with Spitfire XIs, then the standard PR version. They would be painted overall in a dark blue colour known officially as 'PR blue' to provide maximum camouflage for these fast, high-altitude but unarmed aircraft. It would be a Spitfire XI flown by Major W.L. Weitner that would fly the first PR sortie to Berlin on 6th March 1944.

Major Walter L. Weitner of 14th squadron, 7th Photo. Group, flew over Berlin on 6th March 1944 after the Eighth's first heavy bombing mission. (USAF)

For the Group's sorties mounted during the month of June 1944 in support of the Normandy landings, it was awarded a DUC. With the appearance of Me 262s, the number of aircraft missing in action increased and from January 1945 it was supplied with its own P-51s to act as escorts. The 7th flew over 4,250 sorties and more than three million photographs were taken for the loss of 58 aircraft, including five P-51s. There is a fine propellor memorial near the site of Mount Farm airfield in memory of the Group – 'The Eyes of 8th USAAF'.

As far as meteorological information was concerned, the Eighth's 18th Weather Squadron maintained a detachment at each operational airfield to provide weather data to the crews; the detachment would also pass local weather information to its headquarters. In the summer of 1943, with the increasing rate of operations, additional and more current weather reports were needed, especially from the east Atlantic where most of the weather fronts originated. With the agreement of the RAF just four B-17s were detached to St Eval in Cornwall under Captain Adam Podjowski, to operate alongside the RAF's No 517 squadron. The crews would fly long-range Met. flights to the Azores coded *Sharon* and to the south-west of Ireland known as *Allahs*.

In the following month the Flight was doubled in size, and in April 1944 when it was based at Watton it was designated the 652 Bomb Squadron (Heavy). At the same time the 802nd Reconnaissance Group (Provisional) was activated with the addition of two squadrons, 653rd and 654th (Light), each equipped with Mosquito PRXVIs – a high-altitude PR model provided with a pressurised cabin. The former squadron was engaged in weather flights over enemy territory as well as being directed to specific targets. The other squadron was largely involved in photographic reconnaissance, both by day and night, and later its crews would be detailed to operate ahead of the main bomber formations to distribute 'chaff' – the American equivalent of the RAF's 'window'; its purpose was to interefere with the enemy's radar detection devices. From July 1944 the heavy squadron used B-24s for its long-range Met. sorties but they were not so effective at high-altitude where the weather data was mainly collected and towards the end of the year it reverted to B-17s. In total the squadron completed over 1,700 Met. sorties for the loss of just two aircraft.

P-51 of 2nd Scouting Force (338 squadron, 55th Fighter Group). (via T. Browning)

They were not the only meteorological units used by the Eighth. As its bombers made longer strikes into Germany it was realised that there was an urgent need for more immediate weather information as the forecasted conditions could often change quite dramatically during the course of an operation. Colonel Budd J. Peaslee, who had been a commander of a B-17 Group (384th), had the notion of using P-51s to operate as 'target weather scouts'. The scouting aircraft would seek out high cloud or other adverse climatic conditions along the planned route and, if necessary, plot a clearer course. The 'scouts' would also be able to give warning of enemy fighter formations and this information could be transmitted back to the bomber leaders on a special radio frequency.

Colonel Peaslee persuaded General Doolittle to consider his idea and he used P-51Ds of the 355th Group at Steeple Morden for the initial trials. The first P-51 scouts were flown by ex-bomber pilots re-trained at Goxhill, as it was considered that they had the best experience and knowledge of the effect of weather conditions on bomber formations. The first scouting mission was launched on 16th July 1944, and in the following month Doolittle authorised the establishment of a scouting force for each Bomb Division. The initial unit, known as the 1st Scouting Force, moved to Honington under Lieutenant Colonel Allison Brooks, an experienced bomber pilot. The other two Scouting Forces, also commanded by ex-bomber pilots, operated from Steeple Morden and Wormingford, flying their first sorties in September. The P-51Ds had no special equipment and the pilots were under strict orders not to get involved in air combat unless directly attacked, but by the end of the war the three Scouting Forces had been credited with 17 enemy aircraft destroyed.

As for air/sea/rescue, for almost two years the Eighth depended solely on the efficient RAF organisation of A/S/R squadrons, its high speed launches assisted by Royal Navy rescue launches. In 1943 the Eighth Fighter Command set up a Direction/Finding centre at its 65th Wing Headquarters at Saffron Walden. Nevertheless the RAF A/S/R squadrons based at Martlesham Heath, Bradwell Bay and Bircham Newton, along with launches operating from Harwich and Great Yarmouth, were mainly involved in the rescue of the Eighth's crews and fighter pilots operating from East Anglian airfields.

In the spring of 1944 it was decided to establish an A/S/R unit to supplement the RAF services, designated 'Detachment B, Flight Section, HQ 65 Fighter Wing', although it would be generally known as the Air Sea Rescue Squadron. It was equipped with 'war weary'

The 5th Emergency Rescue Squadron operated OA-10A Catalinas from January 1945. (USAF)

P-47Ds that had been gathered from Groups throughout the Command. These fighters would be adapted to carry a M-type dinghy pack under each wing, smoke marker flares and a 150-gallon drop tank to give about five hours endurance. Because of the increased weight the aircraft's armament was reduced to two .50 machine guns.

The Unit was based at Boxted, the home of the 56th, and an ex-member of the Group, Major Robert P. Gerhart, was given the command; he had previously been an A/S/R controller at Saffron Walden. Its first sortie was flown on 10th May 1944, and from then on the pilots flew regular missions during the whole period of a combat mission. On 30th June Lieutenant Tucker managed to bring down a V-1 flying bomb, the Squadron's only air victory of the war.

In January 1945 the Squadron moved to Halesworth and was designated the 5th Emergency Rescue Squadron. Towards the end of the month it received its first Consolidated OA-10As or Catalinas, the very distinctive twin-engined amphibian aircraft used successfully by the USAAF on A/S/R duties in the Mediterranean. The aircraft had a range of some 2,500 miles and was manned by a crew of six.

The first A/S/R patrol was mounted on 3rd February and they continued almost daily with March proving to be the busiest month of the war. OA-10As rescued several American and RAF crews as well as a Luftwaffe pilot, but two aircraft were lost. One failed to take off from the sea after making a successful rescue of a crew of a ditched B-24; the unlucky amphibian sank whilst being taken in tow by a launch. Then on the last day of March one was on the sea when it was attacked by an enemy fighter. The crew managed to get away in a lifeboat but they were not picked up for another five days. During March the squadron

196

also received some old B-17Gs, which had been converted to carry the US-designed airborne lifeboat under the fuselage; one was successfully dropped off the Danish coast on the 31st. The last operational patrol was mounted on 7th May when five OA-10As were on patrol to ensure that the crews supplying food to the Dutch people arrived back safely. The squadron completed over 3,500 sorties, the vast majority by P-47s and had lost only one to enemy action.

Of the two other 'specialised' squadrons that operated with the Eighth, perhaps the most well-known was the Night Leaflet Squadron. It originated back in the summer of 1943 when there were plans to equip and train a number of B-17 Groups to join RAF Bomber Command on night operations. The crews of 422nd Squadron of 305th Group at Chelveston were chosen to act as 'guinea pigs', so their B-17s were duly modified and the crews' night-flying training commenced in August. When the project was shelved, rather than waste the crews' valuable night-flying experience, the 422nd was given the task of delivering propaganda leaflets and newspapers over mainly enemy-occupied countries. The first leaflet operation went out on 7/8th October to Paris; usually the squadron would dispatch up to six B-17s on its nightly operations. Its Commander, Major Earle J. Aber, was

Major Earle Aber, CO of the Night Leaflet Squadron, and two crew members at Chelveston. (Imperial War Museum)

Leaflets being packed into Monroe 'bombs'. (via Robin J. Brooks)

responsible for much of the expertise, and along with Captain James L. Monroe, the Armaments Officer, was instrumental in the development of a special leaflets bomb (T1 & T2) in 1944. It contained 80,000 leaflets and was time-fused to explode at about 2,000 feet, with each aircraft carrying on average twelve of these leaflet 'bombs'.

In late June 1944 it was redesignated 858th Bomb Squadron and moved to Cheddington, where two months later it formed the 406th Squadron. With a number of B-24s from the 492nd Group being added it became a mainly B-24 force. Particularly after D-Day the squadron was very active in this type of 'psychological' warfare. The leaflets were then largely directed at the German people to try to persuade them that further resistance was useless, and also to foreign workers to urge them to sabotage the German war industries. During the ensuing months the squadron's crews were active over Norway and Germany and on average eight aircraft were dispatched nightly; the crews were dubbed 'Night Owls'!

Although the Squadron dispatched over 2,300 sorties and some 3,730 tons (or 1.5 billion) of leaflets were dropped, only three aircraft were lost in action and perhaps the most tragic was the loss of Lieutenant Colonel Aber. His aircraft, *Tondalayo*, one of its last remaining B-17s, was returning from an operation over Holland on 4th March 1945 when it was shot down by friendly flak near Clacton and crashed into the river Stour; it was the Colonel's 51st mission. He and his co-pilot, 2/Lieutenant Maurice Harper, stayed with the stricken aircraft to guide it away from the populated areas of Harwich whilst the nine crewmen baled out. Fifty-five years later, in June 2000, the wreck of the B-17 was finally located near Wrabness and the remains of Lieutenant Colonel Aber and Lieutenant Harper recovered.

Another unit that operated on purely special operations was the Radio Counter Measures (RCM) Squadron. It had been formed to assist the various RAF squadrons in No 100 (Bomber Support) Group of Bomber Command. This Group used various electronic devices to jam and disrupt the enemy's radio and radar defence systems. In January 1944 a detachment of air and ground crews under Captain G.E. Paris arrived at Sculthorpe to train and work alongside RAF crews, especially those of No 214 squadron, also operating B-17s. In April the USAAF were modifying a B-17G as a prototype RCM aircraft. In May the Eighth's detachment was designated the 803rd Bomb Squadron (Provisional), but Sculthorpe was closed for development and both the RAF and USAAF crews moved to Oulton.

A small number of B-17s had been equipped with 'Carpet' designed to interfere with the German 'Wurtzburg' radar, and 'Mandrel' used against 'Freya'. It was not until 2nd June that the Eighth's crews entered this war of stealth for the first time, on a daylight mission, and their first night operation was made a couple of days later in support of the D-Day operations. It was then considered that B-24s were better suited to the RCM work, in addition to being able to accommodate all the intricate jamming apparatus. By August the squadron, now redesignated 36th Bomb Squadron (Heavy), had nine B-24s and just two B-17s. It moved to Cheddington to operate alongside the Night Leaflet Squadron, although most of its operations would be conducted by day. The crews finally completed their war from Alconbury – over 1,150 sorties with only two aircraft lost in action.

The Eighth became very briefly engaged in the bitter offensive against the German U-boats. Two squadrons of B-24s (330th and 409th of 93rd Group) were seconded to RAF Coastal Command in late October 1942 to operate for about a month on anti-submarine patrols. They were the precursors of an Antisubmarine Group that operated under the aegis of the Eighth from July to October 1943. Early in July the 4th and 19th squadrons of the 479th Group arrived at St Eval in Cornwall directly from the United States. For about a week the crews, under the close direction of their Commander, Colonel Howard Moore, trained with the RAF crews. They mounted their first patrol on 13th July and during their short stay at St Eval the crews were credited with a share in the destruction of three U-boats, *U-558, U-404* and *U-706,* for the loss of one B-24, shot down by U-boat flak.

The two squadrons moved up the coast to Dunkeswell, where they were joined by the 6th and 22nd squadrons. Their brief time at Dunkeswell was not as successful. In the course of over 450 patrols and 8 attacks on U-boats, three aircraft were lost in action mainly brought down by enemy fighters. Their final operation was made on 17th October and then the Group was stood down from anti-submarine duties, which had been transferred to the US Navy. The Group moved to Podington, where it was disbanded on 11th November; most of the crews would then form the nucleus of two Bomb Squadrons – 36th and 406th – to be engaged on very special operations, largely on account of their valuable experience of long-range navigational patrols.

In November the first six crews were sent to RAF Tempsford to gain experience for their new duties – dropping supplies to various groups of Resistance forces in occupied Europe. They operated on behalf of the OSS, the American counterpart of the British Special Operations Executive (SOE). These operations were all part of a grand Allied plan, which was co-ordinated with the SOE. The Americans code-named their special missions 'Carpetbaggers' – a name redolent of post-Civil War days and its opportunist travelling salesmen. The crews were required to make two operational flights with RAF crews of Nos 138 and 161, who were vastly experienced in these clandestine missions, before they went 'live' on their own account. In fact the Americans sent out their first 'Carpetbagger' operation from Tempsford on 4/5th January 1944, led by Colonel Clifford J. Heflin. They would operate first from Alconbury and then later from Watton before moving to Harrington in late March 1944, which became their permanent base.

Their B-24Ds had been specially adapted for their new clandestine role; painted overall in non-glare black, later changed to gloss black as its reflective qualities were thought better for evading searchlight batteries. The nose and waist guns were removed, as well as the ball turret, leaving an opening for a cargo hatch and an exit for parachutists, which became known as a 'Joe Hole' – 'Joe' was the American slang for a secret agent. The waist windows were blacked out and teardrop perspex blisters were added to both cockpit windows to afford the pilots better visibility, extra room was provided internally for the crews, and the fuselage was fitted with plywood flooring to ease the movement of supplies.

Black B-24 'Carpetbagger' leaving Harrington.

Each aircraft was equipped with 'Gee' – the British navigational aid – later replaced with 'Loran', an American-built version. Special radio equipment was installed, 'S-phone', which enabled the crews to communicate with the landing parties on the ground. Also an airborne air/ground homing device known as 'Rebecca' was used, which received radar impulses from a ground set 'Eureka', an aid for the navigators in locating the precise dropping zones. During the night-flights the B-24s would be completely blacked-out save for a small light in the navigator's compartment. Over the dropping zone the aircraft would be flown to within 600 to 400 feet of the ground and at a speed of about 130 mph. The supply packs contained radio equipment, specialised tools, money, forged documents, foodstuffs, clothing, cigarettes etc. Arms and ammunition were usually dropped separately.

On 28th March 1944 the two squadrons were designated 801st Bomb Group (Provisional) under the command of Colonel Heflin, and in the following month the crews began parachuting special agents and *Jedburgh* teams. These three-man *Jeds*, as they were known, usually comprised a British or American officer, along with a French or Dutch officer and a radio operator, all in full military uniform. They would help to train Resistance groups in the use of arms and explosives and also plan and take part in sabotage operations. In May 1944 the crews were active on sixteen nights with the number of successful sorties exceeding 200 for the first time, although three B-24s were lost in action. Leading up to D-Day the pace of operations dramatically increased and the Group had difficulty in meeting the demands of OSS. However, two additions were made to the Group, when 850th squadron came directly from the States, and the 788th was transferred in from 467th Group. By mid-June the Group would have fifty-four B-24s on complement and ultimately some eighty B-24Ds and Hs had been modified for Carpetbagger duties.

During June the first C-47s were allocated to the Group, used to land supplies and passengers, as well as returning with passengers. In July the crews were in action on 27 nights. Nearly five hundred and forty successful sorties were dispatched with over one hundred agents dropped, although on the night of 4/5th, three crews were lost in action with a fourth crash-landing on return. In August it was redesignated the 492nd, inheriting the identity of the Eighth's most unfortunate Bomb Group. The squadrons were also renumbered 856th to 859th. Colonel Heflin left for the States to command a B-29 training unit and was replaced by his deputy, Lieutenant Colonel Robert W. Fish, who had also previously served in the Antisubmarine Group. August had been the busiest month so far – 700 tons of supplies and 227 agents dropped.

Carpetbagger operations over France ceased in the middle of September, although a limited number of operations continued over Holland, Belgium and Denmark, conducted by one squadron, 856th. In December 859th squadron was detached to Italy to operate over northern Italy and the Balkans and did not return to the UK. Also in December the remaining two squadrons would commence night-bombing operations in co-operation with the RAF's No 100 Group. Not until the last weeks of February 1945 were Carpetbagger operations resumed to Holland, Denmark and Norway, and special flights over Germany were mounted during March and April.

In March two new aircraft appeared at Harrington, both employed on special duties. Douglas A-26 Invaders – fast twin-engined light bombers – were considered particularly suitable to drop special agents into Germany. On 2nd March an A-26 crew operating from Watton dropped two agents close to Berlin. Several Mosquito PRXVIs were used on what were coded 'Red Stocking' – the receiving and recording of signals transmitted by Allied agents in enemy-occupied territories and Germany. The Group's final Carpetbagger sorties left on the night 26/27th April for Norway; over 2,800 sorties had been completed with over 1,040 persons delivered behind enemy lines. During these

Careful Virgin – B-17F originally of 91st Bomb Group. Seconded to the 'Aphrodite' project in May 1944, sent out to Mimoyecques on 4th August.

operations twenty-five B-24s were lost and another eight written-off in accidents. Somewhat belatedly in March 1947, the Group was awarded a DUC for its operations during 20th March to 26th April 1945, citing 'the perilous flying conditions and opposition from the close-range enemy ground defences . . . the 492nd BG continued to distinguish itself in special operations involving long flights in enemy territory'.

Perhaps the most bizarre of all the Eighth's special operations was the project code-named *Aphrodite*, which was cloaked in the utmost secrecy. In June 1944 as the first V1 flying bombs fell on southern England, the USAAF decided to activate their own 'guided weapon', battle-worn B-17s with all the armour, turrets, bombing and oxygen apparatus removed before being equipped with radio receiving sets and then filled with ten tons of explosives. The method of operation was for the 'robot' B-17 to be flown manually by a two-man crew until radio contact was ensured with the guide aircraft; the two airmen would then bale out to allow the robot aircraft to be directed onto the target by control from the guide aircraft. The project was authorised for action on 23rd June.

Lieutenant Colonel James Turner was put in charge and he and his team moved into RAF Woodbridge early in July with ten B-17s, a couple of B-24s and eight P-47s as fighter escorts. Because the airfield was used as an emergency landing ground, there was a high risk of one of the damaged aircraft colliding with one of the lethal robot aircraft, and it was wisely decided that it would be safer to move the secret project elsewhere. An empty and secluded airfield at Fersfield, already allocated to the USAAF, was thought to fill the bill. The 388th Group based at nearby Knettishall was given overall control of the satellite base, with Lieutenant Colonel Roy Forrest of its 560th squadron moving into Fersfield.

The two *Aphrodite* missions were launched on 4th August and were directed at 'rocket sites' in northern France. The first went well but the second malfunctioned and the robot bomber landed in a wood near Sudbourne Park in Suffolk with a massive explosion, making a crater over 100 feet in diameter! Two days later two were launched but because of problems with the radio equipment both fell harmlessly into the sea.

The US Navy had also been working on their own rocket projectile and they decided to take a slice of the action; their program was code-named *Anvil*. The Naval Unit launched their first rocket aircraft – PBY-1 (B-24) – on 12th August, directed at Mimoyecques rocket site. The aircraft was piloted by Lieutenant Joseph Kennedy, the eldest son of the ex-US Ambassador and brother of John F. Kennedy, the future President. The robot aircraft headed out towards Southwold and then exploded in mid-air, killing Kennedy and Lieutenant W.J. Willy; the wreckage was strewn over a wide area and the bodies were never recovered.

Another eight *Aphrodites* were dispatched from Fersfield and one pilot, 1/Lt R.W. Lindahl, was killed on 11th September. In November it was decided to move the project to Knettishall, however only four launches were made – two in December directed at the marshalling yards at Herford, both of which missed their targets. The last two were sent out on New Year's Day to a power station at Oldenburg. The first one was damaged by flak and landed short of the town but without exploding, and the other, also struck by flak, landed some miles away from the target. It is fair to say that the project had not been a conspicuous success and its future now became a political matter at the highest level mainly because of the high risk of civilian casualties. The debate continued for several months before the project was abandoned at the end of April.

13
THE RESTLESS SKIES

'Operations continued at a prodigious rate on a vast scale; in the area of the East Anglian bases, it seemed that the sky was never still', writes Roger Freeman in *The Mighty Eighth*. Without doubt July to September 1944 was a frantic time for crews and fighter pilots alike. Over 63,000 bomber sorties were dispatched in eighty missions and almost 50,000 fighter sorties. The Eighth seemed to be revelling in its sheer strength and might, as its aircraft roamed the skies over the length and breadth of France, the Low Countries and Germany. This frenzied period of action was even more remarkable because unfavourable weather on twenty-eight days, either prevented or restricted operations – almost a month lost to the unpredictable north-European climate.

Rail/road targets and airfields in France and the Low Countries were attacked by the heavies and fighter/bombers. V1 sites still demanded attention, and despite the inclement weather the Eighth was in action over Germany on forty days with oil targets now the main priority. It also provided tactical air support for the land forces on a number of occasions, and carried supplies to the airborne forces, as well as 'trucking' vital petrol to the US armies in France; also arms and ammunition were dropped to the Resistance in France and Poland – a veritable maid of all work!

With the increased operations since D-Day, it was decided that the number of missions to constitute a combat tour needed to be raised to thirty-five; this effectively extended a tour to some four to five months. Fighter pilots' tours were extended to three hundred operational hours. Many crews felt, with some justification, that the long and exhausting missions to southern Germany should count as double compared with

B-24M of 576th squadron, 392nd Bomb Group. (USAF)

the relatively shorter and less hazardous missions to France. However, thirty-five missions, irrespective of distance or danger, remained in force for the duration of the war.

It was not until 7th July that the weather relented sufficiently for the Eighth to mount a major strike at oil targets at Lützkendorf, Böhlen, Merseburg and Leipzig, along with several aircraft plants. On this mission the Second Division bound for Lützkendorf and Halle encountered the heaviest Luftwaffe opposition and the 14th Wing in particular suffered from a massed onslaught. It was led by Colonel Leon Johnson, the hero of Ploesti, and his 'old' Group (44th) lost three crews, the 392nd five (two collided over the Dutch coast) but the 492nd caught without fighter support lost twelve B-24s, which brought its losses in action in less than two months to forty-four!

Many B-24s were victims of the Sturmgruppe – IV.(Sturm)/JG 3 based at Salzwadel and led by Hauptmann Wilhelm Moritz. It was a special unit equipped with Fw 190A-8s, *Sturmbocks* or 'Battering Rams'; heavily armoured and equipped with powerful cannons, including the lethal 30 mm MK108; three strikes from its high-explosive shells were claimed to be sufficient to bring down a heavy bomber. The specially selected pilots attacked the bomber formations from astern in tight arrowhead formations and closed in to very short-range. The inception of this fighter tactic dated back to the winter of 1943/4 with the formation of the Sturmstaffel 1 under Major Hans-Günther Kornatzki.

B-17Gs of 532nd and 533rd squadrons, 381st Bomb Group over Essex. Little Guy VE-K lost 26th November 1944. (Smithsonian Institution)

The Fw 190A-8s were heavy and unwieldy and required their own escorts. Although very effective 'bomber destroyers', they were easy prey for the the American fighters. Nevertheless two further units would be formed during July/ August – II.(Sturm)/JG 300 and II.(Sturm)/JG 4.

Although the Eighth lost thirty-seven aircraft on this mission, the escorts claimed seventy-five victories (including nine Fw 190A-8s). The 55th, soon to convert to P-51s, had a successful mission notching up nineteen without loss. One of the finest Fighter Commanders, Colonel Glenn E. Duncan of 353rd with nineteen victories, was posted missing whilst strafing Wesendorf airfield. He force-landed his *Dove of Peace IV*, evaded capture and joined the Dutch underground. Colonel Duncan finally returned to England in April 1945 and resumed command of the 353rd!

On three successive days, 11th to 13th July, industrial targets in Munich were attacked by over 3,000 bombers and 6,400 tons of bombs were dropped. The massive Allach aero engine works and the railway yards were the main targets. A fourth mission planned for the 16th was frustrated by high clouds topping over 30,000 feet, although two hundred and ten B-17s did bomb the Aero engines works. Relatively little fighter opposition was encountered on the operations, only thirteen enemy aircraft shot down, but nevertheless sixty-three bombers went missing. Twenty-four crews found their way to Switzerland, where, in two weeks, a total of thirty-three aircraft would end up, the equivalent of two squadrons.

Bastille Day – 14th July – was the occasion for more than three hundred and fifty B-17s of the First Division engaged in Operation *Cadillac*, the second delivery of supplies to the French Resistance. This time 3,700 containers were dropped at seven zones near Limoges, St Lô and Vercorse. Intelligence sources confirmed that the operation had been most successful; there were no losses in action, although two crews landed near the Normandy beach-heads. Four days later B-24s of the 2nd Division attacked tactical targets to the south and east of Caen in support of British troops, some of whom were only about 300 yards away from the bombardment but no injuries were sustained. On the same day the First's B-17s bombed the experimental stations at Peenemünde and Zinnowitz on Usedom along the Baltic coast. General Spaatz later described this mission as 'the finest example of precision bombing I have ever seen.' The three missing B-17s landed in nearby Sweden.

The now all too familar oil targets at Lützkendorf, Merseburg and Leipzig were bombed on the 20th by over six hundred B-17s. The 91st sustained eight losses mainly from flak and eight fighters were also lost. The Eighth's leading ace, Lt Col Francis S. 'Gabby' Gabreski of the 56th Group known as the 'Mad Pole', was shot down whilst strafing Heinkel 111s at Bassienheim airfield. He spent the rest of the war as a prisoner. Gabreski's total of twenty-eight victories would not be surpassed by any Eighth fighter pilot throughout the war. He served as a fighter commander with the USAF until 1967. The Suffolk County (New York) airport near Westhampton was renamed the Francis Gabreski airport in 1991.

Before the American break-out at St Lô and Pêriers on the Contentin peninsula, code-named *Cobra*, General Omar Bradley, the Commander of the US 12th Army Corps, ordered a large air bombardment of the Wehrmacht's strongly fortified positions. On the 24th July over 1,500 bombers were dispatched but due to persistent ground haze less than one third actually bombed. Despite every care being taken twenty US troops were killed and sixty wounded. Another strike was called for on the following day and almost fifteen hundred crews managed to bomb, dropping some 3,300 tons. From the ground it was 'indescribable. The whole earth was shaking, the air was full of dust and smoke and bits of steel and earth, and the roar of engines overhead went on and on and

Lt Col Francis S. 'Gabby' Gabreski of the 56th Fighter Group – the Eighth's highest scoring fighter pilot with 28 victories in the air and $2\frac{1}{2}$ strafing. (The Mighty Eighth Air Force Heritage Museum)

on . . . The earth looked like the surface of the moon.' Sadly, some 'short bombing' resulted in three hundred and eighty casualties in the US 4th Division of whom one hundred and two were killed, including Lieutenant General McNair, the Deputy Commander. These two operations were the only blemishes in the Eighth's long bombing offensive, although the tragic incidents were not quickly forgotten by US Army personnel.

Merseburg and Leipzig were revisited by B-17 crews on both the 28th and 29th, and twenty-two went missing – the 'Bloody Hundredth' suffered ten losses, their 'jinx' reputation would not die. At least twelve were claimed by 5./JG II, and its pilots remembered it as 'the Day of the Great Shooting Party'! Perhaps more ominous was the first sighting, on the 28th, of a new Luftwaffe fighter – the rocket-powered Me 163B. Pilots of the 359th on escort near Merseburg saw two thick white contrails at about 32,000 feet. The Group's CO, Colonel Avelin Tacon Jr, thought they were 'jet-propelled fighters'.

The following day Captain Arthur Jeffrey of the 479th gave chase to a Me 163. It was seen to go into a vertical dive and after aerial photographs had been examined Jeffrey was credited with the first enemy 'jet' aircraft; after the war German records did not confirm that one was lost. This Me 163 was probably on a training flight from its base at Brandis, just to the east of Leipzig, where 1./JG 400 was equipped with about thirty-five *Komets* and its pilots were working towards operational readiness. The appearance of these new fighters was no surprise to the Eighth, intelligence sources had revealed their existence and indeed a silhouette drawing had been circulated to all Groups. Nevertheless the notion that its fighters would soon be faced with an enemy fighter capable of speeds well in excess of 500 mph did at least provide food for thought!

The month closed with another B-17 strike at industrial targets in Munich, whilst the Second Division was in action over chemical works at Ludwigshafen and the Third's B-24s attacked a couple of French airfields. Once more few enemy fighters were seen and in total sixteen bombers were lost, three due to collisions and a ditching. The Eighth's airmen could be forgiven for believing (or hoping?) that the Luftwaffe was a spent force, indeed the press daily fostered this notion. However, it was about to demonstrate a resurgence of strength, as its battered units retreated from France and were re-equipped for the defence of the Reich. By the end of July over five hundred and fifty fighters, mostly single-seaters, were based in Germany, an 20% increase during the month.

During July there were changes in the Eighth's fighter force. Three P-38 Groups, 20th, 55th and 364th, converted to P-51s, which left just five P-47s and a single P-38 Group; by 1945 the 56th would be the solitary P-47 unit. On 1st August the 92nd Wing of the Third Division mounted its first B-17 mission, and the other three B-24 Groups would have re-equipped with B-17s by mid-September. There was a rumour circulating within the Division that B-24s were being sent to targets

B-17s of the Third Division dropped supplies to French Resistance forces in several operations during June to September. (Imperial War Museum)

where flak was known to be heavy just to get rid of the aircraft 'naturally'! There is certainly no evidence of this happening; in eighteen missions the three Groups lost seven B-24s in action.

The first three days of August saw bridges, airfields, marshalling yards and supply depôts, mainly in France, as the targets for heavies and fighter/bombers. A number of V1 sites were bombed on each day by B-24s and another drop of arms and supplies was made to the French Resistance in south-east France, this one code-named *Buick*. The final supply drop was made on 9th September, coded *Grassy*. In all the missions the bomber losses were slight – eighteen – and for the first time Fighter Command lost more aircraft – twenty in action whilst flying over eighteen hundred sorties.

On 4th August it was a return in strength to strategic targets – oil, aircraft plants and airfields – at Hamburg, Anklam, Bremen, Kiel, Rostock and Peenemünde. Of course losses were heavier – fifteen – and again more fighters were lost, although the pilots claimed sixty-eight in air combat. The 356th had its most successful mission so far, credited with fifteen Me 109s over Bremen for the loss of a P-47.

Two days later Berlin and Brandenburg were on the agenda for B-17 crews, whereas B-24s were directed to a variety of oil targets in and around Hamburg. It was a disaster for the 351st – six out of the eleven crews missing over Brandenburg. The small force (154) bound for Berlin escaped relatively lightly with five missing, quite a contrast with earlier missions to 'Big B'! The 'Bodney Boys' (352nd) were credited with twelve of the thirty-one victories; Captain George E. Preddy in his P-51D *Cripes A'Mighty 3rd*, destroying six Me 109s to bring his tally to twenty-one. He left for the States on leave, where he was feted by the American public. He returned to the Group in October and added to his score.

Seventy-five B-17s of the 95th and 390th attacked the Focke-Wulf plant at Rahmel in Poland and then flew eastwards to land at Russian airfields; the second *Frantic* shuttle mission. They were accompanied by P-51s of the 357th. Escorting the mission as far as Poland were P-51s of 339th and 55th Groups and they completed the longest fighter mission so far – over 1,590 miles or $6\frac{1}{2}$ hours in the air. The *Frantic* force would bomb an oil refinery at Trzebinia in eastern Poland, as well as two Rumanian airfields *en route* to Italy, finally returning on 12th August, after bombing Francazal airfield at Toulouse on their way home.

The luckless 492nd Group flew its final mission with the Eighth on 7th August; it was then disbanded. In barely three months and sixty-four missions, no fewer than fifty-seven aircraft had been lost. It was decided to re-designate the Special Operations Group (Carpetbaggers) the 492nd with effect from the 13th; aircraft and personnel moved either into the Carpetbaggers or other Groups in the Division. Its erstwhile Commander, Colonel Snavely, was given command of his old Group – the 44th. 'The Ringmasters' (491st) moved from Metfield into North Pickenham; earlier in the month one of its airmen, Lt Charles Griffin, had completed his combat tour in just sixty-two days – a record. He had hardly time to enjoy English beer!

The inherent dangers of ground-strafing were made abundantly clear during the month, with the Eighth losing a number of fighter pilots in the large scale strafing and fighter/bomber missions mounted during August. On the 10th fourteen pilots were lost, including Lt. Col

Kyle Riddle, CO of 479th. He successfully evaded capture and returned to command the Group again in November. Two days later eighteen pilots were lost including another Fighter Commander; Colonel Thomas J.J. Christian Jr, of the 361st. He was leading his pilots on an attack of rail targets in northern France when they encountered fierce and accurate flak; the Colonel's P-51, *Lou IV*, received a direct hit and was seen to burst in flames. Christian was a popular and able leader, the only 'West Pointer' to make Fighter Commander. There is a street named in memory of him in Bottisham, as well as a fine memorial lych gate. Another eleven pilots went missing on the 27th; Colonel Cy Wilson, CO of the 20th Group, ditched near the Danish coast, he was rescued and taken prisoner. Col Wilson was the twelfth Fighter Commander to be killed/missing in action. They certainly led from the front.

More tactical air-support was given to the Allied armies on 13th August, as they were breaking out of the Normandy enclave. Both heavies and fighter/bombers attacked coastal batteries, road and rail targets and enemy troop positions over a wide area from Le Havre to Paris. Again more fighters were lost than bombers – thirteen to twelve, but the pilots returned with claims that over seven hundred and seventy enemy vehicles and guns had been destroyed and many more damaged.

Two days later airfields in western Germany and the Low Countries were attacked by over eight hundred and seventy crews. The 'pioneer' Group, 303rd, experienced a torrid time whilst bound for Wiesbaden; its formation was 'suddenly attacked by about two dozen Fw 190s and in a matter of minutes nine B-17s went down.' Another damaged aircraft crashed on approach to Molesworth. As one veteran pilot remarked, 'It wasn't as if it was a major target like Berlin or Merseburg.' The Group had been the victims of II.(Sturm)/JG 300. Also the 446th had a sharp encounter with enemy fighters over Meppel and although its gunners claimed six Me 109s four crews failed to return to Bungay. These losses were the only ones suffered by their respective Divisions. The 364th, which had not long converted to P-51s, claimed ten enemy aircraft.

Oil and aircraft plants in central and south-east Germany were attacked on the 16th by over one thousand bombers, and it was the fate of another two 'veteran' Groups to fare badly. The 91st bound for the Siebel aircraft factory at Halle lost six B-17s and another was salvaged after crash-landing at Halesworth. The 95th suffered four losses over oil targets at Zeitz. The 359th Group that had made the first sighting of a

Man O'War: P-51D of 354th squadron, 355th Fighter Group. Flown by Lt Col Claiborne H. Kinnard Jr. (USAF)

Me 163 in July, again picked out the distinctive thick rocket contrails and 1/Lt Cyril W. Jones claimed and was credited with its destruction. This brilliant young pilot, who gained a victory on his first mission, was lost on his sixteenth mission; he had six air and five ground victories to his name.

Five days of unfavourable weather almost completely grounded the Eighth but time was made up on 24th August when over 1,300 bombers were sent to Brunswick, Merseburg, Weimar, Brüx and Ruhland. Twenty-six were lost, mainly over Merseburg, and for the second time in the month the 306th lost six crews; the Group would incur heavier losses in September. Two bomber missions were mounted on the 25th and 26th to aircraft component plants, oil refineries, fuel stores and chemical works for relatively light losses – twenty-eight in total. Then on the 27th a major operation directed at Berlin was severely hampered by high cloud formations over Denmark and northern Germany and the force was recalled. Many Groups bombed 'opportunity' targets at Esberg and Emden.

Poor weather precluded heavy bomber missions on the following two days but a large fighter/bomber and strafing operation was mounted on the 28th with a smaller one the next day. All Fighter Groups, except the 361st, were in action on the 28th – over eight hundred and thirty fighters; twenty were lost for thirty victories. Major Joe Myers of 78th Group and an ex-P-38 pilot, sighted an unusual aircraft flying far below his flight whilst returning from Brussels. At first he thought it was a B-26 but quickly realised that a B-26 could not travel that quickly! Myers identified it as a 'twin-jet' and as the P-47s closed for the attack, the jet took evasive action and finally crash-landed in flames. Myers and his wingman, Lt Manford Croy, were credited with its 'destruction' – the first Me 262 victory.

On 30th August the Eighth brought its 'Noball' offensive to a conclusion, when some two hundred and ten bombers attacked sites in the Pas de Calais without loss. In just over a year these sites had been bombed on sixty-nine days by over 16,270 bombers for the loss of sixty-three; by September 16th all V1 launching sites in France had been captured. During August two hundred and twenty heavies had been lost, which was the lowest monthly figure since January, but almost the same number of fighters were missing in action – two hundred and eleven; an indication of the increase in the number of fighter/bomber and strafing missions flown.

The first two days of September were unfavourable for bomber operations but on the 3rd gun batteries in the Brest peninsula were bombed by B-17s of the Third, and they returned two days later to attack enemy positions. German forces were stubbornly resisting US ground troops and General Bradley had requested an all-out air offensive, which was mainly undertaken by B-26s of the Ninth Air Force; Brest was not captured by US troops until September 19th.

Two major missions, each involving over 1,100 bombers, were dispatched on the 9th and 10th September to rail and motor industry targets at Mannheim, Mainz, Dusseldorf, Fürth and Ulm. Losses of twenty-one could be considered quite moderate but these two operations can be seen as the lull before the storm for the crews. On the next three days the Eighth sent out over 3,000 bomber sorties for a total loss of ninety. Although this overall figure equates to a 2.9% loss rate, such bare statistics mask the sobering fact that for several individual Groups these missions proved very costly.

On 11th September oil plants at Ruhland, Brüx, Merseburg, Lützkendorf, Misburg and Magdeburg were targeted, and the crews faced the strongest and most determined Luftwaffe opposition since 28th May; it was estimated that over five hundred enemy fighters were in action. Forty bombers went missing and another seven were written-off. The 'jinx' Group, 100th, lost eleven and the 92nd eight. The heaviest B-24 loss was sustained by the 392nd; four failed to return to Wendling.

The air battles were intense and furious in the extreme, and the escorts claimed their highest number of victories so far, one hundred and sixteen in the air and another forty-two on the ground. The laurels went to two Groups, the 352nd with twenty-seven, closely followed by the 359th with twenty-six: the latter was awarded its only DUC for the defence of the bombers over Merseburg. The 339th was also awarded a DUC for its tally of fifty-eight enemy aircraft on the 10th and 11th, many of them on the ground. The Group led by Major Edgar B. Gravette, had come to the aid of the embattled 100th and prevented even heavier losses. Whilst these air battles were raging, B-17s of 96th and 452nd, escorted by P-51s of the 20th Group, attacked oil targets at Chemnitz without loss and continued onwards to land in Russia – the third *Frantic* mission. The force would return five days later after bombing a target in Hungary.

The following day enemy fighters were again out in large numbers and the First Division bore the brunt of their onslaught. The 306th lost nine and the 351st six, with another two crash-landing in Belgium. Sadly the Third's B-17s did not escape the battle; the Eighth's most junior Group, 493rd, sustained the heaviest losses – nine in action with another salvaged. This, the Group's first taste of sustained fighter attacks, proved to be its worst single mission of the war. Fifty-four enemy fighters were shot down by the escorts, the 361st and 352nd each being credited with thirteen.

For the third successive day over 1,000 bombers were out over oil and industrial targets at Merseburg, Lützkendorf and Ludwigshafen. Although most Groups survived with light losses, the 92nd had four crews missing, one landing in Switzerland. Thirty-three enemy aircraft were destroyed, fifteen to the 357th and the 55th was credited with sixteen, which brought its total in ten days to one hundred and six for the loss of nine pilots. The Group's 'purple patch' gained its first DUC.

From the beginning of September the Second Division's B-24s began flying valuable fuel supplies to General Patton's army in France. On the 12th, the 96th Wing (458th, 466th and 467th) was removed from operations to concentrate on these 'truckin'' flights. Many B-24s had been modified to carry extra five-gallon petrol cans. The aircraft carried a crew of five and usually two passengers but no gunners. They landed at three airfields, Chartres, St Dizier and Florennes, which had only recently been captured. Two daily missions were planned depending on the weather, and as night-flying was not allowed, the crews had a stop-over in France. Many managed a quick trip to Paris (liberated on 25th August), returning to their bases with tall tales, war souvenirs and, of course, wine!

These 'truckin'', operations continued until the end of the month. The 458th at Horsham St Faith carried over 720,000 gallons and the 'Rackheath Aggies' some 640,000 gallons. Unfortunately the flights were not completed without fatalities. The 458th lost two aircraft; one

B-24s of 458th Bomb Group over Norfolk: first operation 24th February 1944. (USAF)

crashed at Hellesdon shortly after take-off, killing the crew and one civilian and severely damaging a terrace of houses. The 466th at Attlebridge also lost two aircraft; one crashed at Woodbridge after the crew had baled out. The Wing was back to 'normal' operations on 2nd October.

On 14th September overall control of the Eighth reverted to General Spaatz with General Arnold declared its 'Executive Officer'. Eleven days later new Directives were issued to the USAAF and RAF and Spaatz could be forgiven for a wry smile of satisfaction when he noted that the First Priority was stated as the 'Petroleum industry, with special emphasis on petrol (gasoline) including storage' – at long last his cherished 'Oil Plan' had gained official blessing! The secondary priorities were the German rail and waterborne transport systems, tank and motor transport production plants and depôts.

Also on the 14th changes were made within Fighter Command. Groups were now placed under the control of the three Bomb Divisions. The 67th Fighter Wing with its five Groups was allocated to the First, the 65th to the Second and the 66th Wing to the Third Division. These changes were made to provide a more simplified chain of command and in theory enable easier planning for escort missions. General Kepner had already left Fighter Command, on 1st August he had been appointed the Commander of the Second Division, although

217

he still kept his hand in with fighters. His personal aircraft was a P-51B!

The Eighth, like all the Allied air forces, was called upon to provide air support for the major airborne landings at Arnhem and Nijmegen, known as *Market Garden*. This operation has passed into military history for the courage and valour of all those taking part both in the air and on the ground. On 17th September the four remaining P-47 Groups were given the difficult and hazardous task of destroying the flak batteries in the path of the dropping-zones. The aircraft's heavier fire-power and greater durability were considered essential for this operation. The pilots were briefed to attack from about 2,000/2,500 feet and not to drop their 250 pound fragmentation bombs until the batteries opened fire. They were effectively being used as 'flak bait'! It was strongly emphasised that bombing accuracy was the order of the day.

The four Groups survived this ordeal of fire with relatively light losses – six. Even the B-17s that bombed the area also escaped lightly, just two in action but one hundred and twenty damaged. On the following day it was the turn of the B-24 crews to enter the cauldron of fire. They made supply drops to the airborne troops, flying through heavy and accurate flak at an altitude of 500 feet; seven were lost and half of the two hundred and fifty strong force suffered flak damage. The P-47 pilots in action on this day had to fly even lower than previously because of poor visibility. The 56th lost sixteen P-47s and the 78th lost five pilots. P-51 escorts had a good day – thirty-three victories – of which the 357th accounted for twenty-six for the loss of two pilots.

Patrols of the area were made by the fighters on both the 20th and 21st September and on the latter day the 56th achieved some revenge for their earlier losses – fifteen victories for the loss of two P-47s. Two days later some five hundred and eighty fighters were sent in 'to neutralize the dropping-zones' before RAF transports re-supplied the beleaguered forces; fourteen were lost but the 353rd claimed fifteen victories. The 'Wolfpack' was awarded its second DUC for its actions on the 18th, and the other Groups, 78th, 356th and 353rd were each awarded DUCs for the missions over the five days.

On 15th September the Eighth had dispatched one hundred and ten B-17s to drop urgent supplies to the Polish underground engaged in a bitter battle in Warsaw. Heavy weather over the North Sea compelled the force to be recalled. Three days later the 13th Wing (95th, 100th and 390th) were able to proceed with the Warsaw supply mission, accompanied by P-51s of the 355th Group. Shortly before reaching

Steeple Morden Strafers (355th Fighter Group) in action! Me 110s being raked with cannon fire. (Smithsonian Institution)

Warsaw the formations were attacked by two dozen Me 109s; the escorts downed four for the loss of two and one B-17 was shot down. The crews dropped 1,248 containers of food, medical supplies and ammunition, although it was later disclosed that many containers fell into enemy hands; the 'Warsaw rising' was put down by the Germans with harsh brutality. The force now flew eastwards to land at Poltava, Piryatin and Mirgorod – the final *Frantic* mission. They bombed marshalling yards at Szolnok in Hungary before returning to the UK on the 22nd. Political difficulties and logistical problems ensured that this was the last 'Russian shuttle'. Although one pilot recalled 'the Shuttle mission was a marvellous experience, one I shall never ever forget.'

During the third week of September bad weather restricted bombing operations but on the 25th over 1,300 bombers were dispatched to the Opau oil plant at Ludwigshafen and a number of railway yards in western Germany. The following day over 1,000 bombers struck rail targets at Hamm and Osnabrück, along with armoured vehicle plants at Bremen – all in accordance with the recent Directives. Several months before, these targets would have resulted in heavy losses but now just nine bombers were missing in the two operations. 1/Lt Urban Drew of the 361st Fighter Group attempted to destroy a Me 262 sighted near Hamm, but he became involved in a prolonged and fruitless pursuit. The jet-aircraft had considerable speed advantage over a P-51 in level flight. Thirty-two enemy aircraft were claimed, of which

B-17Gs of 92nd Bomb Group bombing oil targets at Magdeburg – 28th September 1944.

(National Archives)

twenty-seven Me 109s were credited to the 479th Group in a short but hectic air battle near Münster.

The Group was now commanded by the legendary Hubert Zemke, who since his arrival on 12th August had brought about an amazing effect on the Group's fortunes. On 18th August its pilots were credited with forty-three ground-strafing victories and now with this successful air combat, in which Colonel Zemke claimed two, the 479th was awarded its only DUC. It should be noted that the pilots were also in the process of converting to P-51s; their first P-51 sorties had been just two weeks earlier.

The mission to the Henschel engine works at Kassel on the 27th by over two hundred and fifty B-24s proved to be a disaster of epic and tragic proportions for one Group – 445th. It had already survived a heavy loss on a single mission, back in February over Gotha, but even that would not compare with the catastrophic events of this operation. Thirty-seven crews left Tibenham and when the Group was at the Initial Point, the lead navigator made a slight but critical miscalculation, which resulted in the Group heading away in the direction of Gottingen, some twenty-five miles to the north-east of Kassel. They were now well to the east of the main bomber stream and because of the thick and heavy clouds that persisted for most of the flight, the crews were blissfully unaware of the navigational error. Unfortunately those same clouds afforded excellent cover for the large enemy fighter force waiting to pounce on the isolated and vulnerable Group.

Fw 190A-8s of the II.(Sturm)/JG 4 aided by their escorting Me 109s proceeded to decimate the B-24s. Seemingly within minutes a heavy toll had been taken and it was the 376th squadron of the 361st, led by 1/Lt Victor E. Bocquin, that answered the crews' desperate calls for help. The P-51s probably prevented the complete annihilation of the 445th, although no fewer than twenty-five B-24s had been shot down. One pilot, 1/Lt William Beyer claimed five Fw 190s (another 'ace in a day' pilot) and Lt Bocquin another two; the squadron downed eighteen, creating a new Eighth record. The scene was later described by a surviving bomber pilot as, 'fantastic ... a sky full of blazing aircraft, parachutes, smoke and the debris of battle ... Hollywood couldn't think of anything to match it.' The 445th ultimately lost twenty-eight aircraft, the heaviest loss ever sustained by a Group in a single mission – two hundred and thirty-seven airmen killed/missing.

Yet on the next day (28th) the Group was back in action over Kassel. It had managed to muster ten operational B-24s, and they all arrived back safely. It required a very special courage to sally forth into hostile skies after seeing many of one's comrades plunge to their deaths. And yet so many of the Eighth's bomber crews did just that day after day.

Over four hundred and forty B-17s of the First Division were dispatched to Magdeburg, a city that abounded with strategic targets – such as the Brabag synthetic oil plant at Rothensee, a Junkers aero engine plant, Polte ordnance works and a Krupps tank factory. But it was the oil plant at Rothensee that was the primary target. The original Sturmgruppe – IV.(Sturm)/JG 3 – with its Me 109 escorts attacked the 41st Wing with great determination. The 'Hell's Angels' (303rd) lost eleven crews, and one pilot recalled: 'About fifty Nazi fighters *en masse* coming at us in a solid bunch ... they came again and again from all directions. These guys were like mad men – with but one idea – to knock us down in a suicidal attack.' This equalled the Group's heaviest loss of the war, and it would actually lose only seven crews during the rest of 1944. The Division lost twenty-three B-17s in action, of which six came from the 457th. Some three hundred crews of the Third Division bombed the Leuna plant at Merseburg, and ten B-17s were missing; five from the 388th. It was the Group's heaviest loss for several months. Only one B-24 failed to return from bombing the Henschel factory at Kassel.

Thirty-four were missing in action and another five crash-landed on the Continent. However, it was claimed that thirty-six enemy aircraft had been destroyed, mostly by the fighters; the 479th continuing its run of success, being credited with thirteen and all of their pilots returned safely to Wattisham. The Luftwaffe would no doubt view the two days of action as a notable victory, eighty-six aircraft destroyed and over eight hundred damaged for its loss of some fifty fighters. Although in all truth it could ill-afford to be engaged in brutal attritional battles against such overwhelming odds.

After two such costly missions for the Eighth, the month ended with attacks on marshalling yards in the Ruhr and airfields around Münster. They passed with minimal losses – eight aircraft in total, and this included two B-17s that collided over the North Sea. No enemy aircraft were encountered – a gentle and peaceful end to what had been a period of sustained and unrelenting action. Little did they realise that the bomber losses sustained during September, over three hundred and ten including those salvaged, had reached a peak; henceforth their monthly losses would steadily reduce. Except for several isolated incidents when the Luftwaffe mounted strong and spirited resistance, the battle for air superiority had effectively been won, notwithstanding the emergence of the Luftwaffe's jet-fighters.

14
'WHEN WILL IT ALL BE OVER? BY CHRISTMAS?'

Many of the Eighth's airmen genuinely felt that they would 'be back in the States for Christmas, with the job all wrapped up'. In retrospect such beliefs can be seen as wishful thinking; it was never a realistic prospect. The Allied armies' rapid advances across France had swept them to the borders of Germany but the failure of the airborne landings, stern German resistance and bad weather had brought them to a grinding halt.

Perhaps the airmen's hopes had been fuelled by the knowledge that the Luftwaffe had virtually disappeared from the skies over Germany, at least for most of October. However, the Wehrmacht's offensive in the Ardennes just nine days before Christmas ensured that the victory was still some distance away. Therefore the Eighth faced its third winter in Europe, condemned to operate in weather conditions considered the worst for over half a century. It was only able to mount bombing operations on fifty-six days (60%) during the last quarter of 1944, and even some of those were hampered by poor weather; additionally there was a greater incidence of flying accidents due to heavy cloud, ground fog and freezing conditions.

The crews' first stern test came on 6th October when Berlin was

B-24s of 445th Bomb Group flying to Glinde, Germany on 6th October 1944. All returned. (USAF)

targeted for the thirteenth time. 'Big B' was still firmly ingrained in the memories of most crews and at Great Ashfield, this mission proved to be the 'unlucky 13th' for the crews of the 385th; although in truth there were not many remaining that had flown the traumatic Berlin missions of March and April. The Elkett armaments complex at Spandau to the west of the city was the primary target for four hundred and eighteen B-17s of the Third Division. The 385th was flying at the rear of the 4th Wing, near Nauer, about fifteen miles from the target, when the formation was forced to reduce altitude because of heavy cloud. Lurking above was a strong force of Me 109s and Fw 190s. They made a massed attack on the Wing; one of the Group's squadrons, 549th, bore the brunt of the assault and in a matter of minutes fourteen B-17s were destroyed, ten from the 385th. The rest of the Wing ultimately lost another five. The Third Division lost seventeen with the other two Divisions engaged elsewhere losing only two aircraft. The escorts claimed nineteen victories – one of their best days in October – including a Me 262 destroyed over Rheine airfield by Lt C.W. Mueller of the 353rd.

On the following day when a number of oil targets were attacked by the three Divisions, the 4th Wing again suffered severely near Leipzig.

Umbriago of 579th squadron, 392nd Bomb Group made an emergency landing at Melsbroek airfield, Brussels after being damaged by flak over Kassel – 7th October 1944. (RAF Museum)

It encountered a strong and determined attack from IV.(Sturm)/JG 3, and the 94th lost eight B-17s to add to the four missing over Berlin. But it was the 94th Wing of the First Division, in action over Pölitz near Stettin, that sustained the heaviest losses. Pölitz was known to be strongly defended with some two hundred and seventy heavy flak batteries and they were largely responsible for seventeen missing B-17s – an 11% loss rate! The 351st lost seven crews; four landed in Sweden. Five from the 457th failed to return to Glatton, including the Group's CO, Colonel James R. Luper. The 401st also lost five; a further example of the mounting costs of the oil offensive. Twenty-nine enemy fighters were brought down with the 361st gaining eight, including two Me 262s caught taking-off from Achmer airfield and destroyed by Lt Urban l. Drew, a just reward for his fruitless pursuit of a week earlier. Major R.E. Connor of the 78th was credited with another Me 262 and three pilots of 364th shared in the destruction of a Me 163.

These Me 262s formed the Luftwaffe's first jet-fighter operational unit based at Achmer and Hesepe airfields under the command of the legendary Austrian fighter ace, Major Walter Nowotny, and called the *Kommando Nowotny*. It had a complement of forty Me 262As but probably no more than thirty were operational. During October there were over one hundred sightings of jet and rocket fighters but relatively few air combats.

From 9th to 17th October, weather permitting, the Eighth planned to concentrate its forces on railway targets in western Germany. Three missions were directed at marshalling yards at Mainz, Koblenz and Osnabrück; then, on the 13th, General Doolittle received a Directive to activate Operation *Hurricane*. Its objective was: 'to demonstrate to the enemy in Germany generally the overwhelming superiority of the Allied Air Forces in this theatre ... to apply in the shortest period a maximum effort against objectives in the densely populated Ruhr.' RAF Bomber Command was also fully committed to *Hurricane*. Thus, on three days, the 14th, 15th and 17th, over 3,000 heavies bombed marshalling yards in Cologne – Kalk, Eifeltor, Nippes and Gereon – and dropped some 7,800 tons of bombs in a massive onslaught. Overall the losses were minimal, sixteen all to flak. The absence of the Luftwaffe was highlighted by the fact that although over 1,800 fighters were in action, only two enemy aircraft were shot down.

During the same period a number of smaller operations were directed to strategic targets at Schweinfurt and Bremen along with oil refineries at Wesseling and Rhenania, and it was here that the Luftwaffe was active, albeit in moderate strength. Over Bremen on the 12th, the pilots of 364th and 357th claimed eight victories each. With these successes the 357th passed the 400th mark, helped by five destroyed by Captain 'Chuck' Yeager, recently returned from his escapades in France. On the previous day Lt Col John D. Landers, the 'Tall Texan' or 'Whispering John' to his pilots, had taken charge of the 357th. Another charismatic and brilliant fighter pilot and leader, he had

B-17G of 398th Bomb Group badly damaged over Cologne – 15th October 1944; an example of the durability of the aircraft. (USAF)

Major Donald H. Bochkay of 363rd squadron, 357th Fighter Group lands at Leiston. He was credited with fourteen air victories. (USAF)

previously served in the south-west Pacific with six victories to his name. Landers came to the UK in April to serve with the 55th, and he would later lead the 78th and 361st, the only officer to command three Groups.

Early in October the 353rd converted to P-51s, leaving the 56th and 78th as the remaining P-47 units, who were steadily losing headway compared with P-51 Groups. The 78th's pilots had rarely found themselves in an advantageous position when tackling enemy fighters and in the previous three months they had mustered a 'mere' thirty-four for the loss of fourteen P-47s. However, on the 15th they returned to Duxford with seven victories for the loss of a pilot, their best single mission for a number of weeks. Before the year was out the Group would also re-equip with P-51s.

Only seven missions were possible during the rest of the month, mostly to rail targets and airfields, with scant interference from enemy aircraft. The final operation in October was directed to the oil refineries at Harburg and Hamburg, and also to Merseburg by the Third Division, but this mission had to be recalled due to unfavourable weather.

On this day two celebrated fighter leaders bowed out of the action. On escort to Hamburg Colonel Don Blakeslee, the CO of the 4th, completed what was thought to be his 350th sortie. He had been in action since 1941, first with the RAF 133 (Eagle) squadron. On his return to Debden he was given a desk job; his operational days were over and he was unable to add to his $15\frac{1}{2}$ victories. Colonel Hubert Zemke was flying his 155th and final mission. His P-51 broke up in a severe storm but he baled out and was taken prisoner; his tally was $19\frac{1}{2}$. The 479th also lost two other pilots, Zemke's wingman, Lt D. Holmes, escaped but Lt Col Jim Herren, CO of 434th squadron, was killed.

The month ended, as it had commenced, with another blank day due to bad weather. Bomber and fighter losses during the month, one hundred and eighty-one, were the lowest of the year, as was the number of enemy aircraft destroyed in the air – seventy; in sharp contrast to 460 credited in September. The absence of the Luftwaffe was a little worrying for the Eighth's planners. They were aware from intelligence sources that despite the heavy bombing of aircraft factories, the production of single-seater fighters had increased, so it would appear the Luftwaffe was conserving itself for a grand assault on the bombers. In a few days these fears became fully justified.

November opened on a fairly muted note; two hundred and fifty-six B-17s and B-24s attacked the Nordstein and Buer synthetic oil plants at Gelsenkirchen in the Ruhr and all returned safely. One B-17, *Swamp Fire*, of the 379th achieved a notable record on this operation having completed one hundred missions without a single return for mechanical reasons, a fine testimony to its ground crew at Kimbolton. The aircraft flew another twelve missions before crash-landing on the Continent on 12th December, its operational days over.

Thirty-eight crews from the 94th and 447th were engaged on a special mission – to destroy the Rüdensheim rail bridge over the Rhine to the north of Bingen. They were using a new blind-bombing device, Micro-H, which effectively combined the attributes of Gee-H and H2X. It employed two transmitting stations in Belgium and France. Their signals could be picked up by the airborne H2X equipment and then used to set an accurate course to the target. By the nature of the signals their range was limited to targets in western Germany and the Ruhr; from December onwards the Third Division's B-17s increasingly resorted to Micro-H.

There are many targets that should be inscribed on the Eighth's Roll of Battle Honors – Schweinfurt, Regensburg, Berlin and Marienburg immediately spring to mind – but after the mission of 2nd November, Merseburg also deserves to be so entered. The operation brought about perhaps the largest and most fierce air battle of the war with some 2,100 American aircraft pitted against over four hundred enemy fighters. More than six hundred and eighty B-17s of both Divisions were bound for the Leuna oil plant. The First's 41st Wing was in action over an oil target at Sterkade in the Ruhr, whilst B-24s attacked another oil plant at Castrop-Rauxel as well as rail targets at Bielefeld. It is interesting to note that Sterkade and Caustrop-Rauxel were amongst the first strategic targets to be bombed by the RAF in May 1940.

The Merseburg operation was costly in the extreme, thirty-eight B-17s destroyed with another four hundred and ninety damaged, with the First Division bearing the heaviest losses – twenty-six (11.6%). Two Groups, 91st and 457th, were attacked by Sturm Fw 190A-8s when they were without fighter escort. They lost thirteen and nine respectively, a crippling blow even for a 'battle-hardened' Group like the 91st that had become somewhat inured to heavy losses. By comparison the Third Division fared a little better, twelve in total but five came from the 447th. That one crew returned safely to Rattlesden was largely due to the actions of its mortally wounded navigator, 2/Lt Robert E. Femoyer, a twenty-three year old on his seventh mission.

Femoyer's B-17, *L-Love*, sustained damage from three near misses from flak and he was severely wounded in the back and side by shrapnel. Despite extreme pain and considerable loss of blood Femoyer stoutly refused morphine as he realised that he needed to be alert to navigate the aircraft around the known areas of heavy flak. Unable to sit at his table, he was propped on the floor with his charts and instruments around him. Only when the aircraft was safely over the North Sea on a direct route for their base, did he allow the crew to sedate him. Shortly after Femoyer was removed from the B-17 at Rattlesden, he died. It was not until early 1945 that his selfless devotion to duty and heroism was recognised with the posthumous award of the Medal of Honor.

The scale of the battles that raged above Germany can be gauged by the claims of one hundred and thirty-eight enemy aircraft destroyed, over one hundred to the escorts for the loss of sixteen. Leading the field was the 352nd with thirty-eight, of which its 328th squadron, under Major George Preddy, claimed twenty-eight; both created new records for the Eighth. Also into double figures was the 20th, led by Lt Col Robert P. Montgomery; the Colonel was credited with three as was 1/Lt Ernest Fiebelkorn. Another ex-P-38 Group, the 55th accounted for eighteen. Although a dozen or so Me 163s were sighted, none made serious inroads into the bomber formations.

It was estimated that the Luftwaffe had mounted over five hundred sorties, seventy pilots had been killed and another twenty-eight wounded. On the day it had lost one hundred and twenty fighters, some had been engaged against the Fifteenth Air Force. Without a shadow of doubt it was a severe defeat; according to Professor Williamson Murray in *The Luftwaffe, 1933-45*: 'from 2nd November the

The jet-fighter menace – Me 262As lined up at Lechfeld in late 1944 – a rare sight! (via H. Stevens)

Luftwaffe as a force that could affect the course of the war was through'. Although, on another three separate days during November it would still challenge the Eighth in considerable strength and with great determination.

Six days later (8th) Merseburg was again bombed by the First Division, but the Third's force was recalled because of bad weather. Mercifully just three crews were reported missing, one from the 457th at Glatton, which had suffered previously over this dreaded target. As one survivor remarked, '[It] was one mission that one could count your blessings if you returned safely.' On this day the *Kommando Nowotny* lost at least three Me 262s: one to accidental causes, another was shared by Lt James W. Kenney of 357th and Lt E. Fiebelkorn, and the third was that of its Commander, Major Nowotny, who was shot down and killed by an unknown P-51 pilot. In its short operational existence the *Kommando* had sustained twenty-six losses in action and in accidents. Few Me 262s were sighted over the next couple of weeks as the *Kommando* was disbanded and basically reformed as III./JG 7 in December.

The next day Operation *Madison* commenced, an all-out air offensive on the enemy's strongpoints at Metz, Saarbrücken and Thionville in the Moselle valley, as a prelude to General Patton's major offensive. Over 1,180 heavies attacked tactical targets in the area, dropping 3,750 tons of bombs, and fighters strafed and bombed railway targets behind the enemy's lines. Eleven days later the US 5th Division entered Metz. In the various operations the Eighth lost eight aircraft but many were damaged by accurate and heavy ground fire.

The 452nd Group from Deopham Green encountered particularly severe flak and three B-17s sustained heavy damage. One, *Lady Janet*, piloted by 1/Lt Donald J. Gott with 2/Lt William E. Metzger Jr as his co-pilot, received several direct hits damaging three engines. The intercom and electrical systems were also put out of action; flares were ignited on the flight deck and the fire was fuelled by leaking oxygen. Two of the crew were seriously injured and Gott ordered the crew to bale out. Metzger went to convey the message to the crew and he gave his parachute to one of the gunners because his was damaged. The radio operator was too injured to bale out. Gott decided to jettison the bombs and attempt an emergency landing in France not many miles away. As the aircraft was about 100 feet above the ground, the fire reached the fuel tank and the aircraft exploded killing the three airmen. Both Gott and Metzger were posthumously awarded Medals of Honor. They had only recently arrived at Deopham Green, Gott was only 21 years old and Metzger just a year older.

Airfields at Hanau, Cologne and Wiesbaden were attacked on 10th November and although only four bombers were lost in action, another four that were heavily battle-damaged made crash-landings on the Continent. With France and Belgium liberated more of the Eighth's aircraft would make emergency landings there, previously they might not have made it across the Channel or North Sea. This mission was the last for the 489th Group operating from Halesworth. Since late May 1944 it had mounted one hundred and six missions for the loss of twenty-nine B-24s in action. It had been selected to return to the States to train as a B-29 unit for ultimate redeployment in the Pacific.

Four days, the 12th to 15th, were lost to extremely poor weather conditions, but on 16th November the Eighth was called upon again to provide tactical air support for the ground troops. Operation *Queen* was a co-ordinated Allied bombing offensive to sever road/rail communications behind the German lines between Aachen and the Rhine. Düren and Eschweiler were bombed by over 1,200 aircraft without loss. RAF Bomber Command also dispatched some 1,180 bombers on a daylight raid and Düren was virtually flattened with some 3,120 civilians killed. The planned advance of the US 1st and 9th armies was not too successful. With their tanks bogged down by the wet terrain and artillery units short of ammunition, the subsequent advance was slow and costly.

The weather restricted operations over the next two days but on 18th

November four hundred fighters were sent out on strafing missions against a number of airfields in western and central Germany. The pilots returned with claims of ninety-five destroyed for the loss of seven. Twenty-six were claimed by the 56th, which had the only P-47s in action – a complete change from less than six months ago. The Group's pilots were cheered by their day's action; their arch rival, the 4th, was only credited with a single air victory! However, its pilots and those of the 353rd had a most successful mission over Lechfeld airfield, the Development Centre for jet-aircraft. Fourteen Me 262s were destroyed on the ground and several more damaged, thus delaying the operational entry of III./JG 7.

To the dismay of the First Division's crews, the Leuna plant was detailed on the 21st, and they made the long flight on their own; the Third's B-17s were in action over Hamburg and Sterkade, whilst the Second's B-24 crews had the Rhenania-Ossag oil refinery at Harburg as their primary target. Once again the fearsome corridor of flak batteries at Merseburg and the Luftwaffe took a toll of the crews. Over Merseburg fourteen were lost in action with another four B-17s salvaged after crash-landings on the Continent. It was the Division's most junior Group, 389th, that sustained the heaviest losses. A savage frontal attack by Fw 190s, mainly directed at its 603rd squadron, caused mayhem and six crews failed to return to Nuthampstead; three had been lost in the earlier Merseburg mission. The other two operations resulted in another eleven crews lost in action and two B-24s of the 389th collided during assembly, killing seventeen airmen. It was perhaps some consolation that the fighter pilots had another 'field' day, notching up seventy-three victories with three Groups, 352nd, 359th and 364th being credited in total with fifty-four enemy fighters – another costly day for the Luftwaffe.

Four days later (25th November) the Eighth returned to Merseburg when seven hundred and sixty B-17s were in action. There was deep concern at the Eighth's headquarters when the Groups' operational returns were tabulated, they implied that over fifty B-17s were missing! Subsequently most of these were located at various Allied airfields on the Continent, many bearing the scars of the intense flak barrage. Ultimately eight were acknowledged as lost, and another four salvaged – a moderate loss largely due to no serious enemy fighter opposition. Only nine victories were claimed.

It was quite a different matter the next day when a major operation was mounted to a variety of rail and oil targets to the east of the Ruhr. The Deurag refinery at Misburg on the outskirts of Hannover was attacked by three hundred B-17s and B-24s, and it was this force that encountered a resurgent Luftwaffe, estimated to be over five hundred fighters.

One Group in particular, the 491st, had one of those missions that crews dreaded. Thirty-one B-24s left North Pickenham but shortly into the mission three crews aborted with engine problems. When the bomber stream was above Dümmer Lake, its strength, route and speed were noted by three enemy aircraft shadowing the force. Within the next twenty miles or so a strong fighter force engaged the P-51 escorts, carefully avoiding the bomber formations. Just as the crews were making their approach over Hannover in excess of a hundred Fw 190s and Me 109s struck at the bombers, which were now without escort cover. The 491st at the rear of the formation attracted the most attention and seemingly within minutes fifteen B-24s were shot down and it was only the timely arrival of a number of P-51s that prevented an even greater disaster. With amazing coolness and great tenacity the surviving crews reformed into one formation and carried on to bomb the target. Only eleven of the original twenty-eight crews returned to North Pickenham. For its determination and discipline in the face of such an onslaught the Group was awarded a DUC.

A German pilot of III./JG 301 later described the action: 'The gaps in the Liberator box were clear to see, and after an immediate follow-up attack few bombers were left in the formation. The airspace around us was full of burning and falling aircraft from both sides and the crash sites on the ground below lay close to one another in burning piles.' Another Group, 445th, which two months earlier had sustained even heavier losses on a single mission, was also involved in the carnage, losing five B-24s with another crash-landing at Tibenham.

It was something of a pyrrhic victory for the Luftwaffe; a total of one hundred and thirty enemy fighters were claimed by the gunners and fighter pilots. The 339th was credited with twenty-nine, five Fw 190s to Lt Jack Daniell making him an 'ace in a day' – remarkably, he was on his first mission! The 355th also did well – twenty-one; two pilots, Captain Fred W. Havilland Jr and Lt Royce W. Priest, became aces. The Group's day was only marred by the collision of two P-51s over the North Sea killing both pilots. The 361st and 356th were credited with twenty-three and twenty-one respectively. It was the latter's first real success with their new P-51s.

Battle was resumed the following day (27th) when it was estimated that seven hundred enemy fighters were in action – the largest number ever encountered. It seemed to be a mere side-issue that over four hundred and eighty heavies bombed marshalling yards at Bingen and Offenburg on the outskirts of Frankfurt and all returned without mishap. The day proved once again that the P-51 reigned supreme in the skies over Germany. Ninety-eight victories were recorded in the air for the loss of sixteen pilots. The 357th was in the thick of the action, a total of thirty – four each to its leading aces, Major John B. England and Captains Leonard K. Carson and 'Chuck' Yeager. Both the 352nd and 353rd Groups were credited with eighteen victories.

This was another devastating demonstration of the Eighth's fighter power and although seven hundred and twenty-seven fighters were in action, this was probably only about 60% of its operational strength; each Group now had over eighty fighters on complement. Besides the numerical superiority the Eighth's pilots also had another advantage over their opponents. They were equipped with Berger 'G' suits, which were designed to prevent pilots losing consciousness during aerial combat, sharp turns and steep dives. They incorporated inflatable panels that equalised the pilot's blood pressure and were first trialled by the 339th at Fowlmere. The Americans were also opposed by mainly inexperienced pilots. The Luftwaffe's training schools could not keep up with the ever increasing loss of fighter pilots. Although it had an ample supply of fighters, with 3,000 produced in September, the constant problem was finding pilots to fly them. In just four days in November the Eighth's pilots claimed three hundred and eighty enemy aircraft for the loss of fifty-five – a shattering defeat from which the Luftwaffe would never recover. Its days as a powerful fighter force were almost over.

On 30th November, nine hundred and ninety B-17s were bound for oil targets at Böhlen, Zeitz, Merseburg and Lützkendorf, whilst a much smaller force of B-24s was engaged over marshalling yards at Neunkirchen and Homburg; three B-24s failed to return. The B-17 crews were not so fortunate, twenty-eight lost in action, ten aircraft written-off and over six hundred damaged. The 390th lost seven and the 379th, in action over Zeitz, another heavily defended target, suffered its heaviest loss for thirteen months – six crews. Over one thousand fighters were in attendance but they hardly gained sight or sound of any enemy aircraft.

Matters were a little different on 2nd December. Crews of one hundred and forty-three B-24s bound for marshalling yards at Bingen to the south of Loblenz, were engaged by a strong force of enemy fighters waiting for them to the west of the Rhine. The 392nd was hit particularly badly, losing six out of the eleven destroyed. The escorts only managed to claim four enemy fighters. But it was 'the Wolfpack' (56th) that had a successful day when engaged in a fighter sweep near Cologne. Its pilots returned to Boxted with eleven victories for the loss of three P-47s.

It was probably no surprise that the Eighth's fighters would record another resounding victory over the Luftwaffe when Berlin was attacked on 5th December. Whatever the operational state of the Luftflotte Reich, its Commander, Generaloberst Hans-Jurgen Stummpf knew that he was compelled to expend his strongest force in defence of the German capital. The primary targets for over four hundred and fifty B-17s were the munitions and tank factories at Tegel in the north-western suburbs of Berlin. Twelve B-17s and seventeen P-51s were reported missing but ninety-one enemy fighters were shot down. The 357th, which seemed to go from strength to strength, was credited with twenty-two. A change of commander just three days earlier had not lessened its performance. Indeed Colonel Irwin H. Dregne would lead the Group to even greater successes in 1945.

Over the next five days, as weather permitted, the Eighth mounted bombing missions to Merseburg, Stuttgart, Koblenz, Bielefeld and Bingen. They encountered scant enemy opposition and only five out of 1,720 bombers were lost. With the advantage of improved weather on the 11th, the Eighth mustered its largest bomber force to date – 1,586. A variety of rail targets in western Germany were attacked with 3,900 tons of bombs dropped. No opposition was met and just five failed to return; although the 445th and 491st, no strangers to heavy casualties, each lost two B-24s.

The following day some three hundred and fifty B-17s of the First Division were sent to the Leuna oil plant – the Eighth's eighteenth and final mission to this dreaded target. Since 12th May over 5,000 crews had experienced the traumas of its notorious flak batteries, some 12,700 tons of bombs had been dropped for the loss of one hundred and eighty bombers. On this final operation just one B-17 (from the 487th) was lost. During the night of 6/7th December RAF Bomber Command made their first major raid on Merseburg, when five out of four hundred and seventy-five Lancasters were lost. It was now estimated that over half of the oil plants and refineries in Germany had either ceased production or had been seriously damaged.

Elsewhere on the day some eight hundred and seventy heavies were ranging over rail targets in central Germany and they escaped with just three losses; there was little evidence of enemy fighter activity. The Eighth was not aware that selected units of the Luftflotte Reich were being transferred to airfields in western Germany and placed under the control of the Luftwaffenkommando West to provide tactical air support for the Wehrmacht's last offensive in the West. General von Runstedt launched his Ardennes offensive at dawn on the 16th, with the intention of capturing Brussels and the port of Antwerp and thus dividing the Allied armies in half. The offensive gained the advantage of surprise; it also had the cover of poor weather conditions, which meant that the powerful Allied air forces could not seriously intervene in the land battle for some eight days.

Attempts were made on both 16th and 17th December to attack rail communications to the rear of the battle area but the bad weather reduced both the strength and efficacy of the missions. But on the 19th over 300 bombers managed to attack tactical targets behind enemy lines before the Eighth was grounded for a few days. On the 23rd the weather showed signs of improvement and three hundred and ninety crews bombed railway junctions and marshalling yards for the loss of a single aircraft. However, one hundred and sixty-three P-51s and P-47s conducted a sweep of airfields around Bonn, forty-six aircraft were claimed and ahead of the field was the 56th with thirty-two victories, demonstrating the value of P-47s in this kind of operation, though the Group did lose three pilots.

The forecast for Christmas Eve was most promising with a high probability of clear skies. The Eighth therefore ordered all Groups to mount a 'maximum effort' – any aircraft that could fly should be airborne on the day. As a result 2,046 bombers and 853 fighters took to

Some fifty B-24s of 458th Bomb Group leave Horsham St Faith – 24th December 1944. (USAF)

237

Brigadier General Frederick W. Castle was the highest ranking and last Eighth airman to be awarded the Medal of Honor – posthumously on 24th December 1944. (USAF)

the skies – the largest single operation ever mounted by the Eighth. The 453rd at Old Buckenham gained the record for the largest number of B-24s sent out – sixty-four! Freezing conditions and ground mist caused a number of take-off accidents and two Fighter Groups, 78th and 339th, failed to get off the ground because of fog. The targets for this massive force were airfields, road and rail junctions, communication centres and canals across western Germany with the intention of frustrating the movement of troops and urgent supplies to support the German offensive.

The Third Division would lead this massive force, and Brigadier General Frederick W. Castle, Commander of its 4th Wing, decided to join the leading B-17 of the 487th as co-pilot. He was an experienced pilot and leader, having already completed twenty-nine missions, mainly when in command of the 94th Group. Over Liége in Belgium the leading formation was suddenly attacked by Me 109s, an unexpected ploy as enemy fighters did not normally oppose the bombers over Allied-held territory.

General Castle's B-17 was already lagging behind due to loss of engine power and when it was hit by cannon fire it fell further behind. The B-17 suffered further fighter attacks, which set two engines on fire and the aircraft appeared to be in imminent danger of exploding. Castle took over the controls and ordered the crew to bale out, including the pilot, Lt Harriman. Before the pilot could make his escape, another fighter attack exploded the gasoline tanks in the wing. Castle would not jettison the bombs for fear of injuring Allied troops and Belgian civilians. The stricken aircraft plunged to the ground, killing General Castle and Lt Harriman. Castle was posthumously awarded the Medal of Honor for 'his intrepidity and willing sacrifice of his life to save members of the crew ... in keeping with the highest traditions of the military service.'

Twelve bombers were lost in action, including three from the 487th, and another twenty-three were written-off in emergency landings. Of the seventy-four enemy aircraft claimed, the 357th weighed in with thirty. One of the Fw 190s shot-down was piloted by Leutnant Klaus Bretschneider, a leading ace of the V.(Sturm)/JG 300; he had thirty-one heavy bombers to his name, many at night.

Because of poor visibility over eastern England, most of the First's Bomb Groups were diverted to other Eighth's airfields in East Anglia and thus were unable to participate in the Christmas Day mission. Sadly Major George Preddy of the 352nd was shot down and killed by 'friendly fire' over Belgium whilst returning from a patrol. He had just

B-17Gs of 390th Bomb Group with escort fighters high overhead.

completed his 143rd sortie and had twenty-seven victories, the second highest ace of the war. His Group, along with the 361st, were operating from airfields in Belgium under the Ninth Air Force, in order to be closer to the action. The 479th also lost a P-51 to 'friendly fire' but the pilot survived; its pilots returned with fourteen victories.

For the next five days, as the freezing weather dictated, the crews were fully engaged in attacking road/rail targets and lines of supply and communication to the west of the Rhine. In all these missions just twelve bombers were lost in action but sixteen were lost to landing and take-off operations. Enemy fighters were not particularly evident, although on 27th December when the 364th was sweeping ahead of the bomber formations, its pilots met strong enemy opposition near Bonn. In the sharp battle they accounted for $29\frac{1}{2}$ (Fw 190 shared with a Ninth fighter) for the loss of a pilot; Captain Ernest E. Bankey became 'an ace in a day'. The 364th gained its only DUC for this action.

Two days later a number of B-24s were detailed to attack a bridge over the Rhine in an attempt to prevent the movement of enemy troop reinforcements and supplies. Hitherto the Rhine bridges had been scrupulously off-target as they were needed for the Allied armies' advance into Germany. The Ludendorff bridge at Remagen, which later became famous for the battle to secure it, survived the bombing. Conditions were appalling, heavy cloud and driving rain; even in perfect weather it would have been a difficult task and now, despite the use of radar, it proved impossible.

On New Year's Eve the Eighth returned in part to strategic targets for the first time for two weeks. Whilst 1st and 2nd Division's crews pounded away at rail/road junctions, marshalling yards and supply routes, the 3rd Division attacked oil targets at Hamburg and Misburg. The five hundred or so B-17s faced fierce fighter opposition and sustained all the losses – twenty-seven. Two Groups, 100th and 452nd, had a 'nightmare' mission. The latter lost five crews and the 'Bloody Hundredth', which had had more than its fair share of heavy losses, lost twelve. It was the sixth time that the Group's losses on a single mission reached double figures.

Two of its B-17s were lost in most strange circumstances. *The Little Skipper*, piloted by 1/Lt Glenn Rojohn with 2/Lt William Leek as co-pilot, was hit by flak over the bombing run and it fell directly onto another B-17 in a lower formation. The two bombers remained mostly intact but jammed together and quite amazingly they continued their forward flight, although the lower pilot and co-pilot had been killed in the collision. Lt Rojohn closed down his damaged engines and using the three surviving engines of the lower B-17 and the controls of *The Little Skipper*, managed to keep the two aircraft steady for the surviving crews of both aircraft to bale out. Then Rojohn, aided by Leek, was able to successfully belly-land the two aircraft. Because of this quite remarkable feat of flying, ten of the eighteen crew members survived as POWs.

The Luftwaffe sustained another heavy defeat. The Eighth claimed eighty-seven fighters destroyed, with the 364th again to the fore with twenty-five victories, of which Major George F. Ceullars, its leading ace, was credited with four. Captain Julius Maxwell of the 78th shot down a Fw 190, which took the Group's tally to over four hundred. It was also the final victory with their P-47s, from now on only the 56th would operate P-47s.

Thus 1944 drew to a close, a year in which the Eighth had reached the pinnacle of its strategic bombing offensive. It is probably stating the obvious, considering the record number of operations mounted, that 1944 brought the Eighth's heaviest losses of the war, over a half of its total; 4,300 aircraft had been lost in action and some 29,700 airmen failed to return. It was a high price indeed to pay for achieving air superiority over the enemy's day-fighters and the destruction of the German oil industry. And yet the Eighth's airmen still had another four months of combat before 'the job was all wrapped up'.

15
UPWARDS AND ONWARDS TO VICTORY

During the Eighth's final four months of battle, it operated ceaselessly in the German skies. Its crews pounded what remained of the German railway system, airfields were bombed and strafed, oil targets came under heavy bombardment and on several occasions Berlin suffered under its might. Its fighter pilots harrassed and hunted the Jagdwaffe with grim determination, and inflicted a grievous toll both in the air and on the ground. It was a demonstration on a grand scale of the awesome might and power of the Eighth Air Force. The words of a popular American song of 1942 now seemed highly appropriate: 'Get a load of those guys, high in the skies, Winging to victory'.

From 1945 the Divisions were redesignated 'Air', maybe as a recognition that they were really now Air Forces in their own right. The severe weather in the early months of 1945 posed difficult operational problems. Ice, snow, freezing fog and heavy cloud caused many missions to be cancelled and made life arduous and miserable for the ground crews as they manfully kept the aircraft operational. The abysmal January weather meant that the number of sorties flown was the lowest for nine months.

On New Year's Day over 1,500 aircraft took to the skies for oil and rail targets in western Germany. Ten were lost in action and the 92nd and 305th sustained half the losses. Just twelve crews were acting as a screening force for the First's main attack on railway yards at Henschel. They arrived eight minutes late for the rendezvous with their escorts and the isolated formation was attacked with relish by Fw 190s. Five B-71s were shot down, four from 305th and one from 92nd, another crash-landed in France. The day also brought a rash of accidents on take-off resulting in sixteen fatalities. Perhaps the most tragic occurred at Steeple Morden. *Heats On*, a 91st B-17 from nearby Bassingbourn, crashed onto a P-51 dispersal area shortly after take-off, seven crewmen were killed and several airmen of the 355th were seriously injured.

There was a rather inauspicious start for the Allied air forces on the Continent. At dawn on 1st January the Luftwaffe launched its Operation *Bodenplatte* (Baseplate) when over eight hundred Me 109s and Fw 190s guided by Junkers 88s made a low-level attack on sixteen Allied advance airfields in the Low Countries and France. Despite the fact that many of the fighters were flown by inexperienced pilots, considerable damage was inflicted. Two hundred and seventy Allied aircraft were destroyed and over one hundred damaged, including some of the Eighth's bombers that had landed there previously. The 352nd and 361st were still operating under the Ninth Air Force, and the 487th squadron of the 352nd was just taking-off when the Luftwaffe struck. In about forty-five minutes twelve pilots accounted for twenty-three enemy fighters, and Lt Col John Meyer claimed his twenty-fourth victory to keep him the leading fighter ace serving in the Eighth. The squadron was awarded a DUC for its actions, the only one to be so honoured.

The operation had cost the Luftwaffe dearly, with over two hundred and fifty fighters destroyed and another hundred or so damaged, many as a result of 'friendly' flak whilst returning to their airfields. The loss of pilots was even more critical – over two hundred and thirty killed/missing – including nineteen experienced leaders. It virtually sounded the end of the Luftwaffe in the west and Generalmajor Adolf Galland described it as 'the final dagger in the back of the Luftwaffe ... we sacrificed our last substance'.

Over the next twelve days despite inclement weather eight missions were mounted – some 12,000 bomber and fighter sorties – and seventy-two aircraft were lost in accidents. The difficulties in mounting missions during January are made clear in a report by the 493rd for 10th January: 'It is sincerely hoped that no future mission will be as arduous to get airborne as this Group's hundredth mission ... It had snowed [over six inches] before take-off, making taxiing in the darkness even more trickier than usual with the result that several aircraft became stuck off the hardstands ... After the first planes were

The winter of 1944/5 was severe. B-17G of 327th squadron, 92nd Bomb Group taking-off

from Podington in snow. (Smithsonian Institution)

airborne one crashed and exploded two miles north of the field [Debach] ... another plane had a tyre blow-out on the runway in use ... Regardless of such problems thirty planes were dispatched'; they all returned safely.

The weather relented on the 14th with clear skies throughout northern Europe, and a large strike was launched to oil targets at Magdeburg, Derben and Hallendorf and road bridges at Cologne. Over eight hundred and forty bombers were in action, but the fine weather had also brought the Luftwaffe up in strength. The Third Division was bound for Magdeburg and Derben and on this mission the 390th suffered its heaviest loss of the war. Enemy fighters attacked and in less than thirty minutes seven B-17s from the 390th were destroyed and another two crews failed to return to Framlingham. The Division lost another seven, of which four came from the 487th. If it was any consolation to the 390th, this would the last occasion that the Luftwaffe inflicted heavy losses on a single Group.

Over seven hundred and sixty fighters were engaged in air battles that raged over central and northern Germany and their pilots achieved a resounding victory – one hundred and fifty-five – the largest in air combat ever attained and it would not be bettered. Six Groups especially, including the 20th, 56th, 78th, 355th and 356th, had claims in double figures, with Captain Felix D. Williamson of 56th becoming 'an ace in a day', showing that the P-47 was still a potent fighter. But the honours went to the 357th, the 'Yoxford Boys', who claimed fifty-six for the loss of three pilots. Although the total was later reduced to forty-eight, it was still the highest number of air victories ever on a single mission. The Group was awarded its second DUC and General Doolittle sent a message to Colonel Dregne: 'You gave the Hun the most humiliating beating he has ever taken in the air ... My personal admiration and congratulations for a superb victory'.

There had been scant signs of jet-fighter Me 262s but they were in action on the 14th. One was credited to Lt B.J. Murray of the 353rd and another hit the ground and exploded whilst being hotly pursued by three pilots from the Group. Six days after the great air battles, 1/Lt Dale E. Karger of 357th claimed a Me 262, as did Lt Roland R. Wright. Karger was only nineteen years old and was probably the youngest pilot to become an ace. The Luftwaffe was in the process of forming two new Me 262 units, KG(J) 54, mainly comprising re-trained bomber pilots, and JV 44, under the command of the legendary Adolf Galland. Production of the aircraft reached a peak in February – two hundred and ninety-six – and the Eighth's battle with the Me 262s really began

B-17Gs of 91st Bomb Group dropping their bombs on Berlin on smoke markers - 3rd February 1945. (USAF)

in earnest in March.

On 3rd February Berlin was back on the agenda. It had been almost two months since the Eighth had been in action over 'Big B'. Over one thousand B-17 crews were dispatched to the Tempelhof marshalling yards to the south of the city, whilst four hundred and thirty B-24s were detailed to attack oil and rail targets in Magdeburg. This was the largest bombing operation yet mounted in 1945. Even at this late stage of the war, and despite the heavy bombardment by the RAF and the Eighth, the city's flak batteries were still potent enough to bring down twenty-four B-17s – three each from 306th and the 100th; the latter Group was still suffering over Berlin. Six damaged aircraft, including

Royal Flush piloted by the famous Major Robert Rosenthal of the 100th, force-landed in Poland, which was now occupied by Russian forces. Another famous B-17 was also lost, *Rose of York* of the 306th, which came down in the North Sea with a senior BBC war correspondent, Guy Byam, as passenger. The aircraft had been named by HRH Princess Elizabeth at Thurleigh on 6th July 1944 and was on its sixty-second mission.

Over 2,260 tons of bombs were dropped and the *Mitte*, the central area of Berlin, was devastated. German propaganda proclaimed '25,000 civilian casualties in this terror raid'. Only the 55th claimed any victories – twelve; although the 56th's pilots whilst making a sweep of Friedersdorf airfield, some twenty miles south of Berlin, returned with nine victories.

During February the 92nd were involved in an unusual type of bombing, using 'Disney' rocket bombs. They had been designed and developed by the Royal Navy for penetrating and destroying the heavy reinforced concrete U-boat pens. These 4,500 pounders were fourteen feet long and dropped in the conventional manner from specially designed wing racks, but at an altitude of 5,000 feet the rocket motors were ignited and propelled the bombs at a speed of 2,400 feet per second. On 10th February nine B-17s loaded with 'Disney' bombs attacked the E-boat shelters at Ijmuiden. Subsequent photographs revealed that only one bomb had directly hit the target but the damage was considerable, at least enough to merit another operation. This took place on 10th March against the same target with similar encouraging results. Later in the month (30th) the final 'Disney' operation was sent to U-boat pens at Farge, but by now the Allied air forces were running out of suitable targets!

The attacks on Dresden by the RAF Bomber Command and the Eighth on 13th/14th February have caused endless controversy questioning the morality of the Allied heavy bombing offensive. The facts of the matter are that Dresden was a major road and rail centre, used for supplies and troop reinforcements for the eastern front. It was therefore a valid transportation target, and such targets had been under Allied air attack for many months. It also housed an important optical works as well as a number of radar and electronic factories. It was now felt that with the Russian forces advancing in the east, Berlin, Dresden, Chemnitz and Leipzig were appropriate targets to aid their Russian allies and the decision to bomb Dresden had been sanctioned at the highest level.

However, earlier in January (16th) over one hundred and thirty B-24s had bombed the marshalling yards at Dresden as a secondary target when primary oil targets had beeen frustrated by weather conditions. On 13th February a mission to Dresden's marshalling yards was planned 'with 1,200 to 1,400 bombs' but according to General Spaatz it was postponed because of 'inferior weather'. Thus it was that the RAF made the first *heavy* bombing raid on Dresden on the night of the 13/14th when Lancasters attacked in two waves, dropping over 2,660 tons of bombs which created a firestorm that left most of the city devastated. On the next day three hundred and eleven B-17s bombed the marshalling yards by radar, as the smoke obscured the targets. Over one-third of the 780 tons of bombs were incendiaries, adding to the conflagration. It should be noted that on the same day railway yards at Chemnitz and Magdeburg were also attacked. Then on the 15th because the weather conditions again precluded the bombing of primary oil targets at Böhlen and Ruhland, two hundred and ten B-17s dropped another 460 tons of bombs on Dresden's railway yards. The flak over Dresden was relatively light and losses on the two missions were five, three B-17s fell to Me 262s of 111./JG 7. Estimates of the Dresden fatalities vary between 40,000 to 125,000. In the light of the subsequent controversy it is interesting to note that as early as 22nd February, Henry L. Stimson, the US Secretary of State for War made a public statement: 'Our policy has never been to inflict terror bombing on the civilian population'.

For six days crews and fighter pilots were engaged in bombing marshalling yards and strafing the German railway system. The strafing experts in this field were the pilots of the 55th Group; on two days, 19th and 20th February, they destroyed one hundred and seventy locomotives and were awarded their second DUC. They were led by Lt Col Elwyn G. Righetti, or 'Eager El', who was given command of the Group on 22nd February and became the Eighth's top strafing ace with twenty-seven ground victories. Also on the 22nd a massive Allied air offensive known as Operation *Clarion* was activated; this was coincidentally the anniversary of George Washington's birth!

Clarion had been first planned back in January and was, like the Transportation Plan of 1944, contentious because of the high probability of heavy civilian casualties. The German road and rail system was the primary target but also towns that had not previously been bombed. The Eighth's crews were briefed to bomb from 10,000 feet or below for greater accuracy and there was a concern about the risk of heavy losses due to ground flak. The fighter pilots were given a free hand to strafe targets of opportunity. *Clarion* required good weather and clear skies and this was the case on the 22nd.

Thirteen hundred and seventy-two bombers and eight hundred and seventeen fighters were in action over the length and breadth of Germany, 3,895 tons of bombs were dropped and twenty aircraft were lost in action, including thirteen fighters. Because of the number and the diversity of the targets the Luftwaffe was unable to mount any serious opposition although it was thought that about fifty Me 262s were in action and 111./JG 7 claimed two B-17s and two P-51s but in the process lost six aircraft. *Clarion* was considered a great success – 'The German people received an unforgettable demonstration of Allied air power.'. It was repeated the following day with a slightly smaller force – 1,878! – for the loss of one B-24 and six P-51s, although two B-24s of the 458th collided in cloud and fifteen airmen were killed and a couple of bombers force-landed on the Continent. Only the 364th was credited with seven enemy aircraft destroyed in the air.

Two days later business was back to normal – strategic targets – namely oil plants and refineries at Hamburg and Misburg. By the end of February German oil production had been reduced to 40% of its total capacity and even more dramatic was the fall in aviation fuel down to a mere 5%! The Third Division was detailed to attack the Deschimag U-boat yards at Bremen, which had been first bombed almost two years earlier. There was now a concern about the new XXI U-boats coming into operation. They had new battery-driven electric engines and the revolutionary Schnorkel breathing tubes, which enabled them to remain submerged for long periods, and as such they posed a real threat to Allied shipping. Unlike the first Bremen mission when sixteen B-17s had been lost, only one failed to return on the 24th.

The Eighth's fighters had a particularly good day against the jets on the 25th. Whilst making a sweep of Gielbelstadt airfield, just south of Würzburg, the 55th led by Captain Donald O. Penn, sighted a number of Me 262s taking off and they claimed six. III./JG 7 recorded the loss of fourteen Me 262s; one is known to have fallen to Lt Carl G. Payne of the 4th Group. On the same day the 364th was credited with two 'jets', the new Arado 234 jet reconnaissance/bombers of KG 74; Lts. Eugene Murphy and Richard E. White claimed the Eighth's first victories.

Considering the losses sustained over Berlin earlier in the month, there must have been a certain trepidation when over eleven hundred B-17s and B-24s were dispatched to attack the major railway stations in 'Big B' on 26th February. But just three were lost in action with another two crashing in Russian-held territory. This was the lightest loss yet over Berlin, and it was thought that the flak batteries were experiencing an acute shortage of ammunition. It should be noted that RAF Mosquitos of Bomber Command were visiting Berlin almost nightly with few losses.

Although the European war was slowly and steadily drawing to a conclusion, there was no question of the Eighth easing up. March proved to be the most active month of the war, surpassing even June 1944. Twenty-six missions were mounted and over 30,300 sorties flown and the tonnage of bombs dropped was greater than for any other month. It was notable for the battles with Me 262s, which appeared more frequently and in greater numbers. On 1st March Lieutenants John K. Wilkins and Wendell W. Beaty of the 355th claimed a jet-fighter – a promising start to the month.

On the next day when oil plants at Böhlen, Ruhland and Magdeburg were the primary targets, the Third Division encountered fierce fighter opposition and the leader decided to change to a secondary target – Dresden's rail yards. Another 1,080 tons of bombs rained down on the city. Eight B-17s were lost mainly to Me 262s and the 385th suffered half of the losses; on the previous day two of its B-17s had collided over Belgium killing sixteen airmen – a harsh couple of days for 'Van's Valiants'. Another six bombers were lost by the other Divisions but the escorts exacted ample retribution with sixty-six enemy fighters destroyed. Over one thousand heavies were again in action on the 3rd when oil targets at Misburg, Ruhland, Magdeburg and Brunswick were bombed. Once again more Me 262s were in action and III./JG 7 claimed 'seven bombers and two escorts', though admitting to the loss of seven fighters. Both the 445th and 493rd lost two aircraft to jets, but the 493rd gunners were credited with one Me 262 destroyed, a fairly rare distinction.

With this increased jet fighter activity, on the following day (4th March) the crews were engaged in bombing known jet airfields in addition to certain industrial targets in southern Germany. The Second Division found all of its primary targets cloud-covered, so the crews sought secondary targets mainly at Stuttgart. However, fifteen crews from two Groups thought that they had, quite independently, located Frieburg – a target of opportunity about thirty miles from the Swiss border. Unfortunately they bombed Basle and Zurich in Switzerland. General Spaatz was sent out on a secret mission to Switzerland to present apologies and condolences (there had been twenty-five civilian casualties) and to negotiate financial compensation.

Two prime targets close to Berlin were attacked on 15th March. The German Army headquarters at Zossen, about twenty-five miles south of Berlin, was bombed by five hundred and eighty B-17s and B-24s. The 453rd was given the honour of leading the Eighth, perhaps in recognition of its admirable record. Only one B-24 was lost, it ditched in the North Sea and two force-landed in Poland. To the north of Berlin some six hundred B-17s were in action over the marshalling yards at Oranienburg and they encountered strong opposition from Me 262s. Eight B-17s were lost in action, four from the 447th. Two days later another four B-17s were shot down close to Leipzig by Me 262s of a new Gruppe, II./JG 7, based near Prague.

It was on 18th March that the Luftwaffe mounted its most concentrated and successful jet- fighter opposition. For the first time Me 262s were armed with R4M rockets – a devastating and destructive weapon firing lethal 30mm cannon shells – in addition to their normal armament. Perhaps it was fated that the bomber crews would face this severe test over Berlin. Over thirteen hundred B-17s and B-24s were dispatched to railway stations and tank factories in the city – the Eighth's heaviest mission to Berlin. Poor visibility gave the Luftwaffe the opportunity to attack the formations without fighter escort. The First Division lost at least two B-17s to the jets, and then near Salwadel, about ninety miles from the target, the 13th Wing suffered a furious onslaught losing six B-17s, two from the 390th and three from 'The Bloody Hundredth' – Berlin was still causing the downfall of its crews. Flak accounted for another eight and eleven bombers crashed or force-landed in Poland behind the Russian lines. The Luftwaffe claimed sixteen bombers and two fighters for the loss of two Me 262s. Another costly mission to Berlin and the Eighth had still not finished

B-24Js of 854th squadron, 491st Bomb Group after bombing Achmer airfield - 21st March 1945. (USAF)

B-24Ms of 328th and 409th squadrons, 93rd Bomb Group dropping supplies to Allied troops across the Rhine – 24th March 1945.

with 'Big B'.

There was no respite for the crews as battle was resumed the following day (19th) over Zwickau. This time the 45th Wing had a torrid mission; three B-17s fell to the jets, two from 452nd and another two of its crews landed safely in Poland. The Second Division's B-24s were in action over jet airfields and they were able to bomb their three primary targets in clear visibility, being especially effective at Neuburg where sixteen Me 262s were damaged and one was shot down by the 355th. The 78th Group, now under the command of Col John Landers, had a battle royal with fifty Me 109s and were credited with thirty-two for the loss of five pilots – their best performance with P-51s so far.

On 21st March the Eighth launched a massive assault on jet-fighter airfields; over thirteen hundred heavies unloaded 3,110 tons of bombs on thirteen targets, seven B-17s were lost to jets but the 78th was again in good form, claiming six and another three on the following day. The Eighth's heavy bombardment and strafing of the airfields imposed a terrific strain on the Luftwaffe's operational capacity, many airfields had been put out of action and in some places Me 262s were forced to use the *autobahnen* as temporary runways!

The final phase of the land battle was launched on 24th March with the large Allied amphibious crossing of the Rhine and the airborne landings to the east of the Rhine – code-named *Varsity*. During the day the Eighth launched 1,097 sorties supported by over 1,290 fighters with most Groups flying morning and afternoon missions. Airfields in

Colonel John D. Landers, CO of 78th Fighter Group, in his P-51, Big Beautiful Doll at Duxford – 24th March 1945. (Smithsonian Institution)

western Germany were bombed for the loss of five B-17s. The B-24 crews of the 14th and 20th Wings were given the hazardous task of dropping supplies to the troops east of the Rhine. Each of the two hundred and forty aircraft carried $2\frac{1}{2}$ tons of supplies and the crews were briefed to make the drops from an altitude of 300 to 400 feet and at a speed of about 145 mph to ensure greater accuracy. They faced fierce and heavy ground fire. Fourteen were lost with the 391st sustaining three casualties and two B-24s crashed on the return flights. The fighters claimed fifty-three victories in the air. Well ahead was the 353rd, led by Lt Col Wayne Blickenstaff, with twenty-three; both Blickenstaff and Major Robert Elder became 'aces in a day'.

Heavy cloud hampered the assembly on the following day and both B-17 Divisions were recalled. As the B-24s had already assembled, albeit with difficulty, it was decided to allow the B-24s to proceed to three oil depots in nothern Germany; near Lüneburg, an isolated squadron of the 448th was attacked by Me 262s and four were shot down before the escorts could intervene. The jets did not escape unscathed, four were destroyed.

After a rare day free from operations, the Third Division were

B-24M of 714 squadron, 448th Bomb Group cut in half by a Me 262 near Hamburg, nine airmen were killed – 4th April 1945. (via Robin J. Brooks)

detailed for rail and munitions targets in Hannover on 28th March and all four hundred and eighty B-17s returned safely. The Second Division was granted another day of rest but some four hundred crews of the First were sent out to Berlin, a little to the west of the city. The Spandau and Falkensee tank and munitions factories were the primary targets for this, the Eighth's nineteenth and final mission to Berlin. Unlike most operations to 'Big B', the losses were minimal – two – one each from the 303rd and 401st. The Eighth had lost over five hundred and fifty aircraft in action over Berlin with another hundred or so salvaged due to battle damage, and some 4,400 airmen had been killed or were missing in action – all in a little over twelve months.

It was thought that thirty Me 262s were in action on 30th March when a large operation (1,320) was mounted on U-boat yards at Hamburg, Bremen and Wilhelmshaven – shades of early 1943! Five bombers were destroyed by jets but JG 7 did lose three Me 262s. During the month of March the Luftwaffe recorded the loss of seventy-two Me 262s, of which the Eighth accounted for forty-three although it had probably lost maybe forty aircraft to jets. It was clear that although the Luftwaffe might be on its knees and somewhat starved of fuel it was still not dead and buried, as the coming weeks would show.

The 446th had the misfortune to lose its Commanding Officer, Colonel Troy W. Crawford, in rather bizarre circumstances on 4th April. He was aboard a Mosquito, borrowed from the 25th Group at Watton, supervising his Group's assembly. Because their target was a relatively short haul to Wesendorf airfield near Dortmund he decided to follow behind the formation. When enemy fighters were reported the Colonel decided to move in closer to the bombers for added protection but sadly the Mosquito was misidentified by some gunners as a Me 262 and it was shot down by fire from his own Group! Crawford managed to bale out and was captured. After a couple of weeks spent in a local prison he and forty other Americans made their escape and the Colonel returned to Bungay on 25th April to a hero's welcome!

It was a day full of action. Of the eight hundred and eighty B-17s and B-24s sent to a number of airfields only half of the crews bombed; they had been briefed that unless they had clear visibility they should return with their bombs. Six B-24s and a B-17 were all thought to be victims of Me 262s with the 448th losing three; the illustration vividly shows the destructive power of a Me 262. Captain George Ceullars of the 364th chased a Me 262 for almost two hundred miles before finally destroying it. The 339th was making a sweep of Rechlin airfield when its pilots sighted some jets climbing into low cloud. The P-51s proceeded to destroy five and damage a couple more. One was flown by Major Rudi Sinner, the Kommandeur of 111./JG 7, he was wounded but baled out and took no further part in the war.

On 7th April the Luftwaffe mounted a desperate and suicidal attack on the Eighth's bombers; the day when the *Schulungslehrgang* 'Elbe' (Training Course 'Elbe'), probably better known as the *Sonderkommando* 'Elbe' was pitched into the battle. It was a special unit of volunteer pilots (some three hundred strong) dedicated to ramming the Eighth's bombers or hated *viermöten*. The unit was the brain child of Oberst Hans-Joachim Hermann with the support and encouragement of Göring. Hermann was utterly convinced that jet-fighters offered the Reich's only hope of salvation and by employing his 'Elbe' unit to destroy a considerable number of bombers, it would allow time for the growth of the jet-fighter force. The 'Elbe' was equipped with adapted Me 109Gs, which had been lightened and armed with a single machine gun. The pilots were instructed to make a firing diving attack on their selected target and if that failed to destroy the bomber, they were to ram the aircraft's fuselage to the right of the tail with their wing, which

P-51D of 434th squadron of 479th Fighter Group – equipped with P-51s in September 1944.

should in theory cut the bomber in half and give them the greatest chance of escape. They had been told that their chances of survival were no more than 10%! The 'Elbe' was commanded by Major Otto Köhnke, a veteran pilot from the days of the Condor Legion.

On 7th April over thirteen hundred bombers from the three Divisions were in action over airfields, oil and munitions storage dumps and marshalling yards. It was over Lüneburg that the 'Elbe' first struck, supported by Me 262s and Fw 190s. The leading Wing of the 2nd Division, with the 398th at its head suffered the first attack. The B-24 of the Group's Commanding Officer, Colonel John B. Herboth Jr, was rammed. It collided with another B-24 piloted by the Group's Deputy Leader, Lt Col Walter R. Kunzel, and both aircraft crashed as did the Me 109 but its pilot, Unteroffizier Heinrich Rosner survived. Two B-24s from the 445th were also destroyed probably by Me 262s and three from the 93rd suffered damage from ramming but all returned to Hardwick. One from the 446th was damaged and crash-landed on the Continent.

The largest air battle took place over Celle. By now the 'Elbe' was probably over one hundred strong and had been joined by additional Me 262s. The 45th Wing of the Third Division sustained the heaviest losses with the 452nd losing four B-17s and the 388th three; the 452nd was later awarded a DUC for its determination in the face of the onslaught and its subsequent bombing of Kaltenkirchen airfield. The following Wing, the 13th, lost three B-17s, although four from the 100th were rammed; two managed to return to Thorpe Abbotts. Four B-17s crashed as a result of ramming, two from the 490th and one each from the 385th and 487th. In total the Division lost fourteen B-17s, the gunners claimed twenty-six enemy aircraft. The fighter losses were quite slight considering the intensity of the battles – five – of which two were accidentally shot down by 'friendly' fire. The escorts claimed sixty-four victories including five Me 262s, the 479th claimed eleven, followed closely by the 339th and 353rd with ten and eight respectively. It is estimated that the 'Elbe' lost forty-five Me 109s and perhaps forty pilots killed. It would appear that eight of the seventeen bombers missing in action were as a result of ramming. The 'Elbe' moved to Pocking airfield in south-east Germany and largely as a result of political chaos it never operated again.

Three days later (10th April) the Eighth inflicted a serious and heavy blow on the Luftflotte Reich. Over twelve hundred bombers attacked known or suspected jet airfields accompanied by some nine hundred fighters. Me 262s mounted a valiant opposition and destroyed sixteen bombers, but the 20th Group claimed five jets. In total nineteen bombers were lost with the 487th losing four to flak over Brandenburg. This would be the last occasion that the Eighth's losses exceeded double figures on a single mission. It was the strafing of the airfields that yielded the greatest rewards – over two hundred and eighty ground victories. The 339th claimed over a hundred with Colonel Joe Thury bringing his total to $18\frac{1}{2}$. Their close neighbours at Duxford, the 78th, destroyed fifty-two with Colonel Landers being credited with eight. Records later revealed that JG 7 had lost twenty-nine Me 262s, more than 50% of its operational strength, a blow from which it never recovered; it was the Eighth's most successful day against the jet-fighters. With the heavy bombardment and strafing of its airfields and the steady advance of the Allied armies, the Luftwaffe was forced to move to airfields in southern Germany and Czechoslovakia. The battered remains of JG 7 moved to Rusin near Prague and Galland's JV 44 to Rien close to Munich.

On two memorable days, the 13th and 16th April, the Eighth's fighters notched up over eight hundred ground victories in massive strafing missions. On the 13th the 'Wolfpack' showed the mettle of their P-47Ms claiming ninety-five, with Lt Randall Murphy setting a new record with ten. These victories made the 56th the first to pass the 1,000 mark. Figures were even more impressive on the 16th. The 78th claimed one hundred and twenty-five victories, followed closely by 353rd with one hundred and ten and the 339th returned to Fowlmere with one hundred and eighteen; Captain Robert H. Ammon of the 339th was credited with eleven – a new record. The 'Eagles' (4th),

Towering Titan – B-17G of 365th squadron, 305th Bomb Group. The last B-17 of the First Division to fall to the Luftwaffe. (USAF)

which had spent March on detachment with the 15th Air Force in Italy, claimed almost one hundred and so passed the 1,000 victory mark. A high price was paid for these strafing missions – thirty-nine pilots lost over the two days.

On the evening of 16th April General Spaatz informed Doolittle that the strategic air war was finished, leaving the Eighth to concentrate on 'tactical' targets. The following day it launched its last one thousand bomber mission (1,054) to rail targets in south-east Germany and Czechoslovakia, although only nine hundred and eighty crews actually bombed. The majority attacked marshalling yards at Dresden and Me 262s of III./JG 7 were thought to have destroyed six B-17s. *Towering Titan* of the 305th collided with a Me 262 and crashed near Brux in Czechoslovakia with a total loss of its crew – the last B-17 of the First Division to fall to the Luftwaffe.

It was another successful strafing day – two hundred and eighty aircraft destroyed for the loss of seventeen pilots. One was Lt Col Elwyn Righetti in his P-51, *Katydid*. He was seen to crash-land some twenty miles from Dresden and escape from his aircraft. After the war it became clear that he was not a POW nor indeed was any grave located, so it was assumed that he had been killed by German civilians angered by the Allies' bombardment of Dresden. This fear of retribution at the hands of enemy civilians or troops, especially in the

Nine O'Nine of 91st Bomb Group made 140 missions without a single turnback or 'abort'. Ground crew at Bassingbourn proudly painting the 120th bomb symbol. (Imperial War Museum)

latter stages of the war, was very real and many fighter pilots and crews carried loaded revolvers.

Two days later, 19th April, some five hundred and eighty B-17s were in action over rail targets in southern Germany. It was the last occasion that jet-fighters engaged the Eighth. The Third Division attacking Pirna and Aussig encountered a small force of Me 262s of III./JG 7 and JV 44. They destroyed one B-17 of the 447th and four from the 490th, twenty-five airmen were killed and the rest taken prisoners but were liberated within a matter of days. This was a particularly bitter blow for the 490th, their heaviest loss on a single mission and so near to the end of the war. Indeed the Group had the lowest total of aircraft lost in action – twenty-two – and a third of these were lost in April! The 357th claimed six Me 262s and the 364th on a sweep of Lübben airfield, about fifty miles south-east of Berlin, encountered some particularly rare Fw 190s and a solitary Dornier 217 bomber. Four Fw 190s and the Dornier were destroyed for the loss of two P-51s. Near Letnany airfield in Czechoslovakia the 355th came across about a dozen Me 109s and destroyed seven without loss. Thus in the final battles with the Luftwaffe, it seemed a just and fitting reward and finale that the Eighth's fighter pilots claimed victories over the enemy's three main day-fighters.

The 381st suffered a particularly tragic accident on the 23rd. A week's 'furlough' in Northern Ireland was planned for a number of its airmen, who would also attend a memorial service for President Roosevelt, who had died on 12th April. Each unit at the airfield selected a deserving airman to make the trip. Captain Charles E. Ackerman, an experienced pilot coming to the end of his second combat tour, along with a crew of four and twenty-six passengers left Ridgewell in a B-17 but they never reached Northern Ireland. The aircraft crashed into North Barrule mountain on the Isle of Man killing all thirty-one. The Group had experienced its fair share of adversity during its time in the ETO, but this tragic accident cast 'a heavy black cloud over the base . . . this hit where it hurts most'.

The Eighth's final mission of the war, No 968, was mounted on 25th April to airfields and rail targets in south-east Germany and Czechoslovakia. Just crews of the First and Second Divisions were engaged, the Third Division was stood down. Sadly six B-17s were lost in action all shot down by flak, with two of the 'Pioneer' Groups, 303rd and 305th, along with the 'veteran' Groups the 92nd and 384th, each sustaining a loss. But it was the most junior Group in the First Division, the 398th, that unfortunately lost two crews, although two B-17s from the 379th collided due to battle damage and crashed on the Continent killing nine airmen. It was either by design or sheer coincidence that the 384th was the last Group to bomb a German target, with *Swamp Angel* credited with dropping the Eighth's final bombs. Thus the Group's memorial records the fact that 'The First and Last Bombs dropped by the 8th Air Force were from airplanes flying from Grafton Underwood.' Only one enemy aircraft, an Arado 234, was shot down by 1/Lt Hilton O. Thompson of the 479th near Salzburg; it was his second jet victory – no mean achievement. The Eighth's oldest Fighter Group, the 4th, lost the last fighter to be missing in action but the pilot baled out and evaded capture.

The Headquarters of the Eighth Air Force now declared that there were no longer any German targets worthy of attack. Thus one thousand and forty days since that fateful Independence Day in 1942, at long last 'the job was wrapped-up'; or as the 457th Group's Memorial simply states: *'Fait Accompli'* – 'the task completed'.

16
THE LEGACY OF
THE EIGHTH

The Eighth Air Force's long and bitter bombing offensive ended after almost three years of fighting – a harsh, harrowing and costly battle. Its crews had fought their war bravely, valiantly and with great determination across the daylight skies, facing enemy fighters and flak with equanimity and suffering grievously in the process. Over 26,000 airmen had been killed, some 28,000 became prisoners of war, with another 1,900 seriously injured and over 6,300 aircraft, the vast majority of them heavy bombers, had fallen – a grave and heavy reckoning.

Seventeen Bomb Groups had completed at least 300 missions, with the B-24 crews of 93rd Group leading the field with 396. But it fell to the 91st to gain the unenviable record of losing the highest number of aircraft in action – 197! Nevertheless the Fighter Groups had taken a heavy toll of the Luftwaffe claiming over 9,400 enemy aircraft both in the air and on the ground, with the 56th, flying P-47s throughout the war, destroying the greatest number in air combat – $674\frac{1}{2}$. Its long-standing rival, the 4th, was the highest scoring Group with $1,052\frac{1}{2}$ victories in the air and on the ground.

Although 25th April marked the last heavy bombing mission, many of the Eighth's operational units had not yet completed their own particular war. The 'Carpetbaggers' went out on their last sortie on the night of 2nd/3rd May and the 25th Group, along with the 'Focus Cats' were active on VE (Victory-in-Europe) Day – 8th May. Also on that day the 'Reich Wreckers' (306th) dispatched twelve crews to Germany with leaflet 'bombs'. The crews of the Night Leaflet Squadron soldiered on

Salute the 'Mighty Eighth' – Fait accompli!

Glory Bee of 44th Bomb Group leaving RAF Valley on the way home – May 1945. (Imperial War Museum)

until the end of the month, but now afforded the luxury of P-51 escorts. In early July the Squadron moved to Germany. The 94th Group continued flying 'Nickle" missions into the late autumn, dropping leaflets over former occupied countries and Germany.

During the final week of the European war, 1st to 7th May, ten Bomb Groups of the 3rd Air Division were engaged in six *Chowhound* operations, dropping food supplies to the Dutch people who were on the point of starvation. Crews taking part in *Chowhound* remembered the missions as the most pleasant and rewarding they had flown. Due to a shortage of parachutes, the food was placed in double sacks and dropped from a height of 300/400 feet and some aircraft were fired upon by German troops; the RAF had mounted their first supply flights two days earlier, code-named *Manna*. In total the Eighth supplied over 4,140 tons of food, but sadly these humanitarian missions were not accomplished without fatalities. Two B-17s collided during assembly, a problem that continued to dog the Eighth until the bitter end. On the final mission a B-17 from 95th Group suffered an engine fire on its return and ditched about five miles off the Suffolk coast, sinking almost immediately. Only six of the crew managed to bale out along with one of the six passengers (all from the Photographic section at Horham), and only two airmen were rescued alive.

For a week or so after VE Day the various Groups made a number of 'Trolley' flights or 'Cooks Tours', taking ground personnel to view the damage wrought on German cities. Later, in May, they were engaged in the so-called 'Revival' flights: with a five-man crew, their aircraft would land on old Luftwaffe airfields to pick up and bring back some forty prisoners of war, and they even met old friends whom they thought they would never see again. Over 9,500 POWs, both American and British, returned early to the UK by this method.

On 13th May, the Eighth mounted a Victory flypast over its head-quarters near High Wycombe, later to become the headquarters of its Fighter Command. B-24s of 467th Group, 'The Rackheath Aggies', were given the honour of leading the flypast, in due acknowledgement of its high standard of bombing, considered to be the best in the Eighth. This owed much to the fine leadership of Colonel Albert J. Shower, the only Commanding Officer to lead a Group throughout its service in the ETO.

Now the thoughts of the Eighth's airmen were firmly turned towards home, the question on all their minds would be how soon they would be crossing 'The Big Pond' but this time in the right direction. Some Groups had been earmarked for service in Germany and another four had been designated to take part in 'The Green Project', the movement of US troops from North Africa and southern France. However, the majority of the Groups would return to the United States and of these the Bomb Groups were given precedence and would be the first to leave their airfields.

From the middle of May until well into July over 2,000 heavy bombers and some 41,500 airmen made the journey back across the Atlantic, on what was known as the 'Home Run'. Some aircraft left from Prestwick (where many had arrived) but over 90% departed from RAF Valley in Anglesey, which would become known as 'The Happy Valley'! A B-24 of 389th Group, 'The Sky Scorpions', was the first to leave on 19th May and it landed safely at Bradley Field, Connecticut three days later. There was a tragic accident on 8th June when a B-17 of 509th squadron of the 351st Group crashed into Craig Cwm-Llwydd mountain in North Wales whilst en route for RAF Valley. The ten-man crew and ten passengers were killed.

During the next six months and more, the B-17s and B-24s would find their last resting place in the wide open spaces of the Kingman Army Air Field in Arizona, bordered on one side by the famous Route 66. At one time it was said that there were over 7,000 aircraft covering five square miles of desert. They were arranged in neat and orderly lines to await their final fate – the arrival of the breakers' men — to be

The final resting place of so many B-17s and B-24s. (San Diego Aerospace Museum)

scrapped and melted down, such an inglorious end for the pride of the Eighth!

The ground personnel would leave as they had arrived, by sea. The first two Groups, 389th from Hethel and 445th from Tibenham, left on 30th May and arrived in New York on 8th June. Most of the other Groups would return home in the comparative comfort of the two Queens – *Mary* and *Elizabeth* – and by the end of August, there were just three Bomb Groups and most of the Fighter Groups remaining in the United Kingdom.

On 1st August those airfields still occupied by the Eighth were opened to the British public and they streamed in to see at close quarters the aircraft that had become such familiar sights in the skies overhead. On the following day, the Freedom of the Borough of Cambridge was conferred on the Eighth Air Force, 'in recognition and grateful appreciation of the great part played by that Unit in winning victory for the cause of liberty and justice in the European War ...' Major General William E. Kepner, the Eighth's last Commander in Europe, accepted the honour.

When shipping space became available the various Fighter Groups finally departed during October and November, leaving just three Bomb Groups – 306th at Thurleigh, 95th at Bury St Edmunds and the 100th at Thorpe Abbotts. But by the middle of December all three had departed, the first to Germany and the other two back to the States – the Eighth Air Force had all but vanished from the UK. Their airfields

The handover of Bassingbourn by USAAF – 15th July 1945. (Smithsonian Institution)

were now empty and forlorn. In September 1945 the *Illustrated London News* captured in words and drawings the desolation of these once busy airfields, which had only recently been vibrant with life and energy: '... silence reigns over the once crowded runways ... the large and commodious hangars echo eerily ...' The journalist was moved to quote from *Othello*: 'Farewell ... the big wars that make ambition virtue! ... And, O you mortal engines, whose wide throats the immortal Jove's dread clamours counterfeit, Farewell! ...' Certainly all over the eastern counties, the 'Yanks' had left almost as quickly as they had arrived just a few brief years earlier; although they would, in fact, return in a short while.

The Eighth Air Force, *per se*, had been transferred to Okinawa in the Pacific on 16th July 1945, once again in its short history to become a 'paper' Air Force, without personnel, equipment or combat units but with Lieutenant General James H. Doolittle as its Commander. Although some weeks later two B-29 Groups, 333rd and 346th, were allocated to the Eighth and ready for action, they were too late, and the 'new' Eighth Air Force did not take part in any operations against Japan; thus ensuring that its Second World War reputation and legacy remained firmly with its operations from the United Kingdom.

It was not until 26th February 1946 that Brigadier General Emil Kiel, the Eighth's Fighter Commander, ceremoniously handed over the keys of Honington airfield to Air Chief Marshal Sir James Robb of RAF Fighter Command – the final Eighth Air Force base to be returned to the RAF. As the Stars and Stripes was lowered, marking the end of the Eighth Air Force's presence in the UK – a historic event indeed – alas the English weather had a final say. The last remaining B-17 could not take-off for a ceremonial fly-past because of low cloud!

Now with the battle over and the dust settled, came the time for an assessment of the Eighth's contribution to the final victory and an evaluation of the USAAF's strategic bombing offensive. Winston Churchill wrote in March 1946, 'Before the end we and the United States had developed air striking forces so powerful that they played a major part in the economic collapse of Germany ... full tribute must be paid to the United States Eighth Air Force ...' From the enemy's point of view General Erhard Milch, the State Secretary of the German Air Ministry, maintained 'The British inflicted grievous and bloody injuries upon us; but the Americans stabbed us to the heart'.

As early as November 1944 the US Secretary of State had set up the US Strategic Bombing Survey comprising some 300 civilian 'experts' in addition to over 800 officers and men. They were given the immense task of examining the strategic bombing offensive of Germany and Japan, to assess its efficacy and evaluate and quantify the damage inflicted on the various strategic targets. Indeed it produced 208 detailed reports for the European air war alone, and some of its general conclusions were not universally accepted. Instead of justifying the offensive, which was really the object of the massive exercise, the

Survey rather revealed its limitations. One of the Survey's members, John Kenneth Galbraith, commented, 'Strategic bombing was designed to destroy the industrial base of the enemy and the morale of the people. It did neither.'

This strikes one as a rather simplistic view of what was a most complicated and complex subject. The Survey did show that the strategic bombing offensive was *ultimately* decisive in the final victory. Although it was evident that the bombing did not dramatically reduce Germany's industrial production (by only 9% in 1943), it did, however, successfully prevent the development and expansion as would have been expected from such a highly organised and efficient industrial power. It is fair to say that throughout the war the Allied Chiefs of Staff greatly underestimated Germany's powers of recovery.

The German aircraft industry, which suffered heavily at the hands of the Eighth and RAF Bomber Command, did manage to survive with only temporary reductions in production. But its planned programme of dispersal to escape the bombing onslaught certainly reduced its efficiency. The figure of 36,000 aircraft produced in 1944 was quite remarkable in the circumstances and this has been cited as evidence of the failure of strategic bombing. However, had it been unhindered by Allied bombing, aircraft production would have risen far higher and far faster; after all a target of 80,000 aircraft had been planned for 1945.

There were, however, two strategic targets that were the shining successes of the bombing offensive – transportation and oil. Indeed the British Bombing Survey Unit, a most modest affair compared with the US Survey, concluded that the ultimate destruction of the enemy's communications system was critical to the final victory. Perhaps more dramatic was the Eighth's bitter and costly offensive against the German oil industry, which can be considered an utter and complete victory. From May 1944 to April 1945 over 340 attacks were mounted against oil targets, twice the number made by the RAF. As one historian has recorded '... [it] was a haemorrhage, which drained the lifeblood of Germany's industry and its Armed Forces, especially the Luftwaffe, which brought its war machine virtually to a halt.'

Indirectly the strategic bombing offensive had forced the enemy to employ some two million men on anti-aircraft defences and fire and rescue services, thus preventing them from being used for offensive purposes. It also compelled the German aircraft industry to almost solely concentrate on the production of fighters rather than bombers – defensive instead of offensive. Perhaps the ultimate triumph of the Eighth was the attainment of air supremacy over the Luftwaffe. In this

The entrance to the museum at Pooler, near Savannah, Georgia.

respect the RAF took a rather minor role until after D-Day, as its bombers generally flew at night and destroyed few night-fighters and its Spitfires had limited impact over Germany because of their range. This harsh battle of attrition with the Luftwaffe, historically likened to 'the trench warfare of the First World War', was an essential part of the strategic bombing offensive, it forced the enemy fighters to come up to fight in defence of the homeland. This hard-won victory can be considered the Eighth's major contribution to the victory in Europe.

Such debates and conclusions are the preserve of air strategists and historians reviewing the air war from a safe distance and with the benefit of hindsight. For the 350,000 airmen that served with the Eighth, they were engaged in what to them was a long, harrowing and brutal conflict, in which they lost friends and colleagues; not for them the niceties and debates of whether this or that offensive was worthwhile or justified. They bravely served and fought in what was one of the most famous military organisations of the Second World War and were an important part of what has been recently called 'The Greatest Generation.'

Those of them who managed to survive the ordeal have ensured that the legacy of the Eighth has remained burnished despite the passage of

The Reflecting Pool in the memorial garden at the Mighty Eighth Air Force Museum.

years. The strength of the Eighth's Group Associations in the US with their reunions, newsletters, provision of memorials in the UK and tours of the old airfields, clearly demonstrate that the memory of the Eighth is still very much alive and well. But perhaps their finest memorial is the Mighty Eighth Air Force Heritage Museum at Pooler near Savannah in Georgia, close to where the Eighth was activated in January 1942.

In 1983 Major General Lewis E. Lyle, along with other veterans, began planning a museum and on 14th May 1996 the Museum was dedicated; since that day over a half million people have visited the Museum. It 'honors the courage, character and patriotism embodied by the men and women of the Eighth Air Force from World War II'. It is a most impressive museum, which concentrates on people rather than aircraft and is a splendid repository of the legacy of the Eighth. There is also a fine Memorial Garden, where it is planned to build a traditional English chapel – The Chapel of the Fallen Eagles. For those interested in the Eighth Air Force, its history and traditions, a visit to the museum is a must.

In the UK the Eighth has certainly not been forgotten. The most tangible and poignant reminders are the fifty or so dignified memorials that are dotted around the English countryside, normally adjacent to the Groups' old airfields, their 'adopted' homes; most of which have been erected in the last twenty years. It would be invidious to pick out the most impressive, those illustrated are merely a representative

Selection of Group Memorials.

sample. Many country churches house permanent memories to the Eighth – plaques, stained-glass windows, rolls of honour, books of remembrance, memorial doors, chapels and altars. There are also plaques, seats, gardens, village signs etc, in towns and villages throughout the eastern counties that recall the Eighth's brief presence. Further afield there are numerous memorials to commemorate tragic

274

The Wall of the Missing at the American Cemetery and Memorial at Madingley near Cambridge.

aircraft crashes and acts of bravery.

The 2nd Air Division Memorial USAAF at Norwich, which was funded by Eighth airmen before they left Norfolk, was dedicated in June 1963 and holds a unique collection of records and books relating

275

to the Eighth Air Force. The relatively new American Air Museum at Duxford is a fitting tribute to the USAAF in Europe; the impressive glass sculpture 'Counting the Cost' records the aircraft losses of the Eighth and Ninth Air Forces. There are also a number of small museums that faithfully and vividly recall the operations and exploits of their respective Bomb Groups.

Perhaps the most imposing memorial is the American Military Cemetery and Memorial at Madingley near Cambridge. The cemetery, covering over thirty acres, was originally established in 1944 on land donated by the University of Cambridge; the construction was completed and finally dedicated in July 1956. The number of US servicemen buried here totals 3,812, their graves laid out in a fan shape across splendidly maintained lawns. The impressive 'Wall of the Missing', over 472 feet long, lists 5,125 names. The Memorial has a museum room with a chapel; the ceiling mosaic depicts ghostly aircraft, accompanied by angels, making their final flight. An annual Memorial Day service is held there in May. A visit to Madingley is a most rewarding and humbling experience that cannot be too highly recommended.

Over the years, countless numbers of ex-Eighth airmen have made the emotional and painful journey to Madingley and have returned to the scenes of their wartime experiences. Naturally, with the passing of time, the numbers get fewer. They are now replaced by their children and grandchildren. In 1992 there was a special reunion to celebrate the fifty years that had elapsed since the Eighth first arrived in the UK. From late March through to November there were special events – exhibitions, air shows, displays, concerts, dances, open days, and memorial services – organised throughout the eastern counties, when dignitaries and local people alike welcomed the veterans and their families back, to share this celebration of the Eighth Air Force.

It seems appropriate and most fitting, on completion of this brief history of a truly remarkable Air Force, to recall the verse that appears on the 398th Bomb Group's fine memorial stone at Nuthampstead in Hertfordshire:

'Their wings of silver touched the passing clouds,
Made soft white lines across the azure blue.
But not for them this life we share on earth
They sacrificed that for me and you.'

Appendix A

MAJOR OPERATIONAL AIRFIELDS

1. ALCONBURY (Cambridgeshire)
   4m NW Huntingdon. Built pre-war for RAF (1938).
   Station 102: 93BG: 95BG(Lodger): 92BG: 482BG: 36BS.
   6th September 1942 – 26th November 1945.
   Also Abbots Ripton Depot (Station 547).

2. ANDREWS FIELD (Essex)
   3m W Braintree. Built by US Engineers 1942-April 1943.
   Station 485: 96BG: 322BG.
   13th May 1943 – 16th October 1943.
   Originally 'Great Saling'. Memorial at Great Saling village.

3. ATTLEBRIDGE (Norfolk)
   1m SW Weston Longville. Built 1941-2 for RAF (Richard Costain
       Ltd).
   Station 120: 466BG.
   7th March 1944 – 15th July 1945.
   Village sign and memorial plaque.

4. BASSINGBOURN (Cambridgeshire)
   $3\frac{1}{2}$m NNW Royston. During 1937-8 for RAF (John Laing & Son Ltd).
   Station 121: 91BG: 94BG.
   14th October 1942 – 10th July 1945.
   Memorial museum in old control tower. Mounted B-17 propellor &
       stone on airfield.

5. BODNEY (Norfolk)
   $4\frac{1}{2}$m W Watton. In 1940 for RAF.
   Station 141: 352FG.
   8th July 1943 – 8th November 1945.
   Roadside memorial near airfield.

6. BOTTISHAM (Cambridgeshire)
   6m E Cambridge. In 1940 for RAF.
   Station 374: 361FG.
   30th November 1943 – 10th November 1944.
   Memorial plaque and lych gate in village.

7. BOVINGDON (Hertfordshire)
   2m SW Hemel Hempstead. During 1941-2 for RAF (John Laing &
      Co Ltd).
   Station 112: No 11 CCRC: 92BG.
   July 1942 – 15th September 1944.

8. BOXTED (Essex)
   Langham 3m NE Colchester. During 1942-3 for RAF (W & C
      French Ltd)
   Station 150: 386BG: 56FG.
   10th June 1943 – 23rd October 1945.
   Fine memorial near main runway at Langham.

9. BUNGAY (Suffolk)
   2m SW Bungay. In 1942 (Kirk & Kirk Ltd).
   Station 125: 446BG.
   3rd December 1942 – 20th July 1945.
   Various memorials in Flixton village.

10. BURY ST EDMUNDS (Suffolk)
    3m E Bury St Edmunds. In 1942 (Richard Costain Ltd).
    Station 468: 322BG: 94BG.
    1st December 1942 – 20 December 1945.
    Also known as 'Rougham'.
    Flying Fortress pub on airfield. Memorial in Abbey gardens, Bury St
       Edmunds.

11. CHALGROVE (Oxfordshire)
    $4\frac{1}{2}$m NE Dorchester. Wartime.
    Station 465: 7PG.
    22 March – 1st December 1945.

12. CHEDDINGTON (Buckinghamshire)
    $6\frac{3}{4}$m NE Aylesbury. During 1941-2 (George Wimpey & Co).

Station 113: 44BG: 12CCRC: Night Leaflet Sqn.
11th September 1942 – 21st June 1945.
Memorial at entrance.

13. CHELVESTON (Northamptonshire)
$6\frac{1}{2}$m S Thrapston. In 1941 for RAF (Taylor-Woodrow Ltd).
Station 105: 60TCG: 301BG: 305BG: Night Leaflet Sqn.
12th June 1942 – 9th October 1945.
Memorial plaque on church tower.

14. CHIPPING ONGAR (Essex)
2m NE Ongar. US Engineers August 1942 – July 1943.
Station 162: 387BG.
21st June 1943 – 16th October 1943.
Also known as 'Willingale'.
Memorial museum at Blake Hall.

15. DEBACH (Suffolk)
3m NW Woodbridge. US Engineers 1943 – April 44.
Station 152: 493BG.
17th April 1944 – 10th October 1945.

16. DEBDEN (Essex)
1m N Debden. For RAF during 1935-7 (W & C French Ltd).
Station 356: 4FG.
29th September 1942 – 5th September 1945.
Small bronze memorial in the Army base.

17. DEENETHORPE (Northamptonshire)
9m NNE Kettering. In 1943 (John Laing & Son Ltd).
Station 128: 401 BG.
3rd November 1943 – 9th October 1945.
Fine roadside memorial. Stained glass window at Weldon.

18. DEOPHAM GREEN (Norfolk).
$1\frac{3}{4}$m N Attleborough. In 1943 (John Laing & Son Ltd).
Station 142: 452BG.
3rd January 1944 – 9th October 1945.
Memorial plinth on edge of airfield: plaque outside church at
    Hingham.

19. DUXFORD (Cambridgeshire)
    8m S Cambridge. In 1919 for RAF.
    Station 357: 78FG.
    15th October 1942 – 1st December 1945.
    Memorial plaque near main gate. American Air Museum.

20. EARLS COLNE (Essex)
    4m SE Halstead. In 1942.
    Station 358: 94BG: 323BG.
    12th May 1943 – 16th October 1943.

21. EAST WRETHAM (Norfolk)
    6m NE Thetford. In 1940 for RAF.
    Station 133: 359FG.
    19th October 1943 – 1st November 1945.
    Memorial plaques at Thetford and East Wretham.

22. EYE (Suffolk)
    1m NW Eye. US Engineers during September 1942 – February
       1944.
    Station 134: 490BG.
    26th April 1944 – 1st November 1945.
    Memorial lych gate at Eye.

23. FERSFIELD (Norfolk)
    16m SW Norwich. During 1943-4.
    Station 554: Aphrodite project.
    April 1944 – 18th January 1945.
    Originally 'Winfarthing' (Station 140).

24. FOWLMERE (Cambridgeshire)
    $3\frac{1}{2}$m NE Royston. In 1940 for RAF.
    Station 378: 339FG.
    5th April 1944 – 1st November 1945.
    Stone memorial near airfield site.

25. FRAMLINGHAM (Suffolk)
    3m SE Framlingham. During 1942-3 (Haymills Ltd).
    Station 153: 95BG: 390BG.
    12th May 1943 – 1st November 1945.

Also known as 'Parham'.
Museum in control tower.

26. GLATTON (Cambridgeshire)
    10m N Huntingdon. US Engineers in 1943.
    Station 130: 457BG.
    21st January 1944 – 12th July 1945.
    Memorial in local churchyard at Conington.

27. GRAFTON UNDERWOOD (Northamptonshire)
    $3\frac{3}{4}$m ENE Kettering. During 1942-3 (George Wimpey & Co Ltd).
    Station 106: 15BS: 97BG: 305BG: 96BG: 384BG.
    14th May 1942 – 9th October 1945.
    Memorial stone. Stained glass window in village church.

28. GREAT ASHFIELD (Suffolk)
    10m E Bury St Edmunds. During 1942-3 (John Laing & Son Ltd).
    Station 155: 385BG.
    26th June 1943 – 9th October 1945.
    Memorial altar and plaque in churchyard.

29. GREAT DUNMOW (Essex)
    2m NW Great Dunmow. US Engineers during 1942-3.
    Station 164: 386BG.
    24th September 1943 – 16th October 1943.
    Roadside memorial.

30. HALESWORTH (Suffolk)
    2m NE Halesworth. During 1942-June 1943 (John Laing & Richard
       Costain Ltd).
    Station 365: 56FG: 489BG: 5 Emergency Rescue Sqn.
    8th July 1943 – 25th June 1945.
    Also known as 'Holton'.
    Drop tank memorial. Roadside memorial stone.

31. HARDWICK (Norfolk)
    3m S Hempnall. During 1941-2 (John Laing Ltd).
    Station 104: 93BG.
    6th December 1942 – 25th June 1945.
    Memorial near airfield.

32. HARRINGTON (Northamptonshire)
    5m W Kettering. US Engineers. For RAF in 1943.
    Station 179: 801(P)BG: 492BG.
    28th March 1944 – 9th October 1945.
    Memorial stone.

33. HETHEL (Norfolk)
    3m E Wymondham. During 1941-October 1942 (W & C French
      Ltd).
    Station 114: 389BG.
    11th June 1943 – 25th June 1945.
    Memorial in church at Carleton Rode.

34. HONINGTON (Suffolk)
    2m NW Honington. During 1935-7 for RAF.
    Station 375: 364FG: Also Station 595: 1 S.A.Depot (Troston).
    September 1942 – 26th February 1946 (last to return to the RAF).
    Memorial near guard room.

35. HORHAM (Suffolk)
    4m ESE Eye. During 1941-September 1942.
    Station 119: 323BG: 95BG.
    21st May 1943 – 9th October 1945.
    Unusual 'B-17 Fin' memorial in village.

36. HORSHAM ST FAITH (Norfolk)
    4m N Norwich. During 1939-40 for RAF.
    Station 123: 56FG: 458BG.
    5th April 1943 – 20th July 1945.
    Memorial in Norwich airport terminal.

37. KIMBOLTON (Cambridgeshire)
    $1\frac{1}{2}$m N Kimbolton. In 1941 for RAF (W & C French Ltd).
    Station 117: 91BG: 379BG.
    12th September 1942 – 4th July 1945.
    Memorial near airfield site and in local church.

38. KING'S CLIFFE (Northamptonshire)
    12m W Peterborough. In 1941 for RAF (W & C French Ltd).
    Station 367: 56FG: 20FG.

13th January 1943 – 1st November 1945.
Roadside memorial for Allied airmen.

39. KNETTISHALL (Suffolk)
5m SE Thetford. 1942-3 (W & C French Ltd).
Station 136: 388BG.
23rd June 1943 – 1st November 1945.
Memorials at site and in village.

40. LAVENHAM (Suffolk)
3m NW Lavenham. September 1942 – September 1943 (John Laing & Son Ltd).
Station 137: 487BG.
4th April 1944 – 12th October 1945.
Memorial plaque on control tower and in Market Square.

41. LEISTON (Suffolk)
2m NW Leiston. September 1942 – September 1943 (John Mowlem & Co. Ltd).
Station 373: 358FG: 357FG.
29th November 1943 – 10th October 1945.
Memorial near airfield site, plaque in village.

42. LITTLE WALDEN (Essex)
2m S Hadstock. During 1942 – October 1943.
Station 165: 361FG: 493BG (Lodger).
26th September 1944 – 30th January 1946.
Originally known as 'Hadstock'.
Memorial in old control tower now offices.

43. MARTLESHAM HEATH (Suffolk)
SSW Martlesham. In 1917 for RAF.
Station 369: 356FG.
5th October 1943 – 1st November 1945.
Memorial on old parade ground.

44. MENDLESHAM (Suffolk)
W Wetherup Street. During 1942 – October 1943 for RAF.
Station 156: 34BG.
18th April 1944 – 9th October 1945.
Fine memorial on roadside.

45. METFIELD (Suffolk)
    1½m SE Metfield. During 1942-3 (John Laing & Son Ltd).
    Station 366: 353FG: 491BG.
    3rd August 1943 – 10th October 1945.

46. MOLESWORTH (Cambridgeshire)
    2m N Molesworth. In 1940 for RAF.
    Station 107: 15 BS: 303BG.
    9th June 1942 – 1st July 1945.
    Memorial plaques in airfield buildings and church at Brington.

47. MOUNT FARM (Oxfordshire)
    8m SE Oxford. In 1941 for RAF.
    Station 234: 7PG.
    7th July 1943 – 1st May 1945.
    Memorial and American garden.

48. NORTH PICKENHAM (Norfolk)
    1m W North Pickenham. During 1943-4.
    Station 143: 492BG: 491BG.
    14th April 1944 – 10th July 1945 (last transferred to the 8th).
    Roadside memorial stone.

49. NUTHAMPSTEAD (Hertfordshire)
    5½m SE Royston. US Engineers during 1942-3.
    Station 131: 55FG: 398BG.
    16th September 1943 – 10th July 1945.
    Splendid memorial in *Woodman* pub garden in the village and
      stained glass window at Anstey.

50. OLD BUCKENHAM (Norfolk)
    2m NE Old Buckenham. During 1942-3 (Taylor Woodrow Ltd).
    Station 144: 453BG.
    22nd December 1943 – 28th May 1945.
    Memorial at village community hall.

51. PODINGTON (Bedfordshire)
    2m SE Podington. In 1941 for RAF.
    Station 109: 60TCG: 301BG (352Sqn.): 15BS: 92BG.
    18th August 1942 – 24th September 1945.
    Memorial in local church.

52. POLEBROOK (Northamptonshire)
   $3\frac{1}{2}$m ESE Oundle. During 1940-1 for RAF (George Wimpey & Co Ltd).
   Station 110: 97BG: 351BG.
   13th June 1942 – 10th July 1945.
   Fine memorial stone near old main runway.

53. RACKHEATH (Norfolk)
   1m S Rackheath. In 1943 (John Laing & Son Ltd).
   Station 145: 467BG.
   12th March 1944 – 20th July 1945.
   Memorial in the village and church.

54. RATTLESDEN (Suffolk)
   9m SE Bury St Edmunds. In 1942 (George Wimpey & Co Ltd).
   Station 126: 322BG: 447BG.
   December 1942 – 10th October 1945.
   Memorial at High Town Green.

55. RAYDON (Suffolk)
   3m SE Hadleigh. US Engineers during 1942-3.
   Station 157: 357FG: 353FG.
   30th November 1943 – 20th December 1945.
   Memorials in local church.

56. RIDGEWELL (Essex)
   $7\frac{1}{2}$m NNW Halstead. During 1941-2 for RAF.
   Station 167: 381BG.
   30th June 1943 – 15th July 1945.
   Splendid memorial on airfield site. A memorial museum in former hospital building.

57. SEETHING (Norfolk)
   $1\frac{1}{2}$m S Seething. During 1942-3 (John Laing & Son Ltd).
   Station 146: 448BG.
   30th November 1943 – 6th July 1945.
   Memorials in local churchyard and near Memorial museum in old control tower.

58. SHIPDHAM (Norfolk)
   2m E Shipdham. During 1941-2.

Station 115: 44BG.
10th October 1942 – 25th June 1945.
Memorials at airfield site and in village churchyard.

59. SNETTERTON HEATH (Norfolk)
2½m NE East Harling. During 1942-3 (Taylor-Woodrow Ltd)
Station 138: 386BG: 96BG.
3rd June 1943 – 20th December 1945.
Memorial chapel and stained glass window in local church at
   Quidenham. Nearby memorial museum.

60. STEEPLE MORDEN (Cambridgeshire)
3½m W Royston. In 1941 for RAF (John Laing & Son Ltd).
Station 122: 3PG: 355FG.
26th October 1942 – 1st November 1945.
Impressive roadside memorial.

61. SUDBURY (Suffolk)
2m N Sudbury. In 1943.
Station 174: 486BG
5th April 1944 – 10th October 1945.
Also known as 'Acton'.
Memorial plaques at airfield entrance and in Sudbury.

62. THORPE ABBOTTS (Norfolk)
4½m E Diss. In 1942 (John Laing & Son Ltd).
Station 139: 100BG.
9th June 1943 – 20th December 1945.
Memorial museum in control tower.

63. THURLEIGH (Bedfordshire)
2m NW Thurleigh. In 1941 for RAF (W & C French Ltd).
Station 111: 306BG.
7th September 1942 – 8th December 1945.
Memorial on roadside near airfield site.

64. TIBENHAM (Norfolk)
13½m SSW Norwich. In 1942 (W & C French Ltd).
Station 124: 445BG.
4th November 1943 – 25th June 1945.
Memorial on airfield site.

65. WATTISHAM (Suffolk)
    9m NW Ipswich. In 1938 for RAF (John Laing & Son Ltd).
    Station 377: 479FG: Also Station 470: 4 S.A. Depot (Hitcham).
    12th October 1942 – 15th December 1945.
    Memorial plaque in station headquarters.

66. WATTON (Norfolk)
    2m E Watton. In 1939 for RAF (John Laing & Son Ltd).
    Station 376: 36 & 406BSqns: 25BSqn. Also Station 505: 3 S. A. Depot
        (Neaton).
    4th October 1943 – 15th August 1945.
    Memorial near main gate.

67. WENDLING (Norfolk)
    2m N Wendling. In 1942 (Taylor Woodrow Ltd).
    Station 118: 392BG.
    1st August 1943 – 25th June 1945.
    Obelisk memorial near old runway near Beeston.

68. WESTHAMPNETT (Sussex)
    $1\frac{1}{2}$m NE Chichester. In 1940 for RAF.
    Station 352: 31FG.
    July – October 1942.
    Fine stone memorial at airfield.

69. WORMINGFORD (Essex)
    6m NW Colchester. In 1943 (Richard Costain Ltd).
    Station 159: 55FG.
    16th April 1944 – 10th October 1945.

NOTES

DATES:
Occupation by 8th Air Force units and handover to the Ninth AF or
back to RAF.

MEMORIALS:
Space precludes giving full details of all 8th Air Force memorials. These
can be found in: *8th Air Force Remembered* by George H. Fox.

Appendix B

OPERATIONAL BOMB GROUPS

HEAVY – (In order of first operation)

1. 97th   17th August – 21st October 1942. B-17s. 1st Wing.
   Airfields: Polebrook & Grafton Underwood. (Trsfrd. to Twelfth Air Force.)

2. 301st   5th September – 8th November 1942. B-17s. 1st Wing.
   Airfields: Chelveston & Podington. (Trsfrd. to Twelfth Air Force).

3. 92nd   6th September 1942 – 25th April 1945. B-17s. 1st Wing/Division.
   Airfields: Bovingdon, Alconbury & Podington. 1 DUC & 1 MoH. 'Fame's Favoured Few'.

4. 93rd   9th October 1942 – 25th April 1945. B-24s. 1st & 2nd Wing/Division.
   Airfields: Alconbury & Hardwick. 2 DUCs & 2 MoHs. 'The Travelling Circus'.

5. 306th   9th October 1942 – 19th April 1945. B-17s. 1st Wing/Division.
   Airfield: Thurleigh. 2 DUCs & 1 MoH. 'The Reich Wreckers'.

6. 44th   7th November 1942 – 25th April 1945. B-24s. 2nd Wing/Division.
   Airfields: Cheddington & Shipdham. 2 DUCs & 1 MoH. 'The Flying Eightballs'.

7. 91st   7th November 1942 – 25th April 1945. B-17s. 1st Wing/Division.
   Airfields: Kimbolton & Bassingbourn. 2 DUCs. 'The Ragged Irregulars'.

8. 303rd   17th November 1942 – 25th April 1945. B-17s. 1st Wing/Division.
   Airfield: Molesworth. 1 DUC & 2 MoHs. 'Hell's Angels'.

9. 305th   17th November 1942 – 25th April 1945. B-17s. 1st Wing/Division.
   Airfields: Grafton Underwood & Chelveston. 2 DUCs & 2 MoHs. 'Can Do'.

10. 95th   13th May 1943 – 20th April 1945. B-17s. 4thWing/3rd
            Division.
            Airfields: Alconbury, Framlingham & Horham. 3 DUCs.
11. 94th   13th May 1943 – 21st April 1945. B-17s. 4th Wing/3rd
            Division.
            Airfields: Bassingbourn, Earls Colne & Bury St Edmunds. 2
            DUCs.
12. 96th   14th May 1943 – 21st April 1945. B-17s. 4th Wing/3rd
            Division.
            Airfields: Grafton Underwood, Andrews Field & Snetterton
            Heath. 2 DUCs.
13. 351st   14th May 1943 – 20th April 1945. B-17s. 1st Wing/Division.
            Airfield: Polebrook. 2 DUCs.
14. 379th   29th May 1943 – 25th April 1945. B-17s. 1st Wing/Division.
            Airfield: Kimbolton. 2 DUCs.
15. 381st   22nd June 1943 – 25th April 1945. B-17s. 1st Wing/Division.
            Airfield: Ridgewell. 2 DUCs.
16. 384th   22nd June 1943 – 25th April 1945. B-17s. 1st Wing/Division.
            Airfield: Grafton Underwood. 2 DUCs.
17. 100th   25th June 1943 – 20th April 1945. B-17s. 4th Wing/3rd
            Division.
            Airfields: Podington & Thorpe Abbotts. 2 DUCs. 'The
            Bloody Hundredth'.
18. 389th   9th July 1943 – 25th April 1945. B-24s. 2nd Wing/Division.
            Airfield: Hethel. 1 DUC & 1 MoH. 'The Sky Scorpions'.
19. 385th   17th July 1943 – 20th April 1945. B-17s. 4th Wing/3rd
            Division.
            Airfield: Great Ashfield. 2 DUCs. 'Van's Valiants'.
20. 388th   17th July 1943 – 21st April 1945. B-17s. 4th Wing/3rd
            Division.
            Airfield: Knettishall. 2 DUCs.
21. 390th   12th August 1943 – 20th April 1945. B-17s. 4th Wing/3rd
            Division.
            Airfield: Framlingham. 2 DUCs. 'Wittan's Wallopers'.
22. 392nd   9th September 1943 – 25th April 1945. B-24s. 2nd Wing/
            Division.
            Airfield: Wendling. 1 DUC.
23. 482nd   27th September 1943 – 22nd March 1944. B-17s & B-24s. 1st
            Division.
            (PFF) Airfield: Alconbury. 1 DUC.

24. 401st 26th November 1943 – 20 April 1945. B-17s. 1st Division.
Airfield: Deenethorpe. 2 DUCs.

25. 445th 13th December 1943 – 25th April 1945. B-24s. 2nd Division.
Airfield: Tibenham. 1 DUC.

26. 446th 16th December 1943 – 25th April 1945. B-24s. 2nd Division.
Airfield: Bungay. 'Bungay Buckeroos'.

27. 448th 22nd December 1943 – 25th April 1945. B-24s. 2nd Division.
Airfield: Seething.

28. 447th 24th December 1943 – 21st April 1945. B-17s. 3rd Division.
Airfield: Rattlesden. 1 MoH.

29. 452nd 5th February 1944 – 21st April 1945. B-17s. 3rd Division.
Airfield: Deopham Green. 1 DUC & 2 MoH.

30. 453rd 5th February 1944 – 12th April 1945. B-24s. 2nd Division.
Airfield: Old Buckenham.

31. 457th 21st February 1944 – 20th April 1945. B-17s. 1st Division.
Airfield: Glatton.

32. 458th 24th February 1944 – 25th April 1945. B-24s. 2nd Division.
Airfield: Horsham St Faith.

33. 466th 22nd March 1944 – 25th April 1945. B-24s. 2nd Division.
Airfield: Attlebridge. 'The Flying Deck'.

34. 467th 10th April 1944 – 25th April 1945. B-24s. 2nd Division.
Airfield: Rackheath. 'The Rackheath Aggies'.

35. 398th 6th May 1944 – 25th April 1945. B-17s. 1st Division.
Airfield: Nuthampstead.

36. 486th 7th May 1944 – 21st April 1945. B-24s & B-17s. 3rd Division.
Airfield: Sudbury.

37. 487th 7th May 1944 – 21st April 1945. B-24s & B-17s. 3rd Division.
Airfield: Lavenham.

38. 492nd 11th May 1944 – 7th August 1944. B-24s. 2nd Division.
Airfield: North Pickenham.

39. 34th 23rd May 1944 – 20th April 1945. B-24s & B-17s. 3rd
Division.
Airfield: Mendlesham.

40. 489th 30th May 1944 – 10th November 1944. B-24s. 2nd Division.
Airfield: Halesworth. 1 MoH.

41. 490th 31st May 1944 – 20th April 1945. B-24s & B-17s. 3rd
Division.
Airfield: Eye.

42. 491st 2nd June 1944 – 25th April 1945. B-24s. 2nd Division.
Airfields: Metfield & North Pickenham. 'The Ringmasters'.

43. 493rd 6th June 1944 – 20th April 1945. B-24s & B-17s. 3rd Division.
    Airfields: Debach & Little Walden. 'Helton's Hellcats'.

MEDIUM

1. 322nd 14th May 1943 – 8th October 1943. B-26s.
    Airfields: Bury St Edmunds, Rattlesden & Andrews Field. 1
    DUC. (Trsfd. to Ninth Air Force).
2. 323rd 16th July 1943 – 9th October 1943. B-26s.
    Airfields: Horham & Earls Colne. (Trsfd. to Ninth Air
    Force).
3. 386th 30th July 1943 – 8th October 1943. B-26s.
    Airfields: Snetterton Heath, Boxted, & Great Dunmow.
    (Trsfrd. to Ninth Air Force).
4. 387th 15th August 1943 – 9th October 1943. B-26s.
    Airfield: Chipping Ongar. (Trsfrd. to Ninth Air Force).

FIGHTER GROUPS

1. 52nd 27th August 1942 – 11th September 1942. Spitfire Vs. 6th
    Wing.
    Airfields: (from Biggin Hill & Maydown). (Trsfrd. to Twelfth
    Air Force).
2. 31st 29th August 1942 – 9th October 1942. Spitfire Vs. 6th Wing.
    Airfields: Westhampnett & Merston. Vics. = 2 Air. (Trsfrd. to
    Twelfth Air Force).
3. 1st 2nd September 1942 – 25th October 1942. P-38s. 6th Wing.
    Airfields: High Ercall & Colerne. (Trsfd. to Twelfth Air
    Force).
4. 4th 2nd October 1942 – 25th April 1945. Spitfire Vs, P-47s &
    P-51s. 65th Wing/2nd Division.
    Airfields: Debden & Steeple Morden. Vics. = $583\frac{1}{2}$ Air, 469
    Ground. 1 DUC. 'The Eagles'.
5. 14th 2nd October – 21st October 1942. P-38s. 6th Wing.
    Airfields: (from Ford & Tangmere). (Trsfrd. to Twelfth Air
    Force).
6. 56th 13th April 1943 – 21st April 1945. P-47s. 65th Wing/2nd
    Division.
    Airfields: King's Cliffe, Horsham St Faith, Halesworth,
    Boxted & Little Walden. Vics. = $674\frac{1}{2}$ Air, 311 Ground. 2
    DUCs. 'The Wolfpack'.

7. 78th   13th April 1943 – 25th April 1945. P-47s & P-51s. 65th, 66th
            Wings/3rd Division.
            Airfield: Duxford. Vics. = $338\frac{1}{2}$ Air, $358\frac{1}{2}$ Ground. 2 DUCs.
8. 353rd   12th August 1943 – 25th April 1945. P-47s & P-51s. 66th
            Wing/3rd Division.
            Airfields: Metfield & Raydon. Vics. = $330\frac{1}{2}$ Air, 414 Ground.
            1 DUC.
9. 352nd   9th September 1943 – 3rd May 1945. P-47s & P-51s. 67th
            Wing/1st Division.
            Airfields: Bodney, Asche & Chievres. Vics. = $519\frac{1}{2}$ Air, 287
            Ground. 2 DUCs.
10. 355th   14th September 1943 – 25th April 1945. P-47s & P-51s. 65th
            Wing/2nd Division.
            Airfield: Steeple Morden. Vics. = $365\frac{1}{2}$ Air, $502\frac{1}{2}$ Ground. 1
            DUC.
11. 356th   15th October 1943 – 7th May 1945. P-47s & P-51s. 65th, 67th
            Wings/1st Division.
            Airfield: Martlesham Heath. Vics. = 201 Air, $75\frac{1}{2}$ Ground. 1
            DUC.
12. 55th   15th October 1943 – 21st April 1945. P-38s & P-51s. 66th
            Wing/3rd Division.
            Airfields: Nuthampstead & Wormingford. Vics. = $316\frac{1}{2}$ Air,
            $268\frac{1}{2}$ Ground. 2 DUCs.
13. 359th   13th December 1943 – 20th April 1945. P-47s & P-51s. 66th,
            67th Wings/ 1st Division.
            Airfield: East Wretham. Vics. = 253 Air, 98 Ground. 1 DUC.
14. 358th   20th December 1943 – 30th January 1944. P-47s. 66th Wing.
            Airfield: Leiston. Vics. = 1 Air.
15. 20th   28th December 1943 – 25th April 1945. P-38s & P-51s. 67th
            Wing/1st Division.
            Airfield: King's Cliffe. Vics. = 212 Air, 237 Ground. 1 DUC.
16. 361st   21st January 1944 – 20th April 1945. P-47s & P-51s. 66th,
            67th, 65th Wings/2nd Division.
            Airfields: Bottisham, Little Walden, St. Dizier, Chievres.
            Vics. = 226 Air, 105 Ground.
17. 357th   11th February 1944 – 25th April 1945. P-51s. 66th Wing/ 3rd
            Division.
            Airfields: Raydon & Leiston. Vics. = $609\frac{1}{2}$ Air, $106\frac{1}{2}$ Ground. 2
            DUCs.

18. 364th 3rd March 1944 – 6th May 1945. P-38s & P-51s. 67th Wing/ 1st Division.
Airfield: Honington. Vics. = $256\frac{1}{2}$ Air, 193 Ground. 1 DUC.
19. 339th 30th April 1944 – 21st April 1945. P-51s. 66th Wing/ 3rd Division.
Airfield: Fowlmere. Vics. = $239\frac{1}{2}$, $440\frac{1}{2}$ Ground. 1 DUC.
20. 479th 26th May 1944 – 25th April 1945. P-38s & P-51s. 65th Wing/ 2nd Division.
Airfield: Wattisham. Vics. = 155 Air, 279 Ground. 1 DUC.
'Riddle's Raiders'.

OTHER OPERATIONAL UNITS

1. 7th Photo. Group. 28th March 1943 – 8th May 1945. F-5s, Spitfire XIs & P-51s. 325th PC Wing (Recon.).
Airfield: Mount Farm Chalgrove. 1 DUC.
2. Special Operations Group. 5th April 1944 – 26th April 1945. B-24s, C-47s, Mosquito XVIs & A-26s. 1st Division.
Airfields: Alconbury, Watton & Harrington. 1 DUC. 'Carpetbaggers'.
3. Night Leaflet Squadron. 7/8th October 1943 – 31st May 1945. B-17s & B-24s. 1st Division.
Airfields: Chelveston, Cheddington & Harrington.
4. 15th Bomb Squadron (Light). 4th July 1942 – 2nd October 1942. Boston 111s (DB-7s). 1st Wing.
Airfields: Grafton Underwood, Molesworth & Podington. (Trsfrd. to Twelfth Air Force).
5. 5th Emergency Rescue Squadron. 10th May 1944 – May 1945. P-47s, OA-10As & B-17s. 65th Wing/2nd Division.
Airfields: Boxted & Halesworth.
6. Radio Counter Measures Squadron. 3rd June 1944 – May 1945. B-17s & B-24s. 1st Division.
Airfields: Sculthorpe, Oulton, Cheddington & Alconbury.
7. 25th Bomb Group (Reconnaissance). 22nd April 1944 – 23rd July 1945. B-17s, B-24s, Mosquito XVIs. 325th PC Wing (Recon.)
Airfield: Watton.

Select Bibliography

During my research I have consulted many books and articles, together with numerous histories of individual Groups and also many memoirs written by serving Eighth Air Force airmen. I list some of them below with my grateful thanks to the authors, especially Martin Bowman and Roger Freeman. It was Roger who coined the phrase 'Mighty Eighth' when, in 1970, the first edition of his classic work on the subject appeared.

Adams, Michael C., *The Best War Ever: America & World War II*. John Hopkins University Press, 1994.

Air Ministry, *Target: Germany: The USSAF's Official Story of the VIII Bomber Command First Year over Europe*, HMSO 1944.

Anderson, Christopher J., *The Men of the Mighty Eighth: The US Air Force 1942–1945*. G.I. Series 24, Greenhill Books Ltd, 2001.

Baker, David, *Messerschmitt Me 262*. The Crowood Press Ltd, 1997.

Bishop, Cliff T., *Fortresses of the Big Triangle First*. East Anglia Books, 1986.

Bowman, Martin W., *Castles in the Air: The Story of the B-17 Flying Fortress Crews of the U.S. 8th Air Force*. Patrick Stephens, 1984.
  Four Miles High. Patrick Stephens, 1992.
  USAAF Handbook 1939-45. Sutton Publishing, 1997.

Bowman, Martin W. and Boiten, Theo., *Raiders of the Reich: Air Battle Western Europe 1942-45*. Airlife 1996. Reprint 1997.

Caine, Philip D., *Spitfires, Thunderbolts and Warm Beer: An American Fighter Pilot over Europe*. Brassey's Inc, Virginia, 2000.

Cooke, Ronald C. & Nesbit Roy C., *Target: Hitler's Oil: Allied Attacks on German Oil Supplies, 1939-45*. William Kimber, 1985.

Craven, Wesley Frank, & Cate, James Lea (Editors), *The Army Air Forces in World War II. Vols 1-6*. University of Chicago Press, 1948-51.

Crosby, Harry, *On a Wing and a Prayer*. Robson Books, 1993.

Doolittle, Gen. J. H. with Glines, Carroll V., *I Could Never Be So Lucky Again*. Bantam, New York, 1991.

Ethell, Jeffrey & Price, Alfred, *Target Berlin, Mission 250: 6th March 1944*. Jane's Pub. Co. 1981.

Fox, George H., *Eighth Air Force Remembered*. ISO Publications, 1991.

Freeman, Roger A., with Alan Crouchman & Vic Marslen, *The Mighty Eighth*. Macdonald & Jones, 1970.

The Mighty Eighth War Manual. Jane's Pub. Co., 1984.

Freeman, Roger A. with Alan Crouchman and Vic Manslen, *The Mighty Eighth War Diary*. Jane's Pub. Co., 1990.

Freeman, Roger A. & Osborne, David, *The B-17 Flying Fortress Story*. Arms & Armour, 1998.

Goldberg, A., *A History of the US Air Force 1907–1957*. D. Van Nostrand Co Inc, 1957.

Goodson, James A., *Tumult in the Clouds*. St Martin's Press, 1983.

Holmes, Harry, *The P-51 Mustang*. Tempus Publishing Ltd, 1990.

Infield, Glenn, *Big Week: The U.S. Air Force vs. the Luftwaffe*. Pinnacle Books, New York. 1974.

Johnson, Robert S., *Thunderbolt*. Rhinehart, 1948.

Larde, D.A., *From Somewhere in England: The life & times of 8th A.F bomber fighter and ground crews in Second World War*. Airlife 1991.

LeMay, Curtis & Kantor, McKinley, *Mission with LeMay*. Garden City Press, New York, 1965.

McFarland, Stephen & Newton, Wesley P., *To Command the Sky: The Battle for Air Superiority over Germany 1942-44*. Smithsonian Institution Press, 1991.

Middlebrook, Martin, *The Schweinfurt-Regensburg Mission: American Raids on 17th August 1943*. Allen Lane, 1982.

Murray, Williamson, *The Luftwaffe, 1939-45: Strategy for Defeat*. Brassey's Washington, 1995.

Neillands, Robin, *The Bomber War*. John Murray, 2001.

O'Neill, Brian D., *Half a Wing, Three Engines and a Prayer: B-17s Over Germany*. McGraw-Hill, 1998.

Price, Alfred, *The Last Year of the Luftwaffe*. Arms & Armour, 1994.

Rust, Kenn C., *Eighth Air Force Story*. Historical Aviation Album. Sunshine House Inc., 1978.

Sherry, Michael S., *The Rise of American Air Power: The Creation of Armageddon*. Yale University Press, 1987.

US Government, *US Strategic Bombing Survey*. Governement Printing Office, Washington, 1947.

Weir, Adrian, *The Last Flight of the Luftwaffe: The Suicide Attack on the Eighth Air Force, 7th April 1945*. Arms and Armour, 1997.

Wells, Ken, *Steeple Morden Strafers, 1943–45*. Egon Publishers, 1994.

INDEX

BOMB GROUPS

FIGHTER GROUPS

OTHERS